Emma's World:
A World War II Memoir

Emma's World:
A World War II Memoir

by Ilene W. Devlin

Emma's World: A World War II Memoir

ORDERING INFORMATION: Additional copies may be obtained from the author: ilenewd@me.com or 210-854-6593.

ISBN – 978-1-7357340-3-3

Cover schoolhouse photo courtesy of the Nodaway County Historical Society, Maryville, Missouri.

DEDICATION

To Mom and her life's goals.

PREFACE

Emma' World: A World War II Memoir is a work of narrative nonfiction. Its foundation is published research, oral family history, personal diaries from 1938–1944, and over 500 letters written between two people in love. The story was composed with admiration and respect for the northwest Missouri area and its people, plus a fascination with a period in history, World War II, that altered the entire globe and all of its cultures. The book's focus is life goals, perseverance, and family.

The names of public figures and places have been retained. Other names have been altered to preserve privacy.

ACKNOWLEDGEMENTS

To Mom, who never realized what an extraordinary life and times she lived.

To Jan Kilby, whose professional advice and devoted friendship encouraged me to write. Thanks for having faith in my writing attempts.

To my editor, Lillie Ammann, for her expert guidance in refining my writing.

To all my teachers, especially in English, who fueled my imagination through the world of books with their unlimited travel through time and space, I thank you for the journey.

To all U.S. military veterans and support personnel who gave so much during World War II.

To those on the World War II home front, who waited anxiously for the war's end.

Chapter 1

Cautiously, Emma eased open the back door. At the halfway point, she slipped through the opening and quietly pulled the door shut behind her. Her brother Owen kept everything on the farm in perfect working order but often forgot to oil the kitchen door hinges, which squealed if the door was opened quickly. Emma didn't want the others to wake too soon—she wanted this morning to herself.

Her deep exhale surprised her, for she hadn't realized she had been holding her breath. She took a moment to relax her tense muscles.

Striding across the screened in back porch, Emma slowly opened the door. She held onto the frame as she shut it. How many times had she dashed across the porch, shoved open the screen door, and let it slam behind her as she ran outside to play in her scarce free moments? Her mother had always scolded her for making so much noise.

Emma stood on the step. *Shoot! I forgot my sweater!* A waft of predawn air chilled her bare arms and legs and her body through her cotton dress. After daybreak, the late August sun would overheat the day. Then she would change into her better clothes, preparing for her new life.

Today is so special. I want this first part just to be mine. I want to remember every sensation, to make a mental image I'll always have. This is my world, the only place I've lived. After today, will I wish I was back here?

She stepped onto the narrow sidewalk, knowing the layout of the yard and farm buildings by heart. Even in the near darkness, she could envision the farm.

The back door was the only entrance used. All the neighbors came there, hollering hello through the screen. Behind her, the farmhouse front door faced west to the dirt county road. The road extended north for two miles to the graveled county road, leading west four miles into Barnard.

Across the yard to her right, a small pasture ran along a narrow dirt lane. From spring until fall, the yearling calves were fattened there, to be sold before winter. Eleven Angus calves lay with sleepy eyes, waiting for more sunlight before moving.

The dirt lane ran east nearly a mile, butting against the raised railroad bed. Crossing the tracks, it disappeared into a corn field. Emma had ridden her horse along the lane countless times, listening to the gentle whisper of the breeze through the tall grasses and watching for rabbits darting across her path that could startle her horse.

Emma strolled east down the sidewalk. With the pale sliver of sun peaking over the horizon, she could distinguish the mound of the root cellar on her left. Seven wooden steps descended into the earth. The cellar held wooden shelves filled with pint, quart, and half-gallon jars of vegetables, fruits, and meat that her mother Edith, sister-in-law Melinda, and she had canned. Each year, Emma dusted the cobwebs from the walls and jars. She waited until a truly scorching summer's day to complete the job, enjoying the cool mustiness of the cellar's interior.

The root cellar also protected her family several times a summer when severe storms battered the gently rolling northwest Missouri farmland. She still remembered the cellar shuddering when a near-tornadic wind had blown over the huge elm tree. Luckily, the tree fell toward the road, just missing the house. Neighbors had helped Owen saw and stack enough firewood to last all winter.

Down the sidewalk on the right was the outhouse. While a necessary structure, Emma never lingered there. Each bedroom had its own chamber pot, which had to be emptied every morning. In the summer, the small enclosure was stuffy, hot, and attracted wasps building nests in the eaves. In winter while she was seated on the wooden bench, the frigid air assaulted her behind. *Someday, maybe we'll have an indoor bathroom.*

The concrete walkway ended shortly beyond the outhouse. On her left, Emma could barely see the long garden rows. Owen plowed the large plot each spring. The women hoed the ground smooth and planted lettuce, peas, green beans, carrots, potatoes, tomatoes, and sweet corn. Most of this year's garden crops had already been picked and canned. Only the potatoes remained, and shell beans were drying on the vines. She had spent many sweat-soaked hours in the garden to grow food to feed her family through the harsh Missouri winters.

To her right, the clothesline ran in two long sections. The women washed once a week and were thankful they had a gas-powered washing machine. They hand cranked the wet clothes through a wringer before jamming wooden clothespins over them on the lines. Afterward, the ironing took hours more. *I love clean, smoothly ironed clothes, but I wish there were an easier way to get them!* thought Emma.

Ahead, Emma could just see the fence posts surrounding the cattle feed lot. In winter, her brother placed the loose hay in wooden troughs for the cattle and horses to eat. In summer, the beef cattle, milk cows, and two horses munched and grew plump on fresh grass in the east-west pasture that paralleled the dirt lane. Owen regularly checked all fencing to ensure none of the animals could escape and possibly be killed on the road. Severe weather could ruin the family's crops, so livestock represented a key financial security.

Emma had always admired fence posts. Their bases were jammed into the ground, solid footing that dared the world to move them. Tornado-force winds would be required to knock them down. Fence posts stood silently, providing their essential service of keeping things in or out of their protection zone. Only many years of ice, snow, and rain could rot their strength. *I hope I will be able to face the life's challenges half as well.*

Crossing her palms on top of a post, Emma rested her chin on her hands and her elbows on the wood cross bars. She closed her eyes. As dawn's light increased, animals began to stir. Across the dirt lane, a quail called the first bob-white, bob-white of the day from inside the cornfield. To the west, another quail answered from the soybean field.

She heard the gentle rustle of corn leaves. The summer's heat dried the corn stalks tan and shriveled the kernels. In fall, men would pick corn from morning until dark, twisting ears off stalks by hand, trying to finish before any rain could moisten the ears or a strong wind could blow down the brittle stalks.

To the north lay the farm driveway. Beyond stood a three-sided shed for machinery and a one-car garage with a door that rolled to one side.

Behind the buildings lay the hog lot, with sows in small individual sheds to protect them from the summer's heat, since hogs could not sweat. In spring, the sows were kept enclosed when they were ready to give birth and afterward until the baby pigs had grown bigger so the coyotes could not get them.

A few hungry sows were already lifting the hog feeder lids to reach the feed inside. When they were finished, the lids slammed shut with a tin bang.

A little northeast of the garage rose the large barn where Owen stored hay. This year's weather had been good with an early hay crop and enough rain for a second harvest. Emma could smell the sweet earthy aroma of hay curing in the loft. Their farm animals would have enough feed to last through even a rough winter. Last year, a hailstorm had nearly destroyed the second hay crop, and her brother had worried about feeding his animals through the winter.

The center barn door was usually left open. A few semi-feral cats sat in the doorway each morning warming their ears. A paddock lay next to the barn. Each morning, six milk cows sauntered in just as the sun rose. In Emma's mind, she could hear their first mooing of the morning, demanding to eat the special grain that awaited them while they were being milked. A short ramp led up from the paddock and into the milking section of the barn. As soon as Owen opened the Dutch door at the top of the ramp, each cow walked into its own stall where a vertical wooden bar locked the cow's head in place while Owen and Melinda milked.

The two horses usually arrived in the paddock, hoping for attention and oats. When Emma was little, her father would saddle a horse for her to ride in the paddock while he milked.

Opening her eyes, Emma enjoyed the edge of sun enlarging over the railway bed. If the dirt lane was too muddy in springtime, Emma would ride the half-mile-long pasture. *I love the feeling of the wind blowing through my hair. I wonder how long it will be before I get to do that again?*

Soon, Owen and Melinda would be rising. Farm folks worked from daylight until dark each spring and summer day. Cows to milk, animals to feed, food to can, clothes to wash, neighbors to help, and Sundays to visit had run through Emma's world like a steady river of activity. Now all that would change for her.

What have I done? I wanted this so badly, but now I'm scared. Emma almost gave in to tears. She felt excitement at the adventures coming, yet loneliness at separating from her family. Her emotions began to swing from one extreme to the other.

Emma looked around her, turning in a circle to capture every scene. *I wish I had a camera. At least I could have photographs of my home to take with me.* But she didn't. Her mind would have to embed the colors, sounds, and scents on its own.

She had spent that Friday and Saturday nights on the family homestead. This would be the last time she lived in her childhood home before her future dreams began.

Oh, Dad, I wish you were here!

Chapter 2

Daniel Trotter studied his heavily pregnant wife Edith as she eased into her kitchen chair. He could tell from her panting and exhausted expression her time to deliver the baby was near. Edith was almost forty years old, and Daniel knew it should be her last pregnancy.

As he glanced around the kitchen table, his thoughts slipped back to their first baby. Rose had been born twenty years ago, the beginning of their family. Although Daniel had hoped for a boy, he was happy his wife came through okay with the help of the local midwife. The baby had arrived in the early morning hours, first squalling around sunrise. Edith and Daniel had taken that as a good sign, healthy lungs and a beautiful start to a new day.

But Rose never grew. She remained puny with little energy. Within two months, she died. Edith took the news badly, feeling she had let Daniel down. Daniel was more circumspect. He had been a farmer all his life. Many young creatures were killed by predators like coyotes or hawks, died from natural deformities, or just got sick and expired. While he never understood the reasons why such things happened, he just accepted they did.

Looking around the table at his sons waiting for him to signal to start eating, Daniel's thoughts again drifted into the past. With the next four babies, Edith had done better producing hearty boys. Daniel thoroughly believed men should raise the boys after age eight, and women should raise the girls.

Daniel took his fatherly duties seriously. His dad, Wilson, had been reared in a stern household, so Daniel did the same with his boys. After all, boys would get into nothing but trouble without proper guidance and firm examples of parenting. Now Daniel was proud of his four achievements, but he never thought to ask them how they viewed his methods of child rearing.

At seventeen, Robert stood six feet two inches, lanky and muscular. His crooked slow grin could soften Daniel's heart. With a matching careful, considered way of talking, his words led people to listen to what he had to say. Also, he was the most obedient to Daniel's commands. Rarely did Bob openly defy Daniel, but the boy kept his thoughts to himself, so Daniel never understood him too well. Bob had the makings of a good farmer, and Daniel felt he would buy his own farm someday and prosper successfully.

Next had come Jacob, now fourteen. He was going to be as tall as Bob, muscular, but with a slightly bigger body build. His chest and arms were thicker, strengthened by strenuous farm work. Jacob's only weakness was his eyesight. He could barely see the end of a row he was plowing and could read only headlines in newspapers. Thus, Jacob found schooling harder, although his intellect was sharp. Usually he had an even temper, but Jacob could get frustrated at the antics of his two younger brothers and cut loose verbally to put them in their proper places.

Michael, age seven, produced the most mischief. If the boys got into any serious shenanigans, Mike had instigated them. His body build indicated he would follow Jacob's path as he grew, already developing muscles from farm chores. But Mike was also the fussiest about his hair and appearance, using his natural charm to sway people his way. Daniel foresaw trouble with girls as Mike matured, and Daniel needed Mike to focus on learning farm duties. Mike also was the biggest influence on his youngest brother.

Owen was four and adored all his brothers, but Mike the most. Owen's grin would spread from ear to ear when he was happy. He wanted to go to school, for he enjoyed learning. Owen kept saying he wanted to read everything he could, once he got to school and learned to read. Owen, too, seemed destined to be tall and lanky, with the Trotter big feet and hands. He would need them for farming, earning his living from the land.

Daniel's father and grandfather had been farmers. Probably a lot of other ancestors had been the same. The life was hard but gave a man satisfaction when the day was done and he could look over his fields to see his efforts producing good crops and livestock. Having a large family would always prove a dilemma. Having more mouths to feed meant more and harder farm work. But a small family, especially if the children turned out to be girls, meant the man of the house had all the work to do with no hope of future relief.

A heavy sigh from Edith broke his reverie, returning his focus to the table. Reaching for the plate of sliced roast beef, Daniel thereby signaled his starving boys they could begin eating. Each boy grabbed whatever food dish was in front of him and helped himself, taking only his fair share and leaving enough to pass to the others. After farming all day, he and the boys were hungry. The roast beef, boiled potatoes, green beans, and homemade bread would abate hunger pangs for a while. The last of Mom's cookies served as dessert, and the boys hoped she would make more tomorrow. Or maybe she would bake some pies. Fresh cow's milk washed down the food. Edith took smaller portions, and Daniel could tell she was not feeling well, for she usually had quite an appetite after her daily duties.

As he stuffed a bite of beef into his mouth, Daniel returned to his thoughts. *I hope this sixth baby is a boy. With Bob nearly grown and probably soon to find a wife, he'll be leaving the farm. The other three are too young to be much help for a while, although Jacob can pick up more of his share of the work. Mike and Owen are just too young yet, but soon Mike can feed the livestock.*

Yes, he would make sure his boys became farmers. They were bright students in school, when they got to attend, usually full-time only when they were under age fourteen. After fourteen, or younger if they were tall and strong, Daniel needed them home to bring in the fall harvest. When that was done around October, then he let them spend more time in classes. Sometimes the older boys had to miss school to help if an early spring allowed planting. Crops had to be in by late spring or they wouldn't have enough time to mature, especially if an early frost hit. In any case, Daniel knew a good farmer needed no more than an eighth-grade education, just enough to read and write and do basic math to keep the farm records.

Daniel's dad had started him on farm work when he was ten. When Daniel left home, he had rented farmland to support his new wife. Times had been hard, but Edith had not complained. Reared to be a farmer's wife, she knew the challenges. Her mother and several generations before had been farmers' wives. Finally, he had scrimped together enough money for a down payment on their current eighty acres of land.

At fifty years old, Daniel was beginning to feel the effects of a lifetime of hard work. His back and butt knew hard pounding as he rode the metal plow seat with two horses struggling to pull the blades through soil each spring. He had planted seeds by hand and later with a horse-pulled planter, with his feet and ankles twisting and rebalancing constantly while walking to stay upright over the uneven plowed ground. Arm muscles had become steel bands as they restrained the taut reins to control unruly horse or mule teams. As he twisted his body to lift and toss loose hay onto wagons, his back had taken a beating. Tossing the hay into barn lofts tested his arms and back.

He thought of other tasks farming required. Daniel had struggled to pull calves out of the womb to help cows having a difficult birthing process.

His thighs and shins had been kicked by various angry animals, luckily never breaking a bone. If bones had been cracked, he had ignored the pain and kept on with working.

How many thousands of ears had his hands twisted, then jerked, off dry, tough corn stalks, tossing each ear high overhead into a horse-pulled wagon? Later those same ears had to be shoveled into the corncrib, piling ever higher to store them for winter use. When grain was needed, his right arm had cranked the manual corn sheller's handle too many times to count, while his left hand fed corn ears one at a time into the sheller's gaping metal mouth.

Many scoop shovels of grain had been hoisted into feed troughs. Many calves castrated. Many farm animals treated for cuts or some kind of disease.

Daniel needed boys to become young men quickly to help him. How long he could keep providing for a family of six, soon to be seven, he didn't know. But he did know they depended on his efforts. He understood he was luckier than some men who only had daughters, thus no one to help the men as their families grew in size. He had remained thankful for good health, even when others had been down with illnesses.

Thinking back to the winter of 1918 to 1919, he recalled the number of people locally who had contracted and died from that blasted influenza epidemic. Daniel blamed the war for moving so many people around the world. If more people had just stayed home, the flu wouldn't have spread so far or so fast. *Too many people just thinking they had to be somewheres else, instead of where they belonged,* he mused. When the flu had arrived in Barnard and vicinity, he had kept his family members on the farm. He had to risk going to town for supplies once in a while, but his family had been spared getting sick. He would pass farms with quarantine flags flying near the road to warn people to stay away. Weeks passed, and still flags had flown in the area. He had not heard the final count of how many died locally, but the graveyards had too many tombstones with a death date of 1918 or 1919.

No, people needed to stay where they were born and be what they were intended to be. Several local young men had gone to that damn war. Some had been killed. Some came home briefly, but then had the notion they wanted to live in a city and had left the farm forever.

First of all, they should never have left the farm, because the government needed farmers to provide food for people, grain for livestock, and horses and mules for the military. If nobody stayed on the farm, how would people live? Farmers were important people, and young folks needed to understand

8

that. The war had spread too many new ideas about how to live and act.

The only good result Daniel saw from the war was the increased development of machinery. Now in 1921, new tractors and farm equipment had been designed. Crop and livestock prices had been good during the war. Daniel had saved some money, putting more into the bank to pay down his farm's mortgage. Still in debt, but with good crops, he would be over the worst in ten or fifteen years. Yes, he might even be able to buy a used tractor before too long.

Sounds of hungry boys talking pulled back Daniel's thoughts. He looked around the small kitchen. The wood-burning stove sat in the southeast corner, with a wood box to its left. To the stove's right, a south window with feed-sack curtains brightened the room. The sink had a hand pump for well water, and a drainpipe leading outside to a large wooden barrel. The outside rinse water could be used to clean dirty tools or a boy's filthy feet. Reused water spared sometimes-scarce well water during drought seasons. They did not have an icebox, so cooked food was eaten completely at each meal if it could not be safely stored. Daniel hated to see good food deposited in the slop bucket along with the potato peelings to be fed to the hogs. The pie safe had belonged to Edith's mother, and probably her mother before her. Another shelving unit held canned goods for current use. Other jars remained in the storm cellar until needed.

His family was healthy, getting stronger, but would soon have another mouth to feed. One boy would soon leave the homestead. Another, hopefully, was about to be born to take his place and would still be around to do some farm work when Daniel reached sixty. Maybe this last baby would be a good thing.

Once more, Daniel studied Edith's face. She had eaten little and looked even more tired than when she sat down.

"Bob, after dinner, I want you to ride over to Mrs. Britton's. Ask if she could come over for a couple of days to help Edith. She'll understand," instructed Daniel.

"But, Dad, it's already dark out. Can't I go in the morning?" moaned Bob.

A sharp glare from his father halted Bob's argument. A halfmoon would provide plenty of light the horse needed for the two-mile round-trip ride.

"Just do it," Daniel demanded. "And, Jacob, you and Mike do the dishes tonight. Owen can clear the table. And be careful and not break anything.

Your mother's gonna lie down for a while."

More quiet groans emerged from the other three boys. Boys didn't do dishes; that was women's work.

"We need a sister to do stuff like that," remarked Owen.

Daniel ignored the remark, hoping it would not influence the baby's choice of sex. Girls were not what Daniel needed.

With a grateful look, Edith slowly rose from her chair. Holding the table's edge to get her balance, she carefully turned and headed for the downstairs bedroom. Yes, she needed to lie down, just for a little time to regain her strength. Maybe the baby would wait a few more days until she wasn't so tired, but Edith doubted it.

Bob grabbed his hat, jamming it on his head. He managed to shut the back door with enough force to register his protest over the night ride, but not enough to get himself rebuked by his father. After the long day's work, Bob was dog tired and wanted to go to bed. They had worked until nearly sundown, then milked cows and fed livestock. Dinner was usually eaten at nearly dark, so everyone was ready for bed soon afterward. Now his ride would take him at least an hour, maybe more if Mrs. Britton wanted to talk before he left. "Oh, well, get it over with," he muttered to himself, heading for the corral to saddle the horse.

Owen began clearing the table, carefully stacking the dishes to the right of the sink. Jacob grabbed a potholder, lifting the teakettle from the stove where it was always kept warm. He poured hot water into the dishpan and added powdered soap.

"I hate getting my hands dried out from this dish water," he groused. "My hands are dry enough from being in the sun all day. Now I have to do dishes!" Luckily for him, his father had gone to the small living room to sit in his rocking chair before Jacob's comments could be overheard.

"Yeah, that's what big brothers are for," intoned Mike, who ducked as Jacob threatened to throw the wet dishrag at him. "I am here to serve as your dryer tonight, sir."

Jacob glared at him but turned to get the task done. Jacob washed and Mike dried each dish and pan. Owen wiped the table clean while the other two rattled the dishes. When done, they stacked the dishes carefully on the cupboard shelves, ready for breakfast tomorrow morning.

Before they left the kitchen, the boys gathered their bath towels and washrags. They cleaned their faces, upper bodies, and even behind their ears, preparing for bed. Without being reminded, they brushed their teeth with tooth powder and stored their brushes with the handles down in a cracked coffee mug.

"We're done, Dad," announced Jacob.

"Say goodnight to your mother, then off to bed," replied Daniel. The small radio played country music. Daniel leaned his head back and closed his eyes.

After knocking on the bedroom door, her sons trudged into the room and kissed their mother good night. Even they could see how tired she was, but she smiled at each of them.

"Have sweet dreams, boys," wished Edith. "I'm sorry I didn't feel up to helping more this evenin'."

"Oh, that's okay," Mike replied. "We were glad to help."

Edith smiled at the little white lie, and Mike knew she understood their feelings.

The three boys opened the stairway door and climbed to the second floor. While Mike and Owen shared a room, Bob and Jacob each had his own bedroom. Each small bedroom had no heat and one window, plus a chest of drawers and a rack to hang clothes. The late November evening would prove chilly, almost cold enough to require bed warming stones. Mom's handmade quilts kept them cozy as they slept. Each room had a chamber pot, which the boys emptied in the outhouse each morning.

Only sleeping hours were spent in the bedrooms unless someone was ill. Otherwise, everyone rose before sunrise to milk cows, feed livestock, and separate the milk and cream. Mom fixed a hearty breakfast of eggs, ham, gravy, biscuits, and homemade jam. The family would consume everything, then the menfolk would head to the fields and the younger boys would do chores.

No one had bothered to explain to the boys about Edith's pregnancy. Children did not need to learn about such things until they were about to marry, even though farm kids often saw animals giving birth. Owen had never been in close proximity to an expectant woman before, and Mike couldn't remember Owen's birth. Bob and Jacob knew Edith was expecting, but that was a woman's problem and no concern of theirs. The older two understood one more person would crowd the small house, but they voiced no opinion on the subject, neither would their parents have discussed it with them.

By the time Bob returned, the only light in the house was a small kerosene lamp in the kitchen. Everyone else had gone to sleep. Bob cleaned up, headed upstairs, and dropped into bed.

Chapter 3

Edith's labor pains began around four in the morning, and her water broke soon after. She tried to keep her groans quiet, so she would not wake the four sleeping boys. For bad pains, she grabbed an extra pillow and yelled into it. Daniel tried to comfort her the best he could, though he felt helpless to ease her suffering.

Mrs. Britton arrived before sunrise. She knocked softly at the back door, and then just walked in like neighbors did. The kitchen kerosene lamp burned low, so she knew Daniel was up.

"I'd a feeling I'd better get over here early," she remarked. "You got water boiling and some clean towels?

Daniel looked at her, letting out a long sigh. "This ain't my first baby, you know. Course, they're ready. I been up since early hours."

Mrs. Britton let the remark pass, as she could see the strain on Daniel's face. He was a good man, hardworking and loyal. But sometimes she felt he was a little stern and strict about his way of getting things done.

"I'll slip in and see Edith. We'll see how long that baby's gonna take to join this family."

Edith's pale, sweat-drenched face lay against the homemade feather pillows. "Oh, Wilma, thanks for coming over. I sure like having another woman here."

Grabbing Edith's outstretched hand, Wilma gave it a reassuring shake. "Between me and you, we've had enough babies to field a baseball team. This one will just add a spare player. So you just ease back and let me take care of you for a while."

By sunrise, the boys roused upstairs. Daniel could hear their footsteps overhead.

"You boys stay upstairs for now. I'll bring you some breakfast," he instructed.

"But I'm hungry now," whined Owen. "Why can't I come down there and eat at the table? It's cold up here."

"Just put on your clothes and get back in bed. I'll get you some food soon as I can."

Daniel could hear more complaints, but he knew the boys would obey. Bob and Jacob would figure out what was going on downstairs, but Mike and Owen would not understand and would certainly be too noisy for Edith's comfort now.

In the kitchen, Daniel started breakfast. He wasn't the cook Edith was, but he could rustle up something to fill five hungry bellies. Taking a skillet from the shelf, Daniel set it on the stove. He grabbed the poker, lifted the iron lid, and jabbed the coals inside the stove. Next, he opened the side door and added two chunks of wood to stoke the fire.

The wooden cutting board hung on the wall. Using his best meat knife, Daniel sliced twenty strips of bacon from the large section of meat. He added those to the skillet, knowing from the sizzle how hot the surface was. As the bacon cooked, Daniel reached for the eggs from yesterday. When the bacon was crisp, he dropped the strips onto a platter, then broke the eggs open one by one. He couldn't make over-easy eggs like Edith, but he could scramble a dozen for the five of them. Finally, he cut ten slices of homemade bread, slapped some butter and jam on them, and put the pieces together face-to-face on a plate.

"Bob and Jacob, come to the bottom of the stairs and grab these plates from me." The boys took the plates and forks, heading up the chilly steps. "Now eat your breakfast and stay up there until I tell you otherwise. You have water in your pitchers to drink."

His four sons were hungry enough that they didn't argue. They dove into the food, knowing not to ask too many questions. Daniel headed back to see Edith.

"She's coming along right well," noted Wilma. "You and the boys just go about your business, and I'll take care of Edith. You might send Bob to my house to phone the doctor and let him know it's Edith's time. Doc could drop by if he's in the area."

Daniel gave Edith's hand a squeeze, then turned and headed for the enclosed porch, which had windows replacing the summer screens. He donned his winter coat, hat, and gloves. Returning to the stairway, he yelled up, "When you boys finish eating, bring down your chamber pots and get them cleaned out. And bring your plates. Just get dressed and head for the barn. Don't come back inside. We've got chores to do and cows to milk. We'll let your mother have the house this morning. And, Bob, you ride over to the

Brittons and have them call Dr. Larabee to see Edith as soon as he can."

Pulling on his five-buckle overshoes, Daniel exited the kitchen door and across the porch. He stepped onto the frosted sidewalk and walked toward the barn. The cold morning air brushed his face, now covered with a day's growth of whiskers. He had forgotten to shave this morning with all the worry about Edith.

"Boy, I wish I knew why Dad looked so worried," said Mike. "He sure didn't act like most mornings."

Bob and Jacob exchanged looks, having guessed their mother was having her own problems. "Just do what he says for now," instructed Bob. "You'll understand later."

Mike looked at him sideways, resenting the fact his older brothers always knew more about what was happening in the world than he did. "You always think you know so much."

Owen just watched his brothers. At four years old, he couldn't follow half of what the other three were talking about most of the time. Today was no different.

The boys stacked their plates and forks onto the platter. Bob carried the pile of dishes downstairs, while Jacob brought two chamber pots. Mike carried the pot he and Owen used. The boys placed the dishes carefully in the sink and donned their winter clothes on the porch. Bob, Jacob, and Mike headed for the outhouse to empty the pots, while Owen waited in the kitchen.

"Let's get moving," said Bob. Looking at Mike and Owen, he instructed, "You two get the eggs and be careful about them. Yesterday you broke two and Mom would've been mad if she'd known. Me and Jacob got chores to do."

"I hate those old hens," griped Owen. "They always peck my hands when I try to get those eggs. That hurts even through my gloves!"

"Yeah, I know," replied Mike. "But we need those eggs, or we won't have much for breakfast. I don't like oatmeal, so I'd rather have eggs, even if it means getting pecked. It's just because we're the youngest we got to get those things. But it's better than being older and us having to clean out the horse stalls and hog houses."

Owen made a face. "Yeah, that stuff stinks worse than chicken poop."

By late morning, a new baby girl had joined the Trotter clan. Her lusty yells filled the bedroom and could be heard throughout the small house. Wilma got her cleaned up, wrapping her in the new baby quilt Edith had made.

"She's got dark hair like the rest of 'em," noted Wilma. "And those green eyes and cute mouth. She's got big feet, so she'll be tall as her brothers."

Edith reached for her daughter. She snuggled the baby close to her chest, pulling down the blanket to see her face. Edith was more tired than she had been after her previous babies' births, knowing her age was partly to blame.

"What you gonna name her?" asked Wilma.

Edith looked at her baby. "Me and Daniel had talked mostly about boys' names. He really wanted another boy to help on the farm. So I guess I get to name the girl. I think I'll call her Emma Jean after my two aunts."

"Emma Jean Trotter. That's a good name for a farm girl. Sounds firm and honest," decided Wilma.

"Maybe you better call Daniel. He'll be a wondering what he's got for his new baby."

Wilma nodded, wiped the sweat from Edith's face, and combed her hair. "You wanna look your best when you tell him he's got a girl-child. But he'll like her anyway. You wait and see. When that little one grabs his finger, she'll own him for sure."

Heading for the porch, Wilma donned her coat and scarf and walked to the barn. She spotted Daniel giving the milk cows some extra hay. He had already separated the milk and stored the milk cans underground.

"Hey, Daniel," she called and then laughed. "You better git a move on up to the house. Edith has something to show you."

Daniel looked up, surprised and concerned. He knew the baby would come today but wasn't sure when. He straightened his back and tried to look unconcerned. "I'll head up directly."

Wilma saw through his cool exterior. She knew how much Daniel loved Edith, even if he didn't say so too often. Most men were that way, it seemed.

"What was it—a boy or a girl?"

"You just git to the house and see for yourself," Wilma smiled. "I'm not giving away the surprise."

Women, thought Daniel. *Ask a straight question and see if you get a straight answer.* He plunged the hayfork into a pile and headed for the house.

"You boys stay out here until I call you," he yelled over his shoulder.

Bob and Jacob looked at each other. They had been giving the hogs some grain, while Mike and Owen pumped water into a bucket for the stock cattle. "Okay, Dad. But we're getting plenty cold out here, so let us know when we can come inside and warm up."

Daniel nodded his head and kept moving. He was worried about Edith, this being her sixth baby.

Scraping the mud and manure on the edge of a fence, he moved toward the house. He removed his overshoes and outerwear on the porch, then opened the kitchen door. The scent of food reminded him lunch would be due soon, and the warm air did feel good after the cold morning. He stopped to wash his hands in the basin of water in the sink.

Quietly he moved through the small living room and opened the bedroom door. Edith was resting, holding the baby near her. She looked paler than he had seen her in a long time.

"Edith, you okay?"

"Oh, Daniel, I'll be fine. I'm just tuckered out for now. I'll be up by tonight, you'll see."

"No, you won't," corrected Wilma. "You aren't doing anything for a couple of days. You ain't as young as you used to be."

Daniel agreed. "You stay in bed like Wilma says. We need you healthy."

"Come see your new family member," replied Edith.

Feeling awkward around the tiny baby, Daniel sat by the bed in the chair Wilma moved under him. Wilma smiled at the three of them and quietly slipped from the room.

He looked at the bundled face, all splotchy and pink. "What is it—a boy or a girl?"

Edith hesitated. "She's a girl. I hope you ain't disappointed."

Daniel looked into her worried face. "As long as she's healthy, that's all that matters. You need help around the house as much as I need help on the farm."

Slowly, Daniel extended his index finger toward the baby. Her little right hand was outside the covers. When she felt his finger, she grabbed hold tightly.

"Well, she's got a grip on her, I'll say."

"You should have heard her yell when she got here. She's got good lungs," Edith laughed. Then sobering, she noted, "I hope she makes it and not be like Rose."

Looking into her sad eyes, Daniel replied, "We won't let it happen again. Not twice in one life. That would be too much."

Edith tried to look brave. She truly hoped for a better outcome than her first daughter had had.

"What's her name?"

Edith smiled. "Since we've only talked about boy names, I thought we might call her Emma Jean."

"Emma Jean Trotter. I like the sound."

"The boys won't know what to do with a sister. They'll be too rough on her, especially Mike and Owen until they understand she's just a baby."

"We'll keep an eye on them two rowdies. They're good boys, just being boys most of the time. I'll get Bob and Jacob to keep 'em in tow."

"She'll have to learn to stand her ground. With four older brothers, she'll have to make do on her own two feet," Edith said with a chuckle.

"You git some rest now. I'll let the boys know they can come inside later for lunch," said Daniel.

"Yeah, I could use a little sleep. I'm feeling a bit tuckered out."

Daniel disengaged his finger from Emma's grip and quietly left the bedroom. Wilma was waiting in the living room.

"You just go about your business with the boys. I'll get you all some lunch and holler when it's ready," bossed Wilma.

"I thank you for being with her when her time came. We were both worried about this birth, her being older and all," Daniel admitted.

Wilma just nodded. "You git along and I'll keep an eye on Edith and the little one. That baby'll be letting us know when she gets hungry next. You'll hear her clear to the pasture."

Daniel smiled, donned his winter duds, and left to tell the boys. As he strode across the barnyard, the boys came hurrying to meet him.

"What's going on, Dad?" Owen was the most curious.

"Yeah, why can't we go inside where it's warm?" asked Mike.

"Okay, boys, here's the news. Y'all got a baby sister, and your mom needs some rest right now. We'll go in for lunch, but for now, we'll just keep ourselves scarce and let them be."

Owen and Mike stared at each other. "A sister! What good is she?"

Daniel laughed. "You might be surprised. If she learns to cook like your mom, you might be gettin' pies more often."

The two younger boys thought it over. "Will she be making some soon?"

"No, you idiot," chimed in Bob. "She's just a baby. She won't be doing much of anything for a long time."

Owen and Mike looked disappointed. "Then why've we got to have her?"

Jacob gave them a shove. "You didn't start out full-growed either, you know. You was just babies, too. Me and Bob had to put up with you for forever! Even now you're not much help, being so little and all."

Mike punched Jacob in the side. "Who says we're too little?"

"Okay, boys, let's get to work. This farm don't run itself."

Dr. Larabee arrived by early afternoon. He gave Emma a thorough exam, proclaiming her healthy and a real cutie. Edith, relieved, prayed she could live a long life.

Chapter 4

Emma was the last of the Trotter brood. Being a girl, she was reared to help her mother. Even at a young age, she learned to plant seeds in the garden, water the baby plants as they grew, and pick the vegetables her mom said were ripe. She also set the table.

Emma loved her big brothers, even if they thought she was a pest following them around in their spare time. They were all so tall, and she laughed wholeheartedly when Bob and Jacob would lift her high over their heads and twirl her around.

When she was four years old, Bob announced he had asked his girl Linda Miller to marry him. She had said yes. He was twenty-two, and he and Linda had been dating for a year already.

"I've talked to Mr. Callison. He's gettin' old and wants off his farm, but he don't have any kids to pass it on to. He said I could lease the farm and buy it over time. So I've got a way to make my living. Linda will help, since she's a farm girl and wants to stay that way."

Planning a nice wedding with virtually no cash money was typical for the area. Daniel was working hard to pay off the mortgage, and he counted on the two older boys to help. With Bob leaving soon to handle his own land, only nineteen-year-old Jacob, twelve-year-old Mike, and eight-year-old Owen filled the gap. Soon Jacob would probably be getting married, too.

Daniel shook his head. Although he felt in good health, he realized at fifty-four he would be pushing hard to keep the farm going by himself until Mike got a little older.

Mike loved school, but if Jacob left, Daniel would require Mike's help during the school year. Otherwise, the spring planting and fall harvesting could be a problem. *Well, Mike's gonna be a farmer,* Daniel planned, *so he don't need a lot of schooling.*

Bob and Linda's wedding took place on Christmas day, 1925, a cold clear Friday. Weddings often occurred in winter in farming country. Crops had been harvested, farm work was at its minimum, and the roads usually were frozen so people could travel without getting stuck in the mud.

19

The two families decorated the First Christian Church in Barnard with what bows and candles they could manage. The bride wore a flapper dress, looking very stylish. Bob wore a new suit, looking somewhat shy with all the attention. Emma got to wear her best dress, and she thought the whole affair confusing and fun at the same time.

By evening, the party began to wind down. Most people headed home by dark to care for livestock and do the milking. The Trotter and Miller families had gotten to know each other even better. Bob and Linda prepared to head to their new home.

Bob's brothers and friends began teasing him.

"Hey, Bob, you better get to sleep early tonight. You gotta chore in the morning," yelled one buddy.

"Yeah, Linda looks real tired, so let her sleep in tomorrow. Bob, you cook breakfast," shouted another.

Bob took the jokes in good humor. "Yep, we'll be shutting the lights out soon. It's been a long day, so we'll just mosey on and talk to y'all later."

Everyone laughed and joked as the couple left the church. They threw rice onto the bridal couple, shouting encouragement for their new life together.

Bob had borrowed a friend's car for leaving the church. The Ford now looked more like a junkyard than a wedding carriage with all the old shoes and tin cans tied to the bumper with binder twine. "Just Married" had been written on the back window with white shoe polish. As Bob roared away from the church, the noise could be heard all over the small town.

Emma could hardly hold her eyelids open. She had awakened early from excitement. By night, she didn't want to admit she would gladly go to bed.

Her family, minus Bob, headed home in their old pickup. The three children sat in the back, covered with homemade quilts and their winter clothing. Daniel and Edith rode up front, also swaddled in blankets and huddled together.

"Remember our wedding?" asked Edith. "We got married on Christmas, too."

"Yeah, cold and really snowin' by evenin'. We didn't have far to go to our old rented farm, but we dang near froze gettin' there."

"That was twenty-five years ago. We've sure had a lot to deal with since then," mused Edith.

Daniel nodded. They had lived on three rental farms before he ha scraped together enough cash to put a down payment on their current homestead. He had been a strong young man when he started his married life. He sure didn't feel that way now, but knew he had to keep going to feed the six people left in his family.

Some of Bob's friends followed them home. Edith poked the cook stove fire to make coffee. She brought out some cakes and cookies she had made for visitors.

Bill Winters, a tall, strapping farm lad, had been Bob's best friend for years. "We're gonna treat Bob and Linda real special tonight!"

"You bet!" chimed in Walt Bradley, another farm neighbor. "We're gonna let them get settled in a mite, then give 'em a real chivaree!"

"They'll never forget their wedding night after we get done kidnapping Bob," added Charlie Hatchett. "He won't get much time with his new bride if we can help it!"

Emma stood still in a corner. She heard the words but didn't understand their meaning. Yet she knew her oldest brother was in danger. She kept quiet and listened.

"First, we're gonna serenade them royally. Got fifteen guys comin' with enough metal pot and pans and wooden spoons to raise the dead when we get to hittin' 'em," Charlie bragged. "We're gonna meet about nine at the end of the road leadin' to the Callison place."

"We've got a car and then we're gonna get into the house and we're gonna blindfold him. Then we're gonna drive around till he's lost and leave him deep in some woods. He'll have a hellava time gettin' home in the dark!" Bill promised, laughing loudly.

Emma couldn't take any more. She burst into tears, yelling, "You leave my brother alone! You're mean! You don't hurt my brother!"

She began to hit Bill on the chest with her fists. She was crying and shouting for them not to hurt Bob.

Edith wrapped Emma's arms so she couldn't hit Bill anymore. "Honey, it's okay! The boys are just joking. Lots of weddings have chivarees. Your daddy and I had the same thing done to us. The boys are just gonna make some noise and drive Bob around a little while. Then they'll bring him right back home. He'll be safe, I promise."

Edith looked at the three young men for help. Walt kneeled down to Emma's level.

"Yeah, Emma, we ain't really gonna hurt Bob. We're just gonna tease him and Linda some," promised Walt. "Honest! We won't hurt him."

"We'll have him home in half an hour after we take him for a ride," added Bill.

Charlie nodded in agreement. "We just want to fun 'em a little, that's all, Emma."

Emma stared at the boys with doubt in her eyes. She had known the three all her life, but now she didn't trust them. Wiping her tears with the back of her hand, she stared straight at Walt.

"You give me a pinky swear you ain't gonna hurt Bob?" she demanded.

Walt held out his right little finger, curled it around hers. "I swear we won't hurt Bob or Linda. We'll just tease 'em some, then leave 'em alone to have a nice weddin' night. I promise!"

Emma wiped away more tears, then shook her head. "Okay. Just you remember you promised!"

The boys laughed and headed for the door. Jacob was joining them for the fun.

"Can we go, too?" pleaded Mike. Owen nodded, staring at his dad with pleading eyes.

"You young men want to take responsibility for two young 'uns? asked Daniel.

"Sure, let them come," urged Charlie.

Mike and Owen ran to get their coats. They couldn't believe their dad had agreed for them to go. They weren't going to give him any time to think about his decision. In thirty seconds, they were out the door, running for the car.

"Have them home before too late," Daniel admonished to Jacob. "We got chores to do in the morning."

Jacob nodded and reluctantly headed for the door. The last thing he wanted was to watch his two younger brothers cut into the fun, and the older guys would have to watch what they said and did. Too late to do anything about it now, as the two youngsters were already in the car.

Emma stood with her nose pressed against the window, watching the boys leave. She moaned to herself, *Why am I always too little to do anything? Life just ain't fair.*

Chapter 5

By the time Emma was seven, she had accepted her role as mother's helper in the family. She dearly loved her brothers, but she always ranked the youngest, so she missed out on a lot of their fun.

One early spring afternoon, Mike, fifteen, and Owen, twelve, ran through the yard in a major game of troublemaking. They teased each other relentlessly, sometimes getting under each other's skin. Finally, they raced around the back yard. Mike had a five-buckle overshoe in his hand, threatening to slam Owen with it.

"I'll get you for saying that!" yelled Mike. He swung his arm, and the overshoe accidentally slipped from his grasp. The boot sailed across space and crashed through the kitchen window.

The next thing they heard was a scream of pain. Mike and Owen froze, stared at each other, then raced inside, slamming the screen door. They found Emma with blood streaming down her face. She cried in fright, having trouble seeing for the blood on her hands that she had brushed across her face.

Edith came running from upstairs where she had been cleaning. "What's goin' on?" she demanded. "Oh, my stars in heaven! What happen'?"

She grabbed Emma in her arms, jerked a towel off the rack, and pressed it against Emma's face to reduce the bleeding. She knew head wounds always bled the worst, and she had to find the wound source.

"Steady, Emma," Edith crooned. "Easy now. Let me take a look."

Edith tried to catch Emma's hands to wipe the blood away. Emma kept wailing, more from fright than pain. Finally, Edith could see a cut just under Emma's left eye. A glass shard had sliced through Emma's cheek, just missing her eye.

"You boys get me a clean rag," she demanded. "Right now! Move!"

Mike finally shook off his fright and wet another towel. "Here, Mom," he said as he handed her the towel. "We didn't mean to hurt Emma. It was an accident! Honest!"

"We can't worry about that now. I've got to stop the bleeding," she replied. "Now, Emma, you aren't hurt too bad. Just a little blood. You're gonna be fine."

Edith held the wet towel against the cut. "Mike, you get me the mercurochrome. That'll fix you up, Emma."

Mike grabbed the bottle from the medicine shelf Edith kept in the kitchen.

"Now, Emma, you just relax. The bleeding has almost stopped. It's just a little cut, so this medicine will disinfect the cut and you'll be just fine. I'll even put on one of those sticky bandages to keep the cut shut."

Emma rested her head on her mother's chest. She still hiccupped a little but had nearly stopped crying. She hated to cry in front of her brothers, for she didn't want to seem like a baby.

Mike found a bandage and tore off the wrapper. Edith wiped the area clean, dried it, and stuck on the pad.

"There!" she declared, looking at Emma reassuringly. "You're all fixed up. Now let's wash your hands and clean the rest of your face. We'll change your dress so I can wash out the blood.

"You boys, git the broom and dustpan. You git that broken glass cleaned up right now!"

"Yes, ma'am," was all they could say. They hung their heads and headed for the porch closet. Without a word, they grabbed a waste basket, broom, and dustpan. Carefully, they swept up the broken glass from the linoleum and small rug and dropped it into the basket.

"Now you boys take this wet rag and sweep the area with it. That will pick up any tiny pieces of glass that're left. Then give me the rag," ordered Edith.

By evening, Daniel couldn't help noticing the broken window as he dragged himself back to the house. He had been working hard all day, now dog tired, and the last thing he needed was one more task to do.

"What happened?" he demanded.

Edith replied, "Let Mike and Owen tell you."

Mike and Owen positioned themselves on the far side of the kitchen table.

"It was an accident! Honest! We didn't mean to break the window," pleaded Mike.

"Yeah, Dad, the boot just slipped," added Owen.

"Tell what happened next," ordered Edith.

"Well, the glass cut Emma's face," Mike managed to whisper.

Daniel looked up, concerned about his only daughter. He strode into the living room, where Emma was resting on the couch. One look at the bandage placement, and Daniel could see how serious the cut could have been.

"That cut dang near hit her eye!" he yelled at the two boys. "She could have been blinded!"

Daniel knew about being blinded. In 1896 when he was just twenty-five years old, he suffered a gunshot wound while hunting in the Ozark region of Missouri. A cousin accidentally shot him in the center of his forehead. For twenty-four hours, the doctor thought Daniel would not live, but he survived. After returning to Nodaway county, Daniel had more treatment by Barnard and St. Joseph doctors. The bullet, which was discharged from a large bore rifle, had pierced his forehead and coursed through his brain to lodge in the cerebellum, about an inch and a half from the back of his head. The bullet's entry destroyed the vision of his right eye, but his mental faculties remained unimpaired. He would carry the large bullet in his brain all his life. Dr. Larabee of Barnard contributed an article about the unique injury and the fact Daniel survived to a Chicago medical journal, which published the account.

Daniel almost lost control. He grabbed the two boys' arms, leading them outside. There he gave each of them a good whipping with his belt strap. He wanted them to remember what being careless could cost someone. And they did.

****

The summer of 1929 stayed hotter than usual. Long Branch Creek ceased flowing along the west edge of the long pasture. Pockets of water remained in deeper spots, but no rains came to provide fresh water in July.

"You boys are hot, I know," cautioned Daniel, "but you stay away from that creek. The water's bad this time of year. No swimming, understand?"

"Yes, sir," Mike and Owen agreed.

Yet the hot days just worsened. Finally, Mike looked at Owen. "We gotta cool off somehow. The house is so hot we can't sleep upstairs." They'd been sleeping on the screened-in porch at night.

"Yeah, so?" replied Owen.

"Let's go swimming in the creek. It's got potholes with cool water. We'll keep our heads above water, so we won't have to worry," cajoled Mike.

Owen looked doubtful. "You know what Dad said. We wasn't to go near the creek. He'll be mad."

"Only if he finds out. He's out cutting hay this afternoon. He won't miss us for a bit. Let's go now!"

Mike started across the barnyard to cut through the back paddock. Owen, dragging his feet, followed.

Trees along the creek provided cooler shade. Owen did enjoy even the slight temperature drop that frying-pan hot day.

"Let's walk along until we find a bigger hole with more water," suggested Mike.

They walked over and under brush and trees that leaned into the creek, their roots undercut by spring floods. Finally, they found a good spot.

"Okay, last one in's late for supper," yelled Mike as he discarded his clothes and waded into the waterhole.

"Alright. I'm coming." Owen undressed and followed Mike into the water. The boys could swim a little, enough to float and dog paddle around.

The water was refreshing, and both boys soon were laughing and splashing each other. As Owen swung his arm to grab water to soak Mike, his foot slipped on the side of the waterhole. His head dunked into the stagnant water, and he came up sputtering the dirty liquid out of his mouth.

"Ugh! That's muddy tasting," complained Owen.

"Yeah, you did wash your mouth out that time!"

They played for an hour, judging from the sunlight sliding down the trees. Soon it would be time for them to do chores.

Mike led the way. "We better git dressed and back. We gotta be home before Dad comes in from the field, or we'll git in trouble for sure."

He shook and wiped water off his skin, then donned his clothes. Owen repeated his actions, and the two headed home.

By the next morning, Owen didn't feel well. His face was flushed, and he felt hotter than usual even in early morning.

"Owen, you okay?" his mother asked. "You look too pink. Let me feel your forehead." She pressed her hand onto his head, then looked even more worried. "You've got a fever!"

Owen could hardly sit up at the table. "Yeah, I don't feel so great. Can I lay down?"

"You go lie on the couch. I'll git you some cool wash rags." Edith pointed him to the living room. She pumped some fresh water into a pan, then followed Owen to the other room.

By noon, everyone knew Owen's health appeared seriously in danger. His fever soared higher, without anyone needing a thermometer to record the change.

Emma watched her brother's sweaty face. She could tell from her parents' tone of voice Owen was in danger. At seven years old, Emma tried to act as grownup as her mom to handle the situation.

"Daniel, Owen needs a doctor. He's real sick," worried Edith. "I know the doctor costs money, but I don't know what's wrong. He's never been this hot before."

Studying his son's face, Daniel felt desperate. "Jacob, ride to the Brittons. They got a phone. Have Wilma call the doc and tell him to hurry!"

Jacob raced out the door and saddled the horse. He slapped the reins, and Buster galloped out of the barnyard. In a few minutes, Jacob was sliding off the horse and running to the neighbor's door.

"Hey, Mrs. Britton! It's me, Jacob. Can I come in?"

Wilma dried her hands and turned from the sink where she had been doing dishes. "Jacob, what's your rush about? Come on in and sit a while."

"Can't, Mrs. Britton. Owen's real sick. Can you call the doc in Barnard? We need him out here fast!"

"Good grief! Of course! I'll ring him right now." Wilma dashed into the living room, where the oak wall phone hung. Lifting the receiver off its hook, she swung the crank three times.

"Hey, we're on the line!" shouted a neighbor's voice.

"Millie, this is Wilma. You'll just have to get off right now! I got to call the doctor!"

"Oh, goodness! Who's hurt?"

"Owen Trotter's sick. Now let me ring through!" Wilma knew within one minute of her getting off the phone with the doctor, everyone on the party line would hear about Owen. Millie was a sweet, generous woman but the biggest gossip in the township.

Wilma reached the operator in Barnard, who connected her with the doctor's home. "Yes, the Trotters need you to come quick. Owen's real sick, and they don't know why!"

"Thank heavens the roads are dried out this time of year. I'll get my car and be there soon as I can," Dr. Larabee promised.

"Thank you, Doc. I'll send the word back with Jacob. They'll be looking for you."

Jacob nodded his head, running out the door. He jumped onto the saddle and raced back home.

Wilma wrote a note to her husband and grabbed a pie and some bread she had made. She packed them in a basket and put on her summer sun bonnet. Pulling the door behind her, she started down the steps, walking to the Trotters' house a mile away.

By the time Jacob returned, Owen had severe diarrhea. They had moved him onto the porch, which was slightly cooler. Already, the bed sheets had been changed several times as Owen's symptoms worsened.

After he arrived, Dr. Larabee quickly examined Owen. The doctor studied his thermometer, watched Owen have another spasm, then motioned for his parents to move to the kitchen.

"Owen's probably got cholera," Dr. Larabee announced. Edith gasped and clamped her hand over her mouth to keep from crying out. Daniel turned pale.

"How bad?" asked Daniel.

"Bad enough," Dr. Larabee replied. "Has he been around any bad water lately?"

"Just our well water, and we've all drunk that."

Mike's eyes started to mist up. He hung his head, knowing he had to tell the truth.

"Me and Owen went swimming yesterday afternoon in the creek. I know we wasn't supposed to, but we were gonna keep our heads up and be careful. It was so dang hot, we just wanted to cool off!"

Daniel's face flashed his displeasure. "I told you boys to stay away from there! That water's been stale for weeks! You probably talked Owen into it, and now he's bad sick!"

"I know, Dad," Mike choked out. "I'm sorry. We just wanted—"

"I know what you wanted," Daniel interrupted. "But sometimes you don' know everthin'. Now your brother's seriously ill!"

"What do we do, Doc?" asked Edith, struggling to catch her breath and calm herself down.

"Well, you need to keep his fever down and pump him full of fluids. He's going to get dehydrated from the runs. Give him some chicken broth, as much as you can get him to take. Cold compresses will help. Do you have any ice blocks left from the winter cutting?"

Daniel nodded. "I've got a few in the ground where we store the milk. I'll get some chipped off and brought up." Daniel looked at Jacob, who took a bucket and headed for the icehouse.

"Other than that, we'll just have to wait and see. His fever is 105, which is not good. We've got to get it down and keep some liquids in him."

"All right. I'll get some chicken broth from the cellar and heat it up," Edith replied, glad to have something definite to do.

"I'll be back tomorrow to check on Owen. But just keep him as cool as you can. The next few days will tell."

Dr. Larabee sternly stared at Edith. "You've got to be extra careful. You're handling those soiled sheets. You be sure to wash your hands even more often and don't touch your face until you do. Those sheets have germs on them, and we don't need you getting sick, too."

Daniel and Edith stared at each other. They had lost one child already and wondered if they could handle losing another one, let alone handle the family if Edith became ill. Edith shook her head to clear out the idea.

Daniel frowned at Mike one more time. He inhaled a deep breath to relax himself, then questioned Mike.

"Did you swallow any water?"

"No, sir. I never had my head under water. And I didn't get none in my mouth," swore Mike.

"You got to let us know immediately if you start feeling poorly, you hear! Don't try to hide it if you do, understand?"

"I feel fine. And I'm so sorry about Owen. He just slipped under one time and came up with water in his mouth."

Jacob returned with some ice chips wrapped in burlap to keep them cold. Edith climbed out of the cellar with her arms carrying three quarts of chicken broth she had canned last winter.

Just then, Wilma Britton walked up the sidewalk with her basket. "I'm here to help. Just point me to a job."

"Oh, Wilma, you're an angel. If you'll heat up some broth, I'll get water started boiling to wash these sheets outside."

"You do that," Wilma agreed. "You boys head out of the house and let us women get to work. We'll call you for lunch when we get a chance to make it."

Daniel nodded and motioned for Jacob and Mike to follow him outside.

For the next two days, Edith and Wilma took turns swabbing Owen's forehead with cool rags. They used the ice sparingly, since there wasn't much available. In between, Emma pumped fresh well water to cool him down. By the afternoon of the third day, Owen's fever finally broke.

Dr. Larabee came by early in the evening. After examining Owen, he took Edith and Daniel into the kitchen and shut the porch door.

"Looks like Owen will be all right," he assured them.

Both parents sighed audibly, and Edith leaned against Daniel in relief.

"But," Dr. Larabee cautioned, "there may be one complication for Owen. We don't know why, exactly, but a high fever can sometimes result in a man not being able to have children. We'll have to wait and see, but that might be the case. Owen's fever was high for quite a while, which isn't good."

Edith felt tears sting her eyes, but she wouldn't let them fall. As long as Owen was alive, it was all that mattered to her. "We'll deal with that as we have to. Do we tell Owen, or wait until he's full grown?"

Dr. Larabee rubbed his chin in thought. "He's only twelve now. I think he's too young to understand. Let's wait until he's older. Then, Daniel, maybe you and he can have a talk before he gets serious about a girl."

Daniel considered, then agreed. "We'll just get him better. That's all that matters now."

Chapter 6

The years of Emma's world passed in the quiet flow of farming life. Barren tree limbs grew buds, then leaves, then waved bare limbs again. Fallow fields rested during the winter, then plows tore up the soil, and seeds planted became standing crops to harvest, allowing the fields to rest through another winter. Life followed a mostly predictable course, varied only by weather's storms.

The Trotters never had much cash money. Daniel always managed to pay the farm mortgage, repair his equipment, and buy seeds first before other needs were considered.

By 1930, the Great Depression had deepened, and Daniel confronted the fact he had no funds when property taxes came due. The tax collector visited the farm, where he and Daniel discussed the situation in the barnyard.

"Daniel," began Albert Miller, "you owe the money on your land. And it's due by the end of the year. I don't want to have to foreclose on your property to get them taxes paid. I truly don't." Mr. Miller had known Daniel for years, knew his hard work ethic and large family.

Daniel looked past Al to his barn and pasture. He had worked so darn hard to keep his family afloat, yet a man only had two hands and no control over what government folks did in Washington. Now he was in a pickle and knew it.

"Yep, I do owe it," replied Daniel. "But I just don' have no cash. We're just scrimping by. We got enough to eat, unlike those city folks, because we got our garden and livestock. But we got no cash. Nobody around here does."

Al nodded in agreement. He knew the local folks and how hard they worked. They were good people, the kind a person wanted as neighbors and friends.

Finally, Daniel rubbed his right hand against his chin. "Would you consider taking a cow instead of cash? You could sell her and git probably more than the taxes are due."

Others in the area faced the same predicament since no one had hard currency available. Daniel's trade would not be the first barter Al had taken.

"Well I guess that might do," considered Al. "If you can get her trucked to Maryville to the stock sale next week, I'll be there. You can sign a bill of sale to me, and I'll put her up for auction."

"Can do," replied Daniel. "I'll have the cow there on time somehow."

Al cautioned, "But if the price don't cover the taxes, you'll still owe the balance."

Daniel nodded. "I'll send you one of my best cows. She's had a good quality calf ever' year."

The men shook hands and Al drove away. Daniel breathed a sigh of relief, but he regretted having to part with a good cow.

Nine-year-old Emma had heard everything from the barn. She had been playing inside when Mr. Miller had arrived. Her eyes filled with tears. She knew how proud her dad was and how hard he worked to keep the family fed and clothed. He didn't owe anyone any money for he always paid his bills on time, either with cash or barter. Her pride in him grew as she realized the creative solution he had found for the tax problem. She also felt relieved their home was safe for another year.

****

Life in northwestern Missouri was predictable. People in the Barnard area had always provided others a helping hand when needed. They knew they could be in the same predicament if something happened in their family, so being available to others was just their way of life.

Few people traveled far from home, and many had never been farther than St. Jo, some thirty-two miles south. First, the roads made travel difficult much of the year. Paved roads were scarce, and the farm and county roads were often deep in mud during rainy periods or winter thaws. Second, farm life required someone's presence every day, usually twice a day for milking, at least. Taking a trip overnight meant finding someone to handle the chores when that person also had his own chores to do. If an emergency required leaving town, others would help, but a vacation was considered a luxury few farmers could afford, either financially or from the time commitment.

Jacob married Helen Olsen, a local girl from Bolckow, Missouri, in June 1932. Emma was eleven and thoroughly enjoyed the wedding. That time she understood the fun of a chivaree but was still not allowed to attend the mainly male event. Jacob and Helen settled on a farm one mile west and a half mile south of Highway 71, the paved road west of Barnard that led south to St. Jo and north to Maryville.

Emma grew taller as the years progressed. She followed her brothers in gaining height each year, always being the tallest child in her one-room school. Finally, some of the older boys started their teenage growth spurts, but even at eleven, Emma nearly matched them.

Emma accepted the male and female role definitions without truly stopping to consider them. She helped her mother with housework, gardening, canning, selling eggs and cream, washing, and sewing. Those jobs were what women did.

Yet she wanted more. Since she was little, her dream had always been to become a teacher.

She had started practicing on her dream at a young age. The Trotter family did not splurge on many birthday presents. On her special day, however, she would come to breakfast to find her plate turned upside down. Underneath would be her birthday gift, some small token of love, usually handmade. One year when she was young, the gift was a cloth doll.

Emma set up her own schoolroom in one corner of her small bedroom. Over time, she taught her doll everything Emma herself learned in school. Emma only had the doll, never having a teddy bear to add as another student.

With her goal always in her mind, Emma studied hard in school. She loved learning, doing her homework the best she could. Her parents had little formal education, and her brothers were almost as lacking. Bob and Jacob had finished the eighth grade. Mike and Owen had attended high school as freshmen for one semester, before Daniel decided they didn't need more since they were destined to be farmers. Both Mike and Owen wanted more, for they loved school, too. But Daniel guided the decisions about family males. All of Emma's brothers were very intelligent, but tradition dictated education was of little value when a farmer needed to be in the fields learning the trade.

As she grew into a preteen, Emma thought about her brothers and what they had missed in their schooling.

How do I dare want to go to high school when they never got the chance? Emma chided herself. I know I'm good at school, but I'm supposed to be a farmer's wife. So Dad says. And the only high school is in Maryville, which is fifteen miles away! How would I ever get there?

Chapter 7

Emma wiped her sweating palms against her cotton dress. At thirteen, she had grown taller than her mother, but lanky as her brothers. Even with all the lifting, hoeing, pumping, and other work she did, her upper arms barely had bumps for biceps. Now her slender knees knocked together, and she knew her father would be able to hear them rattle.

Trying to inhale deeply, Emma walked into the living room where Daniel rested in his favorite chair. The two boys had departed for a Friday evening with their friends. Edith still rattled dishes in the kitchen.

Daniel looked up from his paper. His face showed how tired he felt after working in the spring fields until dark. Rains were predicted next week, and he wanted to get the main field plowed before they arrived.

"Dad," Emma said softly as she grabbed the sides of her dress with her shaky hands. "Could we talk a minute?"

Since Emma rarely needed a private conversation, Daniel knew something important bothered her.

"Pull up that chair," he said as he pointed to the straight-backed chair by the small writing desk.

Emma slid the chair beside his and seated herself. Taking a deep breath, she tried to look her father in the eyes and appear much calmer than she felt.

"Dad, I really like school," she began. "I try hard and my teacher says I'm one of her best students."

Daniel nodded his head, watching Emma intently. He could look so serious most of the time, and Emma tightened her hold on her courage to continue with her announcement. She had rehearsed the words for weeks, trying to work out the logic to convince her father to agree to her dream.

"I know that my brothers never went very far in school," she continued, working to keep her voice from quavering. "But, Dad, I really want to go to high school. I want to become a teacher!"

Daniel paused a moment. "But you're going to marry some farmer. What good would all that learning be if you just stayed home on the farm later?"

"Maybe I won't marry a farmer," Emma countered. "I don't know what

I want to do about getting married, but I've always wanted to be a teacher. Most people seem to like me, and I learn really fast in my subjects. I want to share my knowledge with other kids, help them enjoy school, too."

With a sigh, Daniel studied Emma's face. He knew she was smart, and she rarely asked for anything special.

"It wouldn't work," Daniel stated factually. "We live too far from Highway 71, the only road the bus goes on to Maryville. And that's too far away for a young girl to be goin' by herself."

"But I've figured it out," replied Emma. "If I could live at Jacob's house, I could walk the mile and a half to the highway to catch the bus. The Sinclair gas station Criss owns is right on the corner, so I could wait there until the bus came each day."

Her father sighed. "Jacob wouldn't want you living with him and his wife. Helen's got her hands full with the new baby girl."

"But I could help with the baby when I was there. Helen would let me, I know."

"Have you talked to Jacob and Helen?"

"Not yet, but I know they would let me. Please, Dad, I want to be a teacher, and I have to go to high school to become one."

Daniel rested his head against the back of his chair. He looked older than his sixty-four years, even a little pale. He closed his eyes to think, not wanting to accept his only daughter had grown up so fast and had her heart set on something so unusual for a girl in 1935 around Barnard.

When he opened his eyes, he saw Edith standing in the doorway. He knew she had overheard the conversation but would not try to influence his decision, at least not directly. She had her ways to get him to accept her viewpoint sometimes, but she just watched him now.

"There's no cost!" asserted Emma. "The Horace Mann High School is funded by the college, so kids don't pay for anything. They just have to get to the school, and the student teachers from the college do a lot of the teaching. I just have to get there, and the bus is free if I can get to the highway."

If Emma left home, then his fifty-four-year-old wife would be alone with all the work. Mike still lived at home, but Daniel suspected Katherine Newmeyer was going to get him married by next spring, if not sooner. They had been dating for a while, and they seemed like they belonged together. Owen was eighteen, but not dating anyone regularly. All the boys looked a lot alike, six feet or a little taller, lanky but strong, and too good-looking for their own safety when it came to being around females. Still, Edith would have a houseful of three men to tend alone, when she was showing her age, too.

Emma gripped her hands together in her lap. She had run through her prepared speech, and the decision lay with her dad. If he objected, she didn't have a prayer of getting to be a teacher.

Raising his head, Daniel looked at Emma for a long moment. Finally, he made up his mind, which rarely changed once he announced his decision.

"You have to talk to Jacob and Helen. If they're willin' to board you, then you have to agree to work for them while you're there. If they say yes, then I guess you better plan to go."

Clasping her hands to her mouth in surprise, Emma felt tears sting her eyes. She jumped out of the chair, hugging her father.

"Oh, Dad, thank you, thank you!" she cried. "I'll talk to them at church Sunday. I just know they'll say yes. Oh, I'll make you so proud of me, Dad, I really will. I'll work harder than I've ever worked, and I'll make it happen!"

Daniel smiled at her enthusiasm but realized she didn't fully understand what moving away from home might mean. She had only stayed away occasionally for an overnight visit with a girlfriend, or once in a while to stay with Bob and Linda. Jacob lived nearly six miles from the homestead and a mile and a half from the school bus stop. Emma would have a long walk every morning and evening, in all kinds of weather to catch the bus, then have homework and nightly chores to do when she got to Jacob's house.

Edith smiled sadly at Daniel. She, too, knew that Emma's leaving would be harder on her own life, but she and Daniel shared a secret.

****

Daniel hadn't felt well for a long time. Since fall 1934, he had lacked the energy he used to have. Age provided one answer, and being a farmer, Daniel never went to a doctor. Doctors cost money, unless they would barter for home goods or meat, and people usually just took care of themselves.

By early in 1935, Daniel knew something different kept draining his strength more each day. Finally, Edith convinced him to see Dr. Larabee.

After a thorough exam, which Daniel found intrusive, Dr. Larabee announced his decision.

"Daniel, I'm going to send your blood sample to a doctor I know in St. Jo. He'll give me a more definite answer, but I think you have cancer in your groin area."

Daniel's muscles froze and his heart skipped. He knew he felt tired but never considered such a cause.

Dr. Larabee continued. "I know it's not a good diagnosis, but I'm pretty sure I'm right. And it's not a good place to be. There's no cure. The cancer may go fast or slow, I can't say. We'll just have to see."

"Can I still farm?" asked Daniel, dreading the answer.

"If you feel up to it. But at some point, you won't have the strength. And the pain will increase as the cancer progresses. I can give you something when that happens, but it'll make your brain real fuzzy. And it wouldn't be safe to be around farm machinery or animals then."

Daniel tried to catch his breath. How was he going to keep paying off the mortgage if he couldn't farm? Mike was going to get married soon, he felt. Only Owen would be left to do all the farm work alone. At eighteen, that was a load for a young man to carry while being responsible for his mother, too.

As Daniel's mind raced through future obstacles, Dr. Larabee pulled him back to the present.

"Why don't you go home and talk to Edith about it," he suggested. "You two can come up with good answers if you give her a chance. She's got a level head on her shoulders. She'll be there for you, you know."

Daniel had left the office, his mind clouded with fears for his family's livelihood and for facing his own death much sooner than he had hoped. He had never really stopped to think about dying. Yes, he had been through his parents' deaths, but that had been in 1917, years ago. Since then, Daniel had been too busy keeping food on the table and a roof over their heads to worry about death.

Opening the old Ford pickup's door, he climbed onto the seat. His hands grabbed the steering wheel, something solid to hold while his world spun out of his control.

Now he had no choice but to consider what to do. In the last six months, he had truly seen a difference in his health. He got winded, felt more exhausted at the end of each farming day. At least now he knew the cause of his declining energy level.

Daniel thought of Edith being a widow. She would have no income and had never worked away from home. She kept the cream and egg sale money, but those funds would never keep her alive if she were left alone. Daniel had read about Congress discussing some kind of Social Security bill that spring, but he didn't really understand what it was or if it could help Edith or if it would even pass into law.

Yes, he would have to talk to Edith soon. She knew something was wrong, had seen the changes even before he had admitted them to himself. She was a strong woman, even if she looked thin and frail. She had kept house for seven people for years, but Daniel had produced the true family income. Now how long would he be able to work?

Later, Daniel and Edith walked along the dirt county road by themselves. The full moon lighted the path, which they had always enjoyed walking together. Daniel told her what the doctor said, and Edith had cried and held onto him. Then they got down to business.

"I don't know how long I can work," Daniel admitted. "I'm doing okay now, but I can feel I'm slowing down. Do you think Mike will leave soon?"

"Yes, I suspect him and Kate will marry next year. He's been talkin' to old Mr. Anderson about his farm just southwest of Barnard. It's got bottom-land, with some low hills. It's a good farm, if Anderson will sell it to him at a price he can handle."

"I know the place. Mike mentioned he might go work for Anderson this fall. He could learn from him what the farm needs and make himself some cash as a down payment. I've been paying Mike wages when I could, and I think he's been saving some to buy a place."

Edith nodded. "That leaves Owen. Has he said if he wants to stay on the homestead any longer?"

"He seems happy to stay put, but I know young men want to be on their own. I guess I got to ask him if he wants to buy the homestead. If he does, then he could start taking over more work, since I'm not going to be much good pretty soon."

Daniel took a ragged breath, on the edge of crying himself, which he rarely did. "Oh, Edith, how can I leave you alone? What're you gonna do? How're you gonna live?"

Taking his face in her hands, Edith stared hard into his eyes. "Daniel, we've been married thirty-five years! We've buried a daughter, seen everybody through flus and measles and every other illness, and nearly lost Owen. We've always done things together, and we're not going to change that."

She kissed his lips. "If Owen agrees to buy the farm, he'll need someone to take care of the house. I can stay with him, help him out. If he gets married, then I'll decide what to do then. With the farm money from Owen, I can at least rent a little house in Barnard or Maryville. I can sew, and people like my baking. Maybe I'll sell my pies and cakes and such."

Hugging Daniel, she tried to be braver than she felt. "I'll miss you so much! How'll I get through the cold nights without you keepin' me warm? A bed warming stone can't hold me like you do."

Daniel nearly crushed her to his chest. "Oh, old gal, I sure do hate the thought of leaving you alone! But we got four good boys and Emma. They'll take care of you, you'll see. We knew someday one of us would be gone. We just thought it might be a while longer, that's all. We'll just have to work through this. I need your strength now, 'cause mine is about all washed out at the moment."

****

Daniel and Edith talked to the boys, one by one, as they got a chance to do so in private. But they didn't tell Emma. They didn't want her to worry until things got really serious.

Now, watching Emma's huge smile as she hugged Edith and laughingly raced to her room, Daniel knew it had been the right decision. If Emma became a teacher, and Daniel was gone, then she could support herself until she found a husband. She could also help care for her mother, maybe even live with her if Owen got married and Edith had to move away from the farmstead.

Daniel felt one huge worry had been conquered. He would live as long as he could, for Emma needed a father. But if she was living with Jacob and Helen, then she would already be starting to separate her life from his and Edith's. She would be growing into her own young womanhood, maybe sooner than she should, but learning she could count on herself if Daniel was not around. She also had four big brothers who had always looked after their little sister.

Chapter 8

During spring 1935, Emma grew more excited about her upcoming eighth-grade graduation. All year, she had worked extra hard to prove she truly deserved to go to high school. She didn't want her dad to regret his decision to let her attend. Her grades stayed strong, even with her helping out more around the house and farm.

She could tell her father's health had declined. Finally, she cornered Edith.

"Dad looks so thin, and he's not as full of energy. Mom, what's wrong with him?" pleaded Emma.

Edith knew the question would come, but she had delayed bringing it up. "Your dad's very sick," she began. "He's been not feelin' good for a long time, and now he's in a lot of pain, also."

Emma felt her throat constrict, and tears filled her eyes. "You mean he's dying?"

"Yes, I'm afraid so. And there's nothing Dr. Larabee can do for him. We'll just let him be as comfortable as we can."

As she began to cry, her mother gave her a reassuring hug. "He's proud of what you've done, and he knows we'll be okay. But we're sure gonna miss him, won't we?"

Emma felt her world collapsing around her. Although often stern, her father was the family's foundation, even if her brothers were grown men now.

"How much longer will he have?" asked Emma.

"No one knows for sure. We'll just have to keep him here as long as we can."

****

Emma's graduation was planned for April 19, 1935. By then, Daniel had lost ground in his health. He had reduced his farming activities, leaving Owen mostly in charge. Daniel provided guidance on crop planting and harvesting schedules and animal care.

"I'm not going to my graduation ceremony," stated Emma, determination etched on her face. "I want to be with Dad now."

Owen studied Emma. "No, Dad wants you to graduate. You're goin', and I'm drivin' you there and back. You even have a new dress bought, and you look swell in it."

A momentary tiny smile crept onto her face. "But we don't know how long he'll live. I don't want to be gone and maybe him not be here when I get back! I couldn't take that!"

Heaving a sigh to mask his own concern, Owen was adamant. "No, you're goin'. You worked too hard for this, and you're bound to get some certificates for bein' a good student. Dad would come if he could, and Mom will stay with him while we're gone."

Emma looked dubious.

"It's only a couple of hours, and you know you want to go. So just make up your mind you're goin', and I'll be there to represent the family."

Finally, Emma nodded. "But it won't be the same. It won't seem like fun knowing Dad can't come. It just isn't fair he's not going to be around much longer!"

Owen could only agree. They stared at each other, feeling helpless. Owen was nineteen, wanting to feel completely like a grown man, but still having enough of a boy in him to want his father's advice a few more years.

When Dad was gone, Bob, at thirty-two, by tradition as the eldest son would take over the leadership role for the Trotter family. But Bob had been married for nine years already and was buying his own farm. He and Linda were rearing their nearly three-year-old son Doug. Bob had his hands full without worrying about his widowed mother and fourteen-year-old sister.

Jacob had married Helen three years ago and worked his own farm. Their baby Alice was three months old.

Mike had married Katherine two months earlier and had his own farm. The only son left to buy the homestead was Owen.

Owen knew he was the logical person to take charge of Edith's and Emma's care. Squaring his shoulders, Owen headed outside to think.

The fresh air and open spaces helped clear his head. If—no, when—his father died, he would be primarily responsible for his mother's care. He needed to talk to her and decide on a fair price for the farm. Then they needed to agree on a payment schedule, and of course, the other three brothers would have to approve everything. That way, his mother would have some income. He would take care of her for now, but if she wanted to move away from the farm, then she would require money to live.

What of Emma? Jacob and Helen had agreed she could live with them in the fall and go to Horace Mann High School in Maryville. But Emma would have to get herself to and from Highway 71 to catch the bus every day. Jacob would be farming, and Helen had the baby to tend. With an extra mouth to feed, Helen needed Emma to do her share of the work around the house to pay for her lodging. Emma wanted her schooling so badly she had accepted any terms.

Life was getting so complicated. When his brothers still lived at home, the house had been cramped with seven people, and the boys always joked and played tricks on each other. Now, just Owen would be there, with Edith keeping house for the two of them. Emma would come home on weekends if someone could give her a ride from Jacob's to the homestead. Mom will sure miss her, thought Owen.

****

Finally, the day of Emma's eighth-grade graduation arrived. She appeared down the stairs in her new dress, smiling shyly at being the center of attention.

"Come here and show your dad," encouraged Edith. "You look so pretty, and we curled your hair just right."

Emma entered the master bedroom. Her father lay propped on some pillows, trying to smile through his pain when he saw Emma.

"My girl," he gasped, "you do look a sight! So growed up!"

His smile pleased Emma, who replied, "I wish you and Mom were coming. It's not as fun without you. I should stay home tonight. It's not such a big deal."

Daniel frowned at her. "You worked for so long. You got to git that certificate. You'll be happy you went later on; you'll see."

Emma tried to smile for him. "Okay. Owen's going to drive me and be there for the ceremony. Then we'll come right home."

"You go have a good time," her dad whispered. "Your mom and I will enjoy the house to ourselves for once!" he joked.

Emma followed Owen to the old pickup. They drove the dirt road to the schoolhouse, thankful the roads were dry.

The nine students and their parents entered the small building, seating themselves as best they could on the few school benches and extra borrowed chairs. Only three students were actually graduating from eighth grade, but everyone attended to encourage the younger ones to keep going until they, too, could have their proud day.

Brent, Harry, and Emma took the seats of honor at the front of the classroom, right before the blackboard and facing the guests. Miss Kline, their teacher, and Mr. Masters, the township superintendent, sat to their right.

Mr. Masters rose and addressed the gathering. "I want to welcome all of you to the 1936 eighth-grade graduation ceremony. Thank you for coming on such a lovely evening. We're all glad the heat hasn't hit us yet, since they are so many of us here tonight!"

Everyone politely laughed. Mr. Masters tended to prefer long speeches, and the group hoped this evening he might make an exception.

"These fine young people before you have worked hard on their studies. They have walked to and from school in all kinds of weather, have helped out at home, I'm sure, and still have done their homework. We are proud of them and know they will become good citizens of this area. Now, I'm going to turn over the program to Miss Kline."

Everyone clapped louder, glad he had kept his part short for a change. Miss Kline stood, looking a little uneasy in the presence of Mr. Masters.

"Students," she began, looking at the three to her left, "I'm so proud of you. You've been a joy to teach—at least most of the time!" She laughed.

Everyone knew Harry loved practical jokes, which he had managed to pull on every student over the years. Some students took it in good fun, but a couple had reacted with less appreciation.

"Now we're gathered here to honor you for your hard work. I tried to push you to learn as much as you could. I know that some will not have the chance to go further in school, so what you took in here can be added to what you read and learn in the future. So let's get on with the certificates."

Miss Kline announced Brent had received the Citizenship award for his good conduct at school. Mr. Masters had Brent stand, shook his hand, and handed him the certificate plus his graduation degree. The papers, fine linen with fancy writing on them and signed by Mr. Masters and Miss Kline, looked very professional. Everyone clapped appreciatively.

"Next, Harry has been awarded the History award. He has a real talent for understanding the big world and what history has shown us."

Everyone clapped again as Harry grinned and took his two sheets.

"Finally, I have the pleasure to present to Emma the English and Math awards. She also had perfect attendance for the 1934–1935 school year. I'm very pleased to announce Emma plans to attend Horace Mann High School this fall!"

Emma rose, felt herself blushing, and shyly accepted her four certificates from Mr. Masters. She could hear Owen clapping the loudest from the back of the room.

After a few more words from the two speakers, everyone adjourned outside. The mothers had brought refreshments and lemonade, which everyone enjoyed by torchlight. All the parents shook the three graduates' hands, adding words of encouragement.

Also, they expressed to Emma how they hoped her father would get better soon. But Emma could see in their eyes they knew the truth. Everyone accepted her father was dying. The grapevine in a small farming community was more efficient than the best telegraph system in the world. Little news remained secret for long, but it also provided a way for others to offer assistance without having to pry the family with endless questions. Emma understood they were doing their best to give her comfort.

Finally, Owen and Emma said their goodbyes. The old pickup rattled home over the rutted road, with its two passengers sitting quietly in thought.

At home, they cautiously entered, knowing at the late hour of nine Daniel was probably asleep. But to their surprise, Edith met them in the kitchen. On the table lay two wrapped presents and a card.

"Happy graduation!" announced Edith. "Your dad and I wanted to give you a little party of our own. And we wanted you to have something to remember this day."

She gently pushed one of the presents toward Emma. Emma stared at the pretty paper and pink bow. With fumbling fingers, she opened the package. Inside was a new dress, a more grownup-looking dress.

"You'll be goin' to high school, so I made you a new dress to start your freshman year," Edith announced.

Emma, overcome with gratitude, wondered how her mother had managed to find time to sew a new dress. She had been caring for Daniel day and night, as well as handling the house and garden while Emma was gone during school hours. Tears filled her eyes as she hugged Edith.

"Oh, Mom, it's beautiful. It's just perfect. I'll be extra careful with it! Thank you so much!" she managed to say.

Edith beamed with pride. "You deserve it for all your hard work. Now open the other one."

The next box was small, with the same printed paper and tiny pink bow. Emma carefully opened it, then stood still in shock. Inside lay a new watch, something that would have cost her mother dearly, after paying doctor bills and medicine.

"Oh, no, this is too nice!" exclaimed Emma. "This is too expensive!"

Shaking her head, Edith had tears in her eyes, too. "No, Emma, you need a watch to know what time it is so you don't miss the bus to school. You only got one chance to catch it each day, so you got to be there when it comes and when it's time to come home. Your father and I wanted you to have this, so you take and use it!"

Emma stared at her mother. She couldn't stop the tears of joy streaming down her face.

Even Owen was a little misty-eyed, for he knew the work his mother had done every time Emma had been out of the house. Owen had chosen the watch for her when he was in Maryville buying seed. Edith had saved her milk and cream money for weeks to buy the dress material and watch, with Daniel's approval.

"Is Dad still awake?" asked Emma.

"Yes, I woke him when you two got back. He wanted me to. He's heard everything we've said."

Emma ran to her father's bed, saw his smiling face, and gently hugged him. "Thank you so much, Dad! You and Mom shouldn't have done it! You both need the money more!"

Daniel shook his head. "No, you're nearly a grown woman, and you need to look grown up when you go to Maryville. You may be just a farmer's daughter, but you'll look grand goin' to school with those city kids."

At last, everyone said good night, heading to their separate bedrooms. The long day had ended on a delightful, but somewhat sad, note.

Emma felt her childhood had ended that evening. She felt more adult, thinking about heading to high school in the fall. She would make herself another dress this summer, maybe two dresses, if she could earn the money for the material. Then she would have enough clothes for a week at school. She drifted to sleep with happy thoughts for once, just enjoying the moment.

****

Daniel died on Friday, April 17, 1936. Edith, the four boys, and Emma had been in and out of his room all day. Daniel had his family with him as he slipped away in late afternoon. No more pain, no more pills, no more having to stay in bed when he wanted to be outside in the fresh air working his farmland. Daniel's body had finally given out.

The day before, Dr. Larabee had checked on Daniel, shaken his head in sorrow, and told Edith to have the boys come home by the next day. As soon as Bob, Jacob, and Mike had finished morning chores, they arrived quickly at the farmstead.

Edith knew the end was near, but she was bereft when it happened. She had never even dated another man, only Daniel, and now after nearly thirty-six years, he was gone.

The boys hugged her, assuring her they would take care of her. She smiled back at them through her tears but understood they had their own families and farms to manage. They couldn't be there every time she started to cry when she thought of Daniel. That part, she knew, she alone would handle.

By early evening, neighbors appeared bringing covered dishes and desserts and asking what they could do to help. Wilma Britton took over crowd control, directing where to place food and telling folks to come inside and see Edith. Edith gladly accepted her help.

Emma was the odd one out. Her brothers had their wives for support. Owen had the farm to occupy his time. Edith had the well-wishers. Emma was included by everyone, but she still felt so alone.

How can I leave Mom in the fall to go back to school? I've been living with Jacob, so far from her. She's had all the gardening, canning, and housework to do by herself, except when I came home on weekends. Now she'll be so lonely without Dad.

Edith's face showed her aging faster during Daniel's illness, and Emma worried about her health. She just couldn't lose her mother, also!

Dr. Larabee had notified Price Funeral Home in Maryville. They sent a hearse to pick up Daniel's body the next morning. Edith didn't have any cash for a fancy funeral, so they had to settle for a pine box for Daniel. That was hard for Edith to take, wishing she could give him a nice metal casket.

Everyone in Barnard, Guilford, and Bolckow knew Daniel Trotter.

Luckily, the weather held, and the family had an early afternoon service at the Barnard First Christian Church. Then they all trekked to the nearby Barnard Cemetery for the interment. The ladies' church auxiliary supplied refreshments afterward, so it was a long day before the families headed home.

While eating refreshments, friends tried to lighten the mood with stories about Daniel. Such anecdotes helped ease the tension somewhat. Edith held up well, with Emma standing by her side most of the day. The brothers presented a strong front, but Emma could see their loss shining in their eyes. Daniel had been a force in the family, and now the central authority was gone, leaving them to shift positions and restructure the family roles. Edith still provided the senior generation, the source of family wisdom, but the male leadership now fell on Bob. The three other brothers joined him in moving up to the senior male generation positions, which they would have gladly delayed many years had Daniel been able to live.

Even Reverend Porath spoke up. He knew Daniel had always attended church more to please Edith than from a strong religious conviction of his own. Daniel had always figured God knew he couldn't be in church every Sunday because God sent the weather on His pleasing, not Daniel's. Daniel's crops had to be harvested before bad weather came, especially the more delicate hay that wouldn't stand up to a hailstorm. So if God wanted Daniel in church, He should have kept the weather good until midweek instead of making Daniel work on a Sunday because the radio said a storm was going to hit Monday.

Yes, the minister understood farm folks and their needs. He didn't hold it against them when they missed church occasionally. They were good people, for the most part, with the very few real stinkers in the area not being church people anyway. He promised Edith he would be out later in the week to see her.

By late afternoon, the four brothers needed to get home. They had cows to milk, animals to feed, and equipment to check before starting work the next day. They gave each other big bear hugs, speaking of getting by soon to see their mom, took their wives' hands, and headed for their trucks.

Emma followed Owen and her mother to the pickup. They squeezed inside. Edith wanted to go by the cemetery one more time but knew she couldn't handle the emotions if she did. She kept quiet and let Owen head east toward the farmstead.

Times were changing, whether or not any of them wanted new ways.

The family would readjust and move forward. Life and death always formed a part of farm life. Animals lived and died. Crops lived and died. People lived and died. Time would lessen the wounds, never completely heal them.

Emma wished they had owned a camera so she would have had more photos of her father. The few they possessed would have to do. The rest of the pictures she would need to etch into her memory. Her world had changed drastically, and she couldn't imagine what the next version would be.

Chapter 9

In the fall of 1935, Emma had moved most of her clothes to her brother Jacob's house. Every morning, she walked one-half mile north, then downhill one mile east on dirt roads to reach paved Highway 71. A small Sinclair gas station occupied the corner, and two other farm teenagers waited for the school bus to take them into Maryville to Horace Mann High School.

Emma and the other freshmen students had an orientation session on the first day. Then they were released to find their lockers and get to their classes.

Feeling rushed and not wanting to be late for her first class, Emma tossed her coat into the locker, slammed the door, and clicked the lock. Turning suddenly, she started to hurry down the hall when she collided with another girl. Since Emma stood nearly five feet nine inches tall, she didn't see the shorter girl of five feet four inches.

"Oh, my gosh, I'm so sorry!" exclaimed Emma. "Are you okay?"

The other girl started to laugh, her round chest bouncing. "If you knew how many times a day I get jostled at home and school, you wouldn't think about it!" She giggled.

"Hi, I'm Emma Trotter, and I hope you won't hold this first bump against me." Emma returned her laughter.

"No, don't worry about it. My name is Mae Beckett. I'm so new here I can't find my way around this big place. My last school had one room, so I never got lost!"

Emma liked Mae's openness. "Mine, too! We better run for class, but would you like to have lunch together?"

"Sure. See you whenever they let us out for food. I do love to eat," noted Mae, patting her slightly plump hips.

"Okay, see you then."

Over lunch, they discovered more about themselves between mouthfuls of homemade sandwiches.

"I'm living with my second oldest brother Jacob so I can go to high school," explained Emma. "His farm is the closest to the pavement so I can catch the bus into Maryville."

"Yea, I wanted to go to high school, but I had to talk my dad into it," noted Mae. "My mom died when I was thirteen, so I take care of my two younger brothers and two sisters while he farms. Luckily, the youngest one, Billy, started school this fall, so he can walk with the others to the school-house. That lets me free to catch the bus from south of Maryville. Then when I get home, I fix dinner, try to help with their homework, do my home-work, then get everyone off to bed. Dad does all the chores and milking, and most of the gardening."

Emma told about her father's impending death and how she wanted to be a teacher. The two girls managed to get some food into their mouths be-tween talking, then hurried to class.

From that day onward, Emma and Mae became best friends. Because Mae was short and Emma was tall, their friends called them "Mutt and Jeff" after the cartoon characters with the same physiques. The girls took the teasing in good humor, for they both had grown up with family members constantly ribbing them over one thing or another. They also looked forward to seeing each other at school and sympathized with the effort to catch the bus each day.

While Emma didn't usually mind the walk from the farm to the bus stop, the weather made the trek arduous at times. Fall and spring rains turned the road into a mud quagmire. She was forced to walk along the edge in the tall weeds, which whipped mud onto her shoes and legs. In winter, the snow became so deep at times walking became strenuous. She regarded rainy days as the worst, since an umbrella didn't provide enough protection to keep her coat and clothes dry for the long walk. Sitting in class in damp clothes often resulted in sore throats for Emma.

During the coldest weather, Jacob loaned her a pony to ride to High-way 71. A small lean-to at the corner allowed the farm youths to leave their horses sheltered during school hours. Emma truly appreciated the pony on days when the snow was too deep to walk easily or the north winds added frostbite danger. Of course, on those days, the bus often arrived late, so the teenagers tried to stand inside the gas station if the guy on duty didn't mind.

The bus ride sometimes provided adventure. Friday, January 20, 1939, found Emma on the bus heading home on slick roads. The bus slid into the ditch and had to be pulled out by a wrecker and two trucks later that evening. Neighbors driving on the highway gave the children lifts to their side-road turnoffs so they could walk home. Then on January 28, the worst snow of the winter arrived, and roads drifted full. Jacob refused to allow her to go to school, which was the right decision. By the next day, the one and a half miles of road to Highway 71 had been plowed, and Emma found out the bus had not run the previous day. Two days later, school again was canceled due to new snowfall.

On weekends, either Jacob would drive Emma or Owen would pick her up to spend the weekend with Edith on the farm. At both places, Emma helped with chores and studied at night. Since no family member had ever completed high school, no one could help her with homework. She had to figure out any hard topics herself, with the family encouraging her to continue her studies.

Events on the farmstead changed also. Owen announced during the winter of 1937 that he was getting married on March 13, 1938, to Melinda Bell. They held the wedding ceremony at her home, then she moved into the house with Owen and Edith.

The farmstead was crowded with three people there daily and Emma joining them on weekends. The women did chores, washed, ironed, gardened, and tended house. Canning for four people seemed more fun with several hands to speed the process.

Emma also helped with the field crop work where she could. She could sheaf wheat, shuck corn ears, and drive the horse team while Owen worked on planting or other tasks.

Finally, Edith felt the time had come for her to find her own home. With Emma in high school in Maryville and planning to go to college there, Edith decided she would move to that town. Jacob and Mike helped her look at houses the three of them could pool their money to make her down payment. By late January 1939, they purchased a three-bedroom, one-story house at 409 East 6th Street.

Edith agreed to repay Jacob and Mike for the down payment loan from the homestead money she was receiving from Owen. Also, the third bedroom would be rented to single women to supply further funds for house expenses and food. The backyard provided enough space for a small garden, and an apple tree grew by the side of the house.

The move from the homestead to Maryville was scheduled for Saturday, March 4, but the roads became too muddy for loaded pickups to maneuver. By Monday, the roads froze by dawn but would become unpassable by noon.

Everyone arrived early and helped quickly stack packed boxes and furniture on the pickups and in a couple of cars. They made it to the paved highway without getting stuck. That evening, Emma and Edith stayed with friends.

The next day, Emma's spring quarter began, so Edith and relatives began unpacking boxes and arranging furniture. Emma helped that afternoon when classes were over.

Spring travel to school was much more enjoyable in Maryville, even on rainy days. Emma was now able to walk the mile to high school on city sidewalks. No more muddy roads.

Emma had a memorable moment in January 1939. Edith had let her keep the money from selling eggs. Emma had her heart set on having a class ring and proudly made a $1.00 deposit for that memento from her high school days. Late that month, Emma paid the remaining $7.55 and received her ring. Her hard work had paid off.

Emma's studies included typing, shorthand, English, history, science, and sports like volleyball and basketball. In April 1939, she used a little of her savings to pay for her photograph for the high school yearbook. She had lots of friends with whom to attend dances, have overnight at her house, and walk to and from school.

She still got to see Mae, and sometimes on Fridays, Mae was allowed to stay overnight with Emma. Mae's dad would agree to care for the four children while Mae had some teenage time to herself. At other times, Emma stayed with the Becketts, for having fun with the large family made her feel like she had when all of her brothers were still at home.

"Can you believe that we're seniors and gonna graduate in May?" gushed Mae one Saturday. "And you get to give a speech to everyone!"

"Thanks a lot," groaned Emma. "As if I'm not nervous enough now without you reminding me how large the crowd will be. I'm no public speaker. Just because I had a decent grade point, they punish me by handing me that job! Ugh!"

Mae giggled. "But better you than me! At least you're tall enough to be seen over the podium! I couldn't reach the microphone."

On May 1, Emma bought a blue formal at Gates' department store for $2.98. On May 3, her class had its graduation banquet and ceremony at the Maryville Country Club. Emma gave her speech, hoping the podium hid her shaking knees. Friends and family members gave her what gifts they could afford.

Emma couldn't believe she had met her goal of graduating from high school. Now she needed a college degree to become a teacher. But she had no money to attend college.

On June 1, she went to work as a housekeeper for the Melvin Stillers. She helped care for Mrs. Stiller's elderly mother, did dishes, washed clothes, ironed, cleaned the house, sewed, sometimes prepared dinner meals, and canned fruits and vegetables. Her pay was $4.00 per week. Emma was seventeen years old.

By July 1939, the Stillers lowered her wages to $3.00 per week. They hired a second girl, Betsy, to help with the workload. On the evening of July 17, Mr. and Mrs. Stiller, Betsy, and Emma worked in the barn killing fourteen rats using hoes, pitchforks, or thick wooden sticks. By the end of July, Emma quit working for the Stillers.

At her home, Emma cleaned, sewed, helped garden, washed and ironed clothes, canned food, and painted the porch or interior rooms as needed. She sewed quilt blocks together in any spare time.

In early July, Mike and Kate had a little boy they named Thomas, who was quickly nicknamed Tommy. Now Emma had two nephews and one niece to love.

Throughout the summer, Emma worked around the house with her mother. They also visited her brothers and helped with housework and canning at those homes. Of course, the women had fun setting each other's hair and getting ready for Saturday dances in Barnard, Maryville, Hopkins, or Savannah. They also loved the midnight movies in Maryville or Savannah.

At times, Emma worked for other people in Maryville. She sometimes earned seventy-five cents or $1.00 a day for odd jobs. Other times she made fourteen cents per hour. She put everything she could save into her college fund.

Each summer, Emma looked forward to the Barnard Picnic. For four evenings, the town park and rodeo grounds came alive with a traveling amusement show. Carnival rides, a magician, singers, and food booths brought families from all around the area.

"Emma, you better hurry up," urged Kate. "Mike is threatening to leave us girls here if we're not in the car in two minutes!"

Emma grabbed her purse and Tommy's diaper bag. "You got Tommy? I've got his bag!"

Both women glanced around the kitchen to check for any last-minute items, then raced out the back door. Mike had the car doors open, ready for them to slide inside.

That Friday had been so hot during the day, but the setting sun dropped the heat to bearable levels. Her other brothers joined them at the picnic. Emma and her sister-in-law Linda danced on the small portable floor to the country band's music. All the women took turns sitting in the car with baby Tommy, so all the gals could enjoy some fun.

On Saturday, everyone headed back to the picnic for another evening of fun. That time, however, the party got rained out. They settled for card games at home and some homemade ice cream, thanks to Mike hand cranking the freezer.

The following week, the traveling carnival had moved to Ravenwood, twenty miles northeast of Barnard. Emma and Edith rode along with Bob's and Mike's families. A neighbor babysat Tommy. Emma loved to dance, talk with people, and enjoy the general excitement of the flashing carnival lights and music. Those outings formed a wonderful break to forget hard farming life for a while.

Emma visited one brother and his family after another into the fall. Wherever she went, she helped with the housework and chores. Local entertainments were good chances for a young woman to enjoy herself. The county held its annual fox hunt in late August, followed by a horse show that weekend. Bob entered his new colt, but the colt didn't win a ribbon.

As fall began, farming became more hectic. Emma helped Bob dig twenty-six rows of potatoes, for which work she received one bag for her and Edith's use. Crops were drying and nearly ready to harvest. Time seemed to speed up as the workload increased and life outside Barnard grew more ominous.

Chapter 10

In the evenings, Emma and Edith listened to their small radio. The news grew more worrisome each day. Germany had taken over the Czech lands of Bohemia and Moravia in March 1939. Then, on one especially bad Saturday evening, they heard worse news.

"Today, September 1, Germany invaded Poland in an unprovoked attack. Using its blitzkrieg strategy, heavy bombing destroyed Poland's air forces, railroads, communication lines, and munitions dumps. Then massive land forces invaded with overwhelming numbers of troops, tanks, and artillery. We will keep you posted on more breaking news as it occurs!" promised the KFEQ radio station announcer out of St. Jo.

"We don't need another war!" exclaimed Edith. "The last one darn near wrecked the world. So many dead! But Roosevelt said he would keep us out of other people's business."

By September 3, 1939, Great Britain and France declared war on Germany. Now most of western Europe was fighting. The *St. Joseph News-Press* covered the world events with increasing urgency at the potential effect of the European war on America.

The United States responded in November with passage of an amendment to the Neutrality Acts of the 1920s. The new law allowed any country to purchase arms and goods from a neutral United States but prohibited American ships from transporting arms or war materiel. U.S. citizens could no longer travel on vessels owned by warring nations. Congress passed the amendment only after intense debate, clearly showing reluctance to become involved in another war.

Unlike the start of World War I, Roosevelt saw Germany as the openly aggressive adversary. His goal was to assist the Allies, while keeping his country out of the fighting. Roosevelt knew American citizens formed two sides over the European conflict. Isolationists opposed even indirect U.S. involvement. Internationalists claimed helping Great Britain and other countries with aid would keep the United States out of any fighting. Roosevelt walked the fine line between the two groups, but personally felt U.S. involvement in the new world war was inevitable.

****

Emma obtained her first bank loan of \$35 on September 11. She used a little to buy some clothes and supplies. The next day, Emma registered as a freshman at Northwest Missouri State Teachers College and deposited \$23 into her college account.

"Oh, my," she moaned that evening to Edith. "My new shoes wore a blister on each heel walking to school and around campus to get registered. I hope we have bandages so I can cover up those sore spots. I've got entry tests tomorrow, so I've got to walk a lot more!"

Emma took an English test at nine, then came home for lunch. She returned for a psychology test at two. By evening, her exhaustion overtook the adrenaline rush of registering for college at long last and completing two tests.

On Thursday morning, Emma attended her classes to get the names of textbooks and supplies she needed. She tried to study, but often stopped to help Owen get their house fixed up. Edith had a woman who wanted to rent the spare bedroom, and Owen came to make the house and room ready. Mrs. Meads from Hopkins moved in Tuesday.

Emma felt sorry for Mae, who would not be able to attend college, even though her grades in high school were good. No matter how much she wanted to go, she was the mother figure for her four siblings, the youngest only seven. Mae had no time to work a part-time job to make money for school when she needed to help support her family. She got a job in a restaurant during the early morning shift. Her father got the children off to school in the morning, and Mae arrived home in the afternoon when they got out of school and their father was still in the fields.

Throughout the fall, Emma attended classes and studied all day. Then she helped her mother around the house and studied more. On weekends, she attended church, visited her brothers, saw friends, and worked part-time for people needing a spare hand.

College kept Emma busy. She paid for college expenses, like her gym lock that cost \$1.00. Students were required to attend musical assembly and lectures from visiting guest speakers. In her humanities class, 127 students attended, but Emma's grade on her first test was 47, with the highest score in the class being 91 and the lowest 7. She figured the middle wasn't too bad, but not as good as she wanted. She also had physical science, English, education, and gym. On October 5, the freshmen students were herded uptown and had to "button," which meant they had to wear green beanies. Later they all ate dinner at College Park. Students who were to be future teachers got to attend the elementary school rooms at Horace Mann to see what teaching a class would be like in real life. Emma watched the second-grade class. By late October, Emma had passed all her subjects for that six-week period.

On October 10, Emma shelled out seventy-five cents prepayment for *The Tower* yearbook and sixty cents for her photograph to go in it. She carefully hoarded her funds, trying to meet all her college expenses with the bank loan and her part-time earnings.

After he harvested his corn crop, Owen brought a load of corncobs to Edith and Emma to use as fuel for their heating stove. Edith and Emma picked buckets of peas from their backyard garden and dug some potatoes. The other brothers shared extra vegetables and fruits with them, so Emma felt like they were always canning something.

In early November, a new renter moved into the spare bedroom after Mrs. Mead moved out. Mrs. West from Skidmore arrived and paid for a month's time.

The next six-week period had the same class subjects with more advanced readings. Emma also attended a Gregorian chant by the Conception Abbey choir from the monastery, which was founded in 1873 near Maryville. She often studied at the library until five thirty and later hit the books at home from seven thirty until midnight.

For Emma's eighteenth birthday on November 20, Edith gave her $1.00. Owen gave her some fresh fruit, a real treat for that time of year. Mae came over to enjoy some of Emma's cake.

"So you're nearly a Thanksgiving baby," commented Mae, licking frosting from her fingers.

"Only because Roosevelt changed the date!" replied Emma.

In 1939, President Roosevelt had officially proclaimed Thanksgiving Day was to be November 23, the third Thursday in November.

"Don't know what that Roosevelt was thinking," complained Edith. "Thanksgiving was always the last Thursday ever since Lincoln said so in 1863. Don't know why this president had to change it! It won't feel right this year!"

"Yes, a lot of people are mad at him," agreed Emma. "I guess the food will taste the same, even if the date seems wrong."

"People are calling it 'Roosevelt's Thanksgiving' or 'Franksgiving'," replied Edith. "I bet he's gettin' a ton of letters wrote to him!"

Two days later, Edith and Emma wrapped the house water pipes to keep them from freezing. Each day, the temperatures dropped with true winter coming fast.

Since Emma's funds had dipped too low, she sadly decided not to attend college the next quarter. She received a $3.75 tuition refund and turned in everything that belonged to the college. In early December, Emma received her class grades, which were all passes with one honor. Her spirits fell lower as the Christmas holiday season approached because she would not be starting classes in January.

Emma applied at the dime store for work but did not get hired, so she continued doing odd jobs for other people. She was determined to make enough to start back to college by the summer session.

In mid-December, Mike brought them a Christmas tree from the farm. Jacob and Owen then left in Owen's pickup to drive to Detroit, Michigan. Jacob had ordered a new 1940 Dodge car and was going to pick it up from the factory floor.

Emma and Edith decorated the tree. Both were working on handmade Christmas gifts for friends and relatives, plus a few items they bought uptown. Emma mailed holiday cards to her friends and loved shopping with them, even if she didn't buy anything.

Following their family tradition on Christmas Eve, all of Emma's brothers, their wives, and their children stayed overnight at Edith's house. The spare bedroom was vacant at the moment, and extra blankets were laid on the floors to serve as sleeping pallets. Everyone helped with the cooking and caring for youngsters, and they all had fun opening presents Christmas morning. After breakfast, the families left to care for their livestock. The two inches of snow was trampled down by then, and the weather was not as cold. Emma served Christmas dinner for a family in town, making a little money.

On December 30, Jacob came to town and gave Emma a ride in his new car.

"Someday, I'm going to have a car," declared Emma. "Then Mom and I can go visit everyone instead of waiting for rides to your houses. And we won't have to carry our groceries home from the store on foot in the snow!"

Jacob saw the determination in Emma's eyes. "You keep yourself working on your teaching degree. Then you might have enough for a car. They cost more money than just the payment. You got to buy tires and oil and gas and fix anything that decides to break down."

Emma knew Jacob was right. Every time she heard a car dealer advertise on the radio, however, she made two goals of getting a car and her college degree.

Throughout the year in the evenings when Emma was home, she and Edith listened to the Grand Ole Opry and other country music stations on the radio. Edith especially loved Hank Snow's music and Minnie Pearl's homespun wisdom through semi-racy jokes about her love life, or lack thereof. The radio news reports continually updated the worsening situation in Europe.

****

From May 26 through June 3, 1939, Allied forces, mostly British, became trapped along the English Channel in Dunkirk, France. The 300,000 soldiers faced daily shelling and strafing by German forces and extinction unless something drastic happened. The miracle occurred when Churchill called for any vessel that floated and could carry men to cross the Channel under fire. Over 600 boats and ships volunteered, transporting the remaining soldiers back to England.

By late November, the Soviet Union invaded Finland, initiating what it called the Winter War. The Finns were forced into an armistice, leaving the Soviet Union in control of their country.

German U-boats used military tactics to sink unarmed commercial ships in the Atlantic. Even when the Allies traveled in convoys, the U-boats scored a heavy toll. Valuable U.S. supplies sent under the Neutrality Act often arrived on the ocean floor instead of at British ports.

Great Britain's naval blockade of German ports had little effect upon its industrial output. The Allies did not have enough ships to stop the majority of German supply imports.

Missouri farmers, like all U.S. agricultural producers, felt the initial impact of the European war. Farming exports dropped between thirty and forty percent below the yearly average for the previous decade. Grain exports alone fell thirty percent between 1939 and 1940, hurting crop prices and farmers' incomes.

Chapter 11

On January 1, 1940, the temperature dropped to zero, with the next day at ten below. Winter had arrived in a deep freeze blast.

Emma joined her friend Amy at a Maryville Theater matinee of *Drums Along the Mohawk*. "Don't you just love Henry Fonda?" asked Amy.

"I could stand to be his wife," replied Emma. "Living in New York state during the American Revolution was a hard life. They got attacked by everybody—the British, Tories, and Indians. I wonder if that's the way the people in Europe feel, with everybody fighting over their land from all sides."

As cold weather continued, farmers turned their attention to their livestock and repairing fencing, equipment, and barns. Owen butchered a couple of hogs. Linda, Melinda, and Emma prepared the meat for canning.

Their reward was attending a dance Saturday evening. Emma had a great time, not getting home until two thirty in the morning. Everyone also celebrated some friends having a new baby girl the same day.

Mae visited that week. Emma gave her some material for a quilt and bought a raffle ticket for a new housecoat. Mae's church was always holding some kind of raffle to raise money either for the church or now for charities to help European people affected by the war.

"I can't keep the little ones all bundled up at the same time," complained Mae. "As soon as I get all of them in their coats, hats, scarves, mittens, boots and out the door, one of them is ready to come back in. They want to play outside, but it's just too darn cold."

"Yea. My brothers always butcher when it's cold. Owen did last week, and Bob did yesterday."

Mae nodded in agreement. "Pa will kill a cow this weekend. More canning for me, but at least my sister Belle is old enough to help now."

Emma gazed over Mae's shoulder and out the window. "You ever feel left behind?"

"Which way?"

"Well, it seems like most girls we know are going steady with some boy or already married or maybe even having kids by now," Emma mused. "We have so much fun at dances, and the guys like both of us, but neither of us has found anyone we really want to be around long-term."

"I've been around kids so many years now I'm in no hurry to get married and have more of my own," replied Mae. "I'd love to live alone for a while and see what peace and quiet is like in a house. And not have to share a bed with anyone else. And not have to wash other people's clothes and comb their hair and fix their lunches. Just a little peaceful time for myself."

Emma had to laugh. Mae could always see the funnier side of her life. As much as Mae complained about being mother to four siblings, she loved them dearly, as if they were her own children.

"I mean, I really want to get my degree and teach school," continued Emma. "But would it be so bad to have a guy who wants to date me on a regular basis? I know I'm no beauty like some of our friends, but I'm not too bad looking. I just feel like I'm heading into being an old maid."

"Hey, we're both just eighteen. We've got a little time—at least a year—before we get that old-maid label slapped on our foreheads," assured Mae. "Besides, the girls who were so eager to get married may have rushed into it and not got the pick of the litter with their guys. We're just being more selective, waiting for the cream to rise to the top of the jar before we choose."

Emma wanted to agree, but still felt down. Facing Valentine's Day with no one special in her life didn't help her mood.

She continued to work for various people in Maryville. She even shoveled snow from sidewalks for twenty-five cents. Whatever work was available, she tried to accept, determined to get back into college soon.

Often, she stayed with her sisters-in-law, helping them around their houses and finishing chores with her brothers. Sometimes Edith came along to see her grandchildren and her boys. Of course, winter provided the best time to make homemade ice cream with milk from their own cows and family-favorite recipes.

At night, Emma worked on her embroidery projects such as pillow tops, doilies, and dresser scarves, or sewed clothes for herself. Edith made quilts as they listened to the radio. Friends would visit, just dropping in whenever they were in the neighborhood. Living in town made it easier to see other people.

With rent money from the spare bedroom and income from Owen's purchase of the homestead, Edith was able to keep paying the house mortgage. She had no other source of income. President Roosevelt had signed the Social Security Act in 1935. Neither Daniel nor Edith had ever earned wages or paid wage taxes, so she didn't qualify for a Social Security check.

While Emma sometimes felt exhausted from working part-time and helping her family, she never resented it. Emma just worked as hard as everyone she knew. Farming was a tough life. People in the city worked hard, too. All citizens were feeling the stress from the European war news, wondering what the effect would be on their lives and jobs.

Her friends provided outlets whenever Emma had spare time. In mid-March, Amy came by one Saturday.

"Come on!" pleaded Amy. "You'll have fun and learn something new."

Emma looked at her skeptically. "Roller skating looks like fun, but I'm not all that coordinated. I've never done it before."

"Then it's time you started," countered Amy. "The rink is open this afternoon, and you're finally not working. Let's go!"

Emma kissed Edith goodbye, heaved a sigh of determination, and headed out the door. Amy did her best to teach Emma to skate.

"Just take easy glides and move your feet slightly outward. You'll get used to the feeling of rolling," she encouraged.

Emma held onto Amy's arm for balance, gingerly stepping onto the rink's wooden floor. Other skaters whizzed by, seemingly born to skate fast. "Okay, here goes."

With slow, awkward, initial movements, Emma tried to glide from one foot to the other. She wobbled helplessly at times before Amy got her rebalanced.

"My long legs seem disconnected from the rest of me. And the skates feel so heavy on my feet," noted Emma.

"You're doing fine for a first-timer. Just relax a little, and you'll get used to the way the skates feel."

Emma held onto Amy with her left hand and the railing around the rink with her right. Slowly, she began to get the sense of rolling, feeling more in control of her feet. After fifteen minutes, she needed a break.

"I've got to sit down. My legs are using muscles they didn't know they had. They're tired!"

They rested and had a soda from the snack bar. Then Amy insisted Emma get back on the floor. Within half hour, Emma was able to take her own baby glides. After another rest, she was beginning to enjoy the experience.

"Okay, I'm on my own for a while. Just stay nearby, please!" begged Emma.

With a little confidence, Emma skated around the rink. She did begin to relax, feeling the gliding become more effortless. She was enjoying herself, learning a new skill and having fun. Then that darned kid raced by, catching Emma's skate. Down she fell, badly skinning her left knee.

"Oh, if I could get my hands on that boy," moaned Emma.

Amy helped her up and over to the chairs. The rink manager arrived with a wet towel and bandage.

"My knee is really going to hurt tomorrow!"

"Yea, but you looked great right up until you went splat!" laughed Amy, who helped Emma walk home.

Poor Mae came down with mumps on April 12. Emma briefly talked with her by phone, sending her sympathies and telling about learning to skate. Emma had never had mumps, so she decided she shouldn't visit her best friend.

Emma held a private memorial for her father on April 17. He had been dead four years, missing out on so many family events and seeing his grandchildren. She missed his presence every day, wishing he could have lived longer to see how well his family was doing. The four boys were buying farms of their own. Edith was buying her house. Emma had been able to attend some college and planned to go back soon. Life just passed out the wrong cards sometimes, and Daniel got dealt a short-life hand.

By the end of April, Emma battled another head cold. During each year, she always managed to catch several colds. Walking to school and jobs in all kinds of weather weakened her immune system. Also, working in so many houses, she was exposed to whatever illnesses those families had.

All spring and summer Emma worked, often while not feeling well. She helped relatives plant strawberries, rhubarb, and garden plants. She washed, ironed, sewed, cleaned, canned, and baked. She and her family attended church services. Edith's brothers and sisters visited at times, and sometimes Emma's brothers took Edith and Emma to see friends in Savannah or elsewhere. Friends joined them for parties, dances, and movies. Emma attended friends' birthdays, graduations, and family gatherings. Her friends who were married had babies, and other friends had weddings. Fillmore held its summer carnival, and the Barnard Picnic and Ravenwood Picnic were huge successes.

Life continued in its normal Missouri routine for farming communities. Emma's world seemed to reflect that continuity, but the tensions around the globe were invading even the Midwest.

****

The European war escalated. In April 1940, Germany invaded Denmark and Norway. Denmark surrendered the first day and Norway by June 9. Germany also attacked France and neutral Luxembourg, the Netherlands, and Belgium in May. Their small valiant military forces couldn't match the German land and air firepower. On June 10, Italy declared war on France and Great Britain. By June 14, German troops occupied France, forcing the French to sign an armistice. Even Russia took advantage of the unrest to occupy the Baltic States in June and annexed them by August.

From July 10 through October 31, Germany threw its mighty bombs against Great Britain in daily air raids. The Battle of Britain resulted in thousands dead, and people sent their children for protection to countryside towns to live with strangers willing to give them a home. The battle concluded as a British win paid by a heavy loss of life.

The war further expanded that autumn. The Italians invaded Egypt on September 13, causing the British to retreat and regroup. On September 27, Germany, Italy, and Japan signed the Tripartite Pact so attacks on one party would result in the other two countries lending aid. The Axis front now reached nearly worldwide. By October, Italy had invaded Greece from Albania. One more country was now at war against the Axis powers.

****

Emma proudly enrolled in college for her second quarter on September 10, 1940. Edith even gave Emma $25 toward her $100 tuition. The remaining $75 Emma had saved over the past eight months. Her subjects included social science, education, biological science, and gym classes of volleyball and swimming. At last, Emma was back in school, loving the chance to learn and work toward her teaching certificate.

One book she was required to read was *Letters from a Hard-Boiled Half-Baked Son* by George Frederick Miller and William H. Patterson. Published in 1931 and still relevant in 1940, it contained common sense ideas for being a teacher and becoming part of the school's community. She found it fascinating and useful.

On October 2, the college had a Walk Out Day. The older students initiated the freshmen, followed by lunch at College Park where the freshmen gave a program. Emma thought it a lot of fun since she wasn't the one being initiated.

On October 25, Secretary of Agriculture Henry A. Wallace spoke at the Maryville Courthouse as he ran for U.S. vice president. Mike and his family joined Emma to hear him speak.

Throughout the school year, Emma was required to attend lectures at her teachers' meetings that provided practical techniques for becoming a teacher. Her life seemed to be heading where she had dreamed it would go, but tensions around her were growing.

U.S. citizens became one step closer to war involvement on September 16. The Selective Training and Service Act of 1940 passed and required all men between the ages of twenty-one and forty-five to register for the draft, the first peacetime draft in U.S. history. Men whose numbers were drawn from the draft lottery would have to serve at least one year in the armed forces. After that, the men would serve in the reserves for ten years or until they reached age forty-five, whichever came first. After registering, the men would be classified for their fitness for military service based on various criteria.

People now feared Roosevelt could not keep his promise for America to remain neutral and out of World War II. Although the Isolationists were strong, the world situation was forcing change in the States. Americans began to feel Great Britain would not be able to defeat Germany on its own. The U.S. military, still using World War I supplies like rifles and ships, was not prepared for a global war.

Bob, Jacob, Mike, and Owen registered for the draft on October 16. Emma now feared for her brothers' safety and what would become of their families and farms if they were drafted.

She hoped her brothers would be exempted from service. In early 1940, many young men had left their family farms to work in factories producing war materiel needed for the Allies. Farmers found it hard to get help, so the government agreed to some exemptions from service. If a farmer lived on his own farm, operated it alone, and had at least eight milk cows, he could request an exemption. A farmer and his son living on their farm with at least sixteen animal units could apply out. Emma prayed her brothers could stay on their farms, since they all met the first criteria.

Emma and her friends went uptown on October 29 to attend a dance in honor of the "Orphan Battery," the 128th U.S. Field Artillery, 1st Missouri F.A. The unit was leaving soon to serve actively and was the oldest military unit west of the Mississippi River, organized in 1812.

Also that day, the first draft numbers were drawn in Washington, DC. So far, her brothers' numbers had not been picked. People all over the area were nervous about the future fates of their loved ones.

The nation re-elected Roosevelt as president for a third term on November 5, 1940. Wallace became vice president, so Emma had actually gotten to see a U.S. vice president in person.

On Armistice Day, November 11, Emma attended a piano and cello concert presented by Mr. and Mrs. Ernst Bacon. As a member of an early generation of composers who found a style for American music, Mr. Bacon, like Aaron Copeland, could write the American spirit into music. How thrilling to hear someone of his caliber. *I wish I could play piano as well,* thought Emma.

She enjoyed her nineteenth birthday on November 20. She received four birthday cards, twenty cents, a pair of pajamas, and a cake. Her brothers had intended to celebrate with her, but rain made the roads impassably muddy.

Roosevelt's Thanksgiving Day occurred the next day. People were still upset with him for changing the date to the third Wednesday. Edith and Emma ate turkey with friends, then Emma and a college friend went to a matinee. The weather was windy and cool, hinting winter was fast approaching.

Six days after Thanksgiving, Emma had four two-hour quarterly exams in two days to complete her second quarter of college. Later she received her grades, passing every course. She now had twenty hours of college education.

On Tuesday, December 3, 1940, Emma registered for a third quarter. She signed up for social science, biological science, English, music, and physical education. Her PE class worked on social dancing until Christmas, so her dancing improved. She was back doing what she loved, learning.

Her brothers helped Edith with paperwork for her house. Bob made sure the house insurance was in order. Jacob and Edith paid the property taxes, and room rental paid for the mortgage. The family had pulled together to keep their word to Daniel.

Christmas assembly was Friday morning, December 20. Then students were dismissed at noon for the holiday.

Emma talked with Mae over the party line. "I've been Christmas shopping over the last few weeks. I've hunted for bargains, stretching my little money as far as possible. I think I have something for everyone, even if it's just a small gift."

"I know what you mean," answered Mae. "I've been making clothes and homemade candy and such for weeks. I've got something for all four kids and Dad."

On Sunday, the church members gathered for a five o'clock service. Prayers focused on avoiding war participation. Then members who were able held choral singing all over town, adding their voices to the cool early evening air. Afterward they enjoyed a chili supper and each other's company in the safety of their current national neutrality. But nagging worries focused on the coming year and world events.

Bob and Linda hosted the family Christmas Eve dinner, complete with turkey and all the extras. They valued their time together even more that season, with thoughts about the draft and in what way America might become involved with outside forces.

Edith and Emma spent Christmas Eve and Day with Owen and Melinda. The day after Christmas, Owen was feeling flu-like symptoms. Edith, Emma, Helen, and four friends went to a free movie in Maryville to let Owen have the house to rest.

Edith's health also needed attention. Her foot had been hurting for several weeks.

"Mom, you've got to see Dr. Jackson. You can hardly walk from the pain!" encouraged Emma.

"I know you're right," Edith acknowledged, "but doctors cost money! And it's Christmas time. I want to be visiting folks!"

Finally, on December 28, they spent the money to have Dr. Jackson x-ray her foot at the hospital. Two days later, Owen and Melinda went with Emma when Edith had a ganglion cyst removed. Bob and Linda came later to keep Edith company. After staying overnight, Edith was released to be home for New Year's Eve.

Chapter 12

The year 1941 began with rain and clouds turning cold by night. Two friends and Linda stayed with Edith. She was uncomfortable but managed to reassure everyone she was getting along fine. More friends dropped by the next day and planned to stay with Edith on Monday when Emma went back to college. Emma worked hard at school, then cared for Edith when Emma got home.

Emma attended the morning assembly for Religious Emphasis week. At home, she studied and carried in coal for their stove. That evening they heard recordings of President Roosevelt's inauguration on January 20.

"Him getting in this time sure feels different than the other times," commented Edith. "We always expected him to keep us safe. Now it don't feel like anyone can."

Emma stared at the radio. "Surely Hitler will stop being so aggressive soon. He's got so much land under his control. You'd think it'd be enough for him."

In late January, however, the college hosted speaker Roeland Van Cavel from Holland. His lecture contained grim reminders that the Germans showed no signs of slowing their conquest efforts. The audience's mood was solemn as they left the auditorium.

The winter of 1940–1941 brought bad news around Maryville. Two couples each had a baby die, and two adult friends passed away. Bob seemed to be having heart trouble, even at his young age, and the family urged him to see a doctor. Bob resisted the suggestion and felt better by late January. The winter weather always took its toll on people's health.

Emma attended the Morningside Choir concert at the college on January 31. The choir had driven from Sioux City, Iowa—over 200 miles from Maryville. To attempt such a risky trip in late January meant potentially hazardous roads, but they had been lucky with a fairly warm day.

That evening, Edith and Emma listened to the Joe Louis vs. Red Burman fight on the radio. Joe won by a knockout in the fifth of fifteen rounds.

"Can you believe we're hearing what's going on at Madison Square Garden in New York City?" asked Edith. "Why, it's so far away! And the sound is so clear like he's down in St. Jo."

Thursday, February 4, brought cold air and big flakes of snow. Emma attended a pep rally, then went to a free matinee. That evening, she had fun at a college folk dancing party.

The college hosted a Monday duo-pianist concert by Jacques Fray and Mario Braggiotti. They had created a catalog of over 200 original recordings and were the first to play both classical and popular music on the same program. Their fame spread internationally after meeting George Gershwin, who was in Paris to compose *An American in Paris*. Gershwin had launched their careers. In the 1930s, Fray and Braggiotti performed three evenings a week on CBS's nationally broadcast Kraft Music Hall and Radio City Music Hall. Emma had listened to them on the radio, not dreaming she would see them in concert. Being in college had truly opened vistas Emma never imagined possible.

The day before Valentine's, the college announced Horace Mann High School and Northwest Missouri State Teachers College had a measles epidemic. They urged students to monitor their health and stay home if they felt ill.

On February 22, Emma got a call.

"You better get dolled up," said Bob. "We're all going to a barn dance in Shenandoah, Iowa, tonight. We'll pick you up about five."

Emma washed and set her hair, donned her dancing dress, and was ready promptly at five. Edith's foot was still recovering, so she agreed to babysit all three grandchildren.

"Can you imagine driving over fifty miles to a dance?" asked Edith. "Why, a few years ago no one had cars or would dare go that far in winter."

The four brothers and their wives piled into three cars, leaving enough room in one for Emma. They drove through the clear, cool, late afternoon to Shenandoah. At the appointed place, a sign greeted them: "Closed due to frozen water pipes."

"Well, I'll be danged," commented Owen. "We're not gonna waste such dressed up gals on some bad pipes. Let's head back to Maryville. We can make it in time for a movie if we hurry."

The three cars turned south and were lucky the roads were dry. They enjoyed the movie, but still didn't want to head home.

Mike suggested, "Let's go to the Covered Wagon. They've got a live band tonight."

What was left of the evening and into the early hours found them enjoying themselves on the dance floor. Finally, exhausted, they headed back to Edith's. She had put the children to bed, so the three fathers gathered their sleeping children and tucked them into their cars to return home. Emma crashed into bed, falling asleep immediately but happily. What a night out!

On March 5, Edith and Emma spent $2.02 for wallpaper for the northeast room, which Bob, Mike, and their wives helped hang. Another Saturday, they hung paper in the southeast room. The bathroom was next, completed in just two hours. Sharing such tasks created family bonding and gossip time.

Emma finished her quarter on March 6, taking two tests that day. She celebrated with Jacob, Owen, and their wives at a dance. She found out later she had passed all her courses with two honors.

On Monday, Emma borrowed more money from the bank for college and registered for the fourth quarter. Her courses carried nearly the same titles with more advanced topics. More studying, assemblies, and working at home. Dances on the weekends were her only fun break from the routine.

On March 22, Linda and Emma attended the State Convention of the Church Council at the Methodist Church in Maryville. While Edith had raised her family in the First Christian Church, Linda was a Methodist. Local people didn't really care about a person's denomination, as long as the person was good to others.

Bob bought a new 1941 Chevrolet car on March 29. Emma got to ride with them to a neighbor's yard sale. *Someday I'll have my own car,* decided Emma. *Someday!*

As ordinary as the daily routine seemed, the real world kept intruding.

"Sometimes I feel like I exist in a whirlwind," she commented to Mae. "One day things seem normal, and the next turned about-face toward the war."

More local young men received draft notices, and she always feared her brothers' numbers might be called.

****

Germany, Italy, Hungary, and Bulgaria invaded Yugoslavia on April 6, 1941, causing an April 17 surrender. Next, Germany and Bulgaria swept into Greece to support the Italians, with Greece submitting by early June. More countries were at war, putting additional pressure on Great Britain and Free France to battle onward.

****

Emma worked up her courage and approached Superintendent Burr on April 5. She wanted to know if she could teach a school of her own, if one was available for the fall.

Mr. Burr said, "Well, now, I'll ask around. But you don't have your college degree yet, so the chances are slim."

On April 14, Emma applied at the one-room Murphy country school. The board turned her down because she had so few college hours. Emma was discouraged but determined.

Emma kept working part-time to earn more money. She hung wallpaper, painted rooms, cooked, cleaned, and canned.

On May 7, she walked four miles in a Walkathon, coming in sixth of nine participants.

"I guess my long legs paid off in fewer steps per mile than the others," she laughed at the finish line.

May 29 was her last day of college for the quarter. Emma had two tests in the morning and mixed feelings when the quarter ended. She would keep working so she could pay for summer classes. At times, however, her determination waivered, but her goal of becoming a teacher would finally win out and keep her sights on the path ahead.

Her hard work had yielded enough money to pay off the bank loan to date. On June 3, Emma registered for the college summer quarter. She bought herself a new dress on sale to celebrate.

On June 6, Emma took an all-day Teachers Exam at the Courthouse. She was one step closer to becoming a real teacher. Again, she visited Mr. Burr, who sent her to Lone Valley to apply for a fall teaching job. Mr. Burr felt her chances of getting the job were good, because she had passed the Teachers Exam. Her interview was scheduled for the next day.

At nineteen, Emma seemed too young to be a teacher. Doubts crowded her mind as she dressed to meet the school board that afternoon. She felt as nervous as when she had asked her father about attending high school. Her palms were clammy, and her knees knocked.

At two o'clock, Emma entered the Lone Valley one-room schoolhouse.

Four local residents who had been elected to the school board sat at a table in front of the blackboard.

"Come in, come in, young lady," said a man who introduced himself as Mr. Watson. "We've been expecting you. Mr. Burr sent a recommendation along with your transcripts."

"Thank you" was all Emma could say as she sat in the indicated chair facing the four men.

"We just have a few questions for you," continued Mr. Anderson. "Your grades are acceptable, and your Teachers Exam score is good. But you seem a little young."

Mr. Ellison jumped in. "Frankly, we wonder if you have enough courses to be a teacher right now."

"And do you have any experience in actually teaching a classroom?" inserted Mr. Hall.

Emma felt a lump in her throat, but she took a deep breath. "Well, I'll have experience after you hire me!"

Surprised, the four men looked at each other, then laughed.

On Monday, June 23, 1941, Emma was summoned to Mr. Burr's office to sign her first teacher's contract. The Lone Valley school board members had liked her spunk and decided to give her a chance. Emma was officially a teacher at long last.

"Oh, Dad, I wish you could see this contract. You made it happen by letting me go to high school. Thank you," Emma whispered as she walked out of Mr. Burr's office.

The next day, her name appeared in the Maryville newspaper listing her as the new teacher at Lone Valley. Other young women's names were included at the various district one-room schools.

From June through early August, Emma studied harder than usual. She wanted to have all the knowledge she could before facing her first classroom in September. She enrolled in physical education, humanities, and literature.

Emma attended assembly on July 9 at the Student Center. Dr. Andre Baude had practiced medicine at Chatteau Thierry, France, while serving in the French Army until captured by the Germans. He spoke passionately about his experiences and the threats the Nazis posed to the entire world if they succeeded. Once again, global events encroached on remote Maryville, Missouri.

Owen bought a 1939 Plymouth four-door sedan on July 16. Now Emma felt her dream of also having a car might be closer, since she had a real income beginning that fall. But money to finish school remained her first priority.

August 7 found Emma completing two tests to end the quarter. She had done well enough and considered herself as prepared as she could be for teaching in the fall. *What will it feel like to be in front of the classroom instead of seated as a student?*

War news now filled much of the radio airwaves. Every day the radio and newspaper stories sounded increasingly grim. Emma became more apprehensive, as were all her friends and relatives, about the fate of the United States' neutrality.

****

Germany and most of its Axis partners invaded the Soviet Union on June 22, 1941. After quickly overrunning the Baltic States, they laid siege to Leningrad in September. Finland also joined the Axis.

U.S. President Roosevelt and British Prime Minister Churchill signed the Atlantic Charter and released it on August 14. The Nazis threatened to overrun Egypt, which would close off the Suez Canal to Allied access to British possessions in India. The two leaders also felt the Soviet Union would be forced to surrender to Germany. Their final concern was that Japan might try to seize British, French, and Dutch territories in Southeast Asia. The Atlantic Charter spelled out the goals for cooperation between the Allies and the United States, both their respective war aims for World War II and an outline of an international system after the war.

Although Roosevelt hoped the Charter would encourage Americans to allow the United States to enter the war, public opinion remained opposed. Churchill also intended to get the U.S. into the war, or at least to increase its military aid to Great Britain and to warn Japan against Pacific aggression. Although neither leader got what he hoped, the Charter raised British public morale and increased the solidarity between the United States and Great Britain.

****

Emma attended the teachers' meeting at the courthouse on Sunday, August 31. She bought a book sack from a neighbor for $1.00. Most of the day, she spent packing her clothes and belongings she would need while boarding for the school year with Tom and Ruth Roberts. That evening, Owen drove her to the Roberts' house, which was three-quarters of a mile southwest of Lone Valley school.

"Well, Sis," Owen commented as he dropped her off. "You really did it. You should sure be proud of all your hard work. Now don't let those kids take advantage of you!"

Emma laughed. "After growing up with four brothers, I think I can handle anything. At least, I hope I can. But I've never lived away from home before. I'm not sure how I'll like that."

Owen smiled at her. "I'll be by on Friday afternoon to pick you up. You can stay with me and Melinda next weekend. You'll do fine! If anyone picks on you, just pretend they're one of your ornery brothers and give 'em hell."

Ruth Roberts welcomed Emma with open arms. "We're sure glad to have you stay with us. Our boys've all grown, so the spare bedroom upstairs is just awaitin' for someone to use it."

Emma smiled and looked around the small room under the sloping roof eaves. Homemade quilts covered the full-sized bed. A mirror hung above a washstand and pitcher of water. Near the gabled window sat a small desk, chair, and kerosene lamp. Everything was spotlessly clean.

"I'll be very happy here," assured Emma. "I'll just unpack before dinner, if that's alright."

"You just go ahead. I'll holler when the food's ready."

So began the biggest adventure of Emma's life. She was to be a teacher starting Monday morning, September 1, 1941, at Lone Valley. Whether or not she felt ready, she would meet her students at nine o'clock.

Chapter 13

Emma rose at six o'clock. She wanted to eat breakfast and get to the schoolhouse before her students arrived. She had not had a chance to examine the room to see if everything was in order for the new school year. Ruth packed a lunch of a ham sandwich, an apple, and some cookies.

Lone Valley school was located about five miles west of Pickering, the nearest small town. Local folks referred to the area from Pickering to Hopkins as Toad Hollow. Of course, Emma was back to walking to school. This time, she had to go one-quarter mile north, then turn east for a half mile. The building sat on a strip of land between the east-west road on the south side and a small, tree-lined creek. Across the road, a knoll rose to level off before heading southwest to the Roberts' farmhouse. Monday was clear and hot, and the dirt roads were dry, a good day to begin a school year.

She would be making about $2.40 per day, a fortune to her after all the hours she had worked for $3.00 per week. Of the $48.00 per month she earned, she had to pay $20.00 to the Roberts for boarding her.

Arriving at eight o'clock, Emma found the room in good condition. Local residents had cleaned the shelves and desks and swept the floor. She quickly laid out her books, lesson plans, and blackboard chalk. The children would bring their own slates. As she surveyed the room, Emma tried to calm her nerves and act like a grown-up, long-term teacher who could handle anything.

Five boys and one girl had enrolled. Emma felt lucky to have a small class to begin her teaching experience. Mentally, she rehearsed her lesson plans, then kept glancing out the windows to watch for any children.

At a quarter of nine, three boys came strolling down the road. Emma straightened her new dress, checked her hair in the hall mirror, and took a deep breath before stepping onto the front porch.

"Good morning, boys," she called as they entered the schoolyard. "We have a fine day to begin our school year, don't we?"

"Yes, ma'am," answered one. The other two just stopped to study their new teacher.

"You have about fifteen minutes to play before I'll start class. The tree in the corner has a good swing on it and there's a teeter-totter also. Does anyone have a baseball?"

The boys just shook their heads to indicate no ball was available. They sauntered toward the tree, more to distance themselves from the teacher than to take advantage of the swing.

Emma kept smiling. She could see a boy and the girl walking down the road. The last boy was nowhere in sight.

"Good morning," Emma called. "Welcome, and we'll all get acquainted in a little while. I'm Miss Trotter, your new teacher for this year."

The girl looked about six years old and the boy about eight. They were obviously brother and sister, with matching heads of red curly hair. They entered the schoolyard and walked over to the pump that provided the school's water.

At nine o'clock, Emma called them into the schoolroom. "Let's get started. As I said, I'm Miss Trotter. Please sit with you older students on my right, and anyone in first through fourth grades on my left side."

After the five students found a desk, Emma continued. "Please introduce yourselves. Why don't you start?" she said as she smiled at the girl.

Obviously a little shy, the girl took her time in answering. "I'm Mary Sue," she finally replied.

"Nice to meet you, Mary Sue. I see from the records you're in first grade?"

Mary Sue nodded.

"Okay," Emma said as she turned to her brother, "what's your name?"

Billy," Mary quickly and firmly answered for her brother. "He's in third grade."

"Very good!" encouraged Emma. "You both are my youngest pupils this year."

The next boy looked about eleven years old. "I'm Pete. I'm in seventh grade!"

Emma tried to hide a smile. "Well, your records say you should be in sixth grade. But if you can pass some of the seventh-grade tests I can give you, I'll let you skip a grade. Do you think you could pass them?"

Pete smiled sheepishly. "Nope. I guess I better do sixth grade first."

The next two boys looked about thirteen and fourteen years old. They just stared at their desks, pretending not to notice her.

Just then, the sixth student, a boy about fourteen strode into the room.

He was a farm boy from his tall height and muscular build, outweighing Emma by over fifty pounds. His face showed defiance as he ambled to the back of the room and took a seat two rows behind the other boys.

"Good morning," smiled Emma. "We are introducing ourselves. I'm Miss Trotter. Could you tell me your name?" She had his name on her class roster but wanted to see his reaction.

The teenager stared sullenly at Emma. She waited patiently, trying to hide her rising irritation at his impudence.

Finally, he responded. "Bud. And we drove the last teacher away, and we're gonna get rid of you too."

It was stated as a fact, not a threat. The other two older boys giggled and smiled at Bud.

Emma did a quick inhale, kept smiling, and took a moment to decide how to respond. "Well, I'm sorry you did not get along with your previous teacher. Maybe we can start fresh, get to know each other, and things will work out better."

Bud grunted in reply.

Emma continued, turning back to the other two boys. "And your names are?"

"I'm Sam," said the fourteen-year-old.

The boy of thirteen, wanting to look as brave as Bud, spat out, "Call me Kurt."

"Okay. So we have Mary Sue, Billy, Pete, Kurt, Sam, and Bud as we go by class levels. We're going to cover a number of topics this year, and as a new item, we'll be discussing the impact of the war on our community as we study history. I'm sure you've been hearing your folks talk about it and maybe have older relatives who've already been drafted or enlisted. We can work in history, math, and social science as we learn about Europe and our country.

"As most of you know, since we're all in one room, I will be working with the different grade levels one at a time. So while I'm with one set of students, the rest of you will be working on assignments or reading your textbooks. Please do so quietly, so the students I'm working with can concentrate on their new material. Are there any questions?"

Thus, the day began. Emma handed out the precious textbooks, paid for by school district funds, which were barely enough to cover the school's costs. Emma had already been told to limit any expenses, and she had to submit her supply lists to the school board for approval before they administered any funds.

"Each of you will have some textbooks. You're responsible for their care and safe return at the end of the year. If you damage or lose them, you'll have to pay the district for their replacement cost. So please be careful. On rainy days, you'll need to keep them dry."

Surprisingly, Bud made no overt misbehaviors throughout the morning. Emma had good peripheral vision and did notice Bud's many smirks when he thought she wasn't looking. By noon, she had met with each grade level and written assignments on the blackboard.

When she called for lunch time, the students raced from their desks, grabbed their lunch pails from hallway storage bins, and fled outside to eat and play. Emma heaved a huge sigh of relief.

"I made it through half a day!" she muttered. "Now for another half, then several months of days more."

Unfortunately, by day's end, Mary Sue grew frustrated at her first day of school. She didn't like being confined to a seat and paying attention for so long. Even though Emma took pains to be patient with her, Mary Sue began to cry before the last period.

"Just great!" muttered Emma after school. "I made a child cry on the first day of school! Wonder what I'll cause tomorrow."

Tuesday began very wet, with rain most of the morning. Emma walked through mud to school wearing galoshes over her good shoes. *I wonder if the students have overshoes and how muddy the classroom floors will be by the end of the day.* She was responsible for cleaning the entire school and outhouses each day before she left for the Roberts' home. She also had to carry in coal for the stove when the weather got cold.

The second day went well, for the most part. Egged on by Bud, Emma was sure, Pete talked back to Emma once too often. She couldn't let him get control of the classroom, so she moved him to two rows behind Billy for one hour. She kept her calm demeanor, but firmly let it be known such rudeness was not allowed in her classroom. Bud didn't say anything, just kept watching her.

By Wednesday, Emma got a brief break. Under morning threatening skies, Miss Kimberly came to teach music. Emma enjoyed a one-hour break, sitting at the back of the room, preparing for the remainder of the day.

That evening, the Roberts took her to a free movie at Clearmont. Emma appreciated the break and a chance to relax during her first week of school.

September 3 was also Jacob's thirty-fourth birthday. The family was going to celebrate that weekend.

By her fourth day teaching, time seemed to pass faster. Emma managed not to yell when a toad jumped out of the desk drawer when she opened it. She grabbed the poor frightened creature and asked, "Is this anyone's pet?" Then she walked outside to deposit it on the grass, washed her hands in the hall basin, and returned to class. Bud seemed impressed she hadn't panicked.

Emma gratefully watched for Owen's Plymouth to drive into he Roberts' yard Friday afternoon. She had completed her first week as a professional teacher. All students had shown up daily for class, she hadn't been threatened further by Bud, and overall the week had gone pretty well.

As her second week began, Emma greeted three visitors to the school. Parents and school board members would occasionally drop in to observe the teacher. Emma had been warned this might happen by other student teachers at college, but she had hoped such visits would wait until she felt more comfortable teaching the class.

On Wednesday, Emma and her students rode to the fall fair parade. The students enjoyed the outing, and Emma had them write a short essay on what they saw.

Emma started decorating the blackboard for fall the next day. Also, three new pupils began classes: Carrie, age ten; Wilma, eleven; and Nick, twelve. After she got them introduced and settled, classwork resumed as usual.

Bud had not carried out any further aggressions toward Emma. She tried to be her usual friendly self, knowing she had always gotten along well with boys, since she had grown up with four brothers and their friends. Her biggest success with Bud seemed to be at lunch and the brief recesses they took in nice weather.

Emma talked Mike into finding a baseball bat and ball from a family whose boys had grown. The second Monday, she brought the equipment to school, inviting everyone to play baseball at lunch. Bud, Sam, and Pete were one team with Nick, Billy, and Emma on the other side. Bud looked smug as they laid out bases for a small diamond in the school yard. But when Sam pitched a fast ball, Emma drove it over the fence into the hay field, rounding bases for a homerun. Bud even smiled in surprise. Afterward, he seemed to give Emma a little more credit, at least for not being a sissy-type girl.

That evening, Emma and the Roberts listened to President Roosevelt's

Fireside Chat. A destroyer, the U.S.S. *Greer,* traveling in daylight near Greenland and clearly flying the U.S. flag, was torpedoed and sunk by a German submarine. Previously, the U.S. merchant ship SS *Robin Moor* was sunk by a German submarine in the mid-south Atlantic in direct violation of international agreements signed by many nations, including Germany. The passengers and crew jumped into lifeboats hundreds of miles from land. In July 1941, an American battleship in North American waters chased away a submarine trying to attack a ship. Other American-owned ships had been attacked and/or sunk in the past few months from the Atlantic to the Red Sea.

Roosevelt stated clearly such a great nation as the United States would not exaggerate one incident or become inflamed by one act of violence. He firmly stated, however, "It would be inexcusable folly to minimize such incidents in the face of evidence which makes it clear that the incident…is a part of a general plan." He declared the Hitler government was defying the laws of the seas, the recognized rights of other nations, and trying to close the entire Western Hemisphere to all ships except those of the Axis. Roosevelt concluded, "From now on, if German or Italian vessels of war enter the waters, the protection of which is necessary for American defense, they do so at their own peril."

Emma expelled her breath after the speech and understood the gravity of what Roosevelt had proclaimed. She thought about her young students, wondering if they had older brothers who might be in danger if Germany continued to attack American ships and pull the United States into the war.

"What madness to think one country would try to dominate the entire Western Hemisphere, in addition to the European territory it already claimed!" she fumed.

Wednesday, September 17, was Emma's hardest day at school. She had tried to let the students pick their own seat assignments, as long as they were grouped roughly by grade level. Sam and Kurt, however, encouraged no doubt by Bud, had been totally obnoxious all day. Finally, Emma moved them apart permanently, seating them so they had no one within three feet. They were not happy, but they minded her.

On her fourth Monday of teaching, Emma welcomed Mr. Burr. The school district had paid for a piano tuner to repair the old upright piano. Sitting in a school room conditions ranging from melting to freezing, damp to dry, had wrecked the piano's tuning. Now it sounded much better when

Miss Kimberly used it for music classes. Mr. Burr approved of the piano and Emma's teaching ability. Emma had prayed Bud and his two cronies would behave while Mr. Burr was present.

Emma went to Maryville on Saturday, September 27. She made her first bank deposit from her teaching salary, retaining a little cash for expenses. Feeling almost giddy and wealthy with so much money in the bank, Emma allowed herself to buy two pairs of shoes, a hat, and a winter coat.

Each district school was required to hold seasonal programs. Emma had to write a Halloween program, which she composed in the evenings at the Roberts'. She wrote parts for all students, trying to match their abilities to memorize with the number of lines the simple play would have. Emma had never written a play, but she had attended programs as a student and had visited other schools. She managed to get an inspiration and worked on writing the parts for the next two weeks.

On October 9 and 10, school was dismissed. Emma had to attend more teachers' meetings. The sessions covered new teaching methods and curricula and also began to answer questions about emergency preparedness in case of war. Even in rural Missouri, people were becoming concerned about growing world tensions.

The next week, students Pete and Kurt moved away. Emma's class now had only seven students, which made teaching easier. Also, two of Bud's buddies were gone, so fewer mischief makers.

The Halloween play plans progressed well. The students practiced a little each day and made decorations. Emma wrote invitations to parents, school board members, and area neighbors.

On October 28, her first Halloween program drew a good crowd who applauded the students' efforts. Afterward they enjoyed coffee, sandwiches, and pie, all donated by the parents.

Her students had taken their finals the day before the program. Most of them made average or above average scores, which pleased Emma. The district provided the tests, so her teaching efforts had been effective. The students seemed more comfortable with her and tried fewer antics.

The next quarter began November 3, but Emma had not received the new materials yet.

"For today and tomorrow," she announced, "we'll have to alter our plans until our new courses arrive. Let's take a field trip and see what we can find." Her students applauded the chance to get outside in the nice weather.

They mounted fall leaves on paper, painted pinecones, wrote stories, and held spelling bees. The unit arrived late the second day, and Emma studied the materials that evening to prepare to teach them the next day.

Prairie View, the closest one-room school two miles north of Lone Valley, held a community meeting Friday night. Emma and the Roberts attended, and Ruth bought three tickets on a chance to win a free turkey. Edith also bought three tickets from a neighbor. Unfortunately, neither of them won the turkey, but they were happy to support the school's fundraising efforts.

Emma's next project was a Thanksgiving meeting. She was on the Program Committee, which also held a raffle for a free turkey. Sam's mother won the bird, and Lone Valley raised $7.70 from ticket sales.

"Now I can buy a tall Aladdin oil lamp for the school. It's so dark inside on cloudy days," announced Emma.

On Monday, November 24, Miss Kimberly came. After music class, as she tried to drive out of the schoolyard, her car tires became mired in the mud. Emma and her students pushed the car while Miss Kimberly slowly applied the gas, trying not to splatter everyone with mud kicked up by the tires.

"Okay, everybody," ordered Emma, "Wash mud off your shoes and legs before going back inside. Anyone who tracks mud inside gets to clean it up!" No one disobeyed, since they all wanted to finish school as quickly as possible.

For 1941, Thanksgiving on November 20 was also Emma's birthday. Since Roosevelt changed the date in 1939, his decision had become increasingly unpopular. Finally, on November 26, he admitted his mistake and signed a declaration making the fourth Thursday in November the permanent national holiday. The public applauded his change back to the traditional schedule.

With the two fall holidays over, Emma turned her attention to the Christmas program. She wrote her Christmas cards at night and encouraged her students to sell Christmas Seals when they were home or in town. The seals were issued by the National Tuberculosis Association to raise funds to fight the disease, and patrons added the cheery stamps to their letters and packages. The students were taught how to sell the stamps and when to return the money to Emma, who would turn in the funds to Mr. Burr in Maryville.

Emma also bought candy for her students, which she divided in little paper bags. Carrie, Wilma, and Nick were moving before Christmas, so she gave them their cards and candy the first week in December.

Emma had enrolled Lone Valley in the Junior Red Cross program, which was already sending relief supplies to civilians in war zones. Schools were encouraged to produce comfort items, clothing, and gift boxes for children overseas, and to contribute to the National Children's Fund to meet emergency needs. Although families in Emma's area had little spare cash, they were happy to make quilts, coats, or blankets from scrap cloth.

Emma worked on a Red Cross quilt in the evenings, with area quilts auctioned to raise money. Her children also gathered scrap metal to sell. The United States might not be at war, but other countries were and needed help desperately.

Chapter 14

Keeping the country out of war ended Sunday morning, December 7, 1941, when the Japanese devastatingly attacked Pearl Harbor. Many Americans didn't know where Pearl Harbor was, but the fact that U.S. ships were sunk and military personnel and civilians killed was enough to enrage the populace. By late Sunday, President Roosevelt had proclaimed his Day of Infamy speech.

Edith and Emma sat stunned beside the radio. "Well, we're in it now," Edith stated flatly. "My boys may be called to go who knows where soon. Oh, how did this ever happen?" Most Americans asked themselves that same question.

On Monday, Congress declared war on Japan. By Tuesday, over fifteen additional countries did likewise.

President Roosevelt's Fireside Chat 19 declared the Japanese attacks in the Pacific provided "the climax of a decade of international immorality." He called the Axis partners gangsters who banded together to make war on the entire human race. He called on every American man, woman, and child to become partners in the most tremendous undertaking the country had ever faced. Victories and defeats were ahead, but the country would fight, and U.S. forces would win eventually, with the help of the Allies.

Roosevelt warned against listening to rumors, the vast majority of which would be false propaganda by Axis members to spread fear and confusion. He required radios and newspapers to reach the ears and eyes of American citizens and not to publish unverified reports of war efforts.

Vast assembly lines would be expanded in the near future and work seven days a week. The country needed money and materials, and production doubled and quadrupled. Such efforts should not be considered sacrifices, but privileges to defend the United States and defeat an evil Axis. Roosevelt warned of shortages to come with raw materials needed for military production.

Roosevelt said the country had a sacred obligation to the dead, their children, and all the country's children never to forget what happened at Pearl

Harbor. The country was now at war, not for vengeance or conquest, but to make the world safe for its children. The United States would face the dark days ahead knowing the vast majority of humans on earth were on its side, hoping for liberty.

Emma's world became a mental whirlwind of international and national news, then returned to day-to-day life in rural Missouri. Many people she knew had never been as far as than Kansas City, some one hundred miles away. Now they tried to understand where places like the Philippines or Guam might be, let alone countries they had never known before like Croatia or the Balkans. Such distances were outside their understanding, for farm life was a constant local cycle of seasons, crops, and events. Suddenly, local folks were unwillingly involved with the entire world's affairs, something they resented. Yet they felt a small part of the larger war effort.

Cold and snowy Thursday, December 11, arrived. By evening, everyone heard on the radio that Italy and Germany had declared war on the United States. Now America would be stretching its military forces across two vast oceans.

****

On the home front, plans for the Christmas program proceeded. Emma wrote the play, the children practiced their parts, and winter set into the area. She bought a new black dress and four-buckle overshoes. She set hair for neighbor ladies and listened to local gossip and attended dances on weekends. She shopped and wrapped Christmas presents and sent cards.

During the week, Emma graded papers and perfected the Christmas program. On Friday, December 19, which luckily arrived as a warm clear evening, program attendance rose to capacity for the one-room schoolhouse.

Christmas Eve that year reflected the public's mood, warm but misty. Ice coated the roads, but Emma's brothers and their families arrived in Maryville to spend the night at Edith's home. Having so many people in a small space required goodwill by all, but the experience bonded the family especially tightly with the draft looming.

By the next day, a dear family friend left for service after being drafted. Other young neighbors enlisted immediately, rather than wait to be drafted. Most men felt torn between wanting to enlist as a patriotic duty and knowing their families and farms required their attention. With the country at war, farm production had to increase dramatically, so farmers were desperately needed on the home front.

School studies went on as if no war existed. Charlie, eight years old, joined Emma's class on December 29. The snow melted enough so everyone made three big snowballs at recess.

Daily life continued its routine of winter weather, school, studies, community events, and family gatherings. Overlaying all the normalcy, the evening radio war news and daily newspaper updates intruded into their lives. At times, everything seemed unreal to Emma, who felt she switched constantly from being pleasant and encouraging to her students to worrying about what changes loomed ahead that she could not control.

Chapter 15

Emma glanced out the schoolhouse window on January 1, 1942. Huge snowflakes swirled in angry fits, driven by furious winds. The roads had drifted full in places, and Emma dismissed school at one o'clock. She sent the students home with assignments to do in case school was canceled the next day.

"Be careful on the way home. Everyone stay together until you reach your turnoff roads. Bud, you and Sam make sure the younger kids get home safely, will you?"

For once, Bud was agreeable. "I'll get them there. Might have to carry Mary Sue 'cause she's so short," he said with a laugh.

Mary Sue's eyes grew large when she saw how much snow had piled against the schoolhouse steps.

"What about you, Miss Trotter?" asked Sam. "You'd better get goin' too. It's real deep out there."

"I'll leave as soon as I straighten up and restock the coal box. You have a safe walk home. Now get going and watch your steps."

Emma shivered as the freezing air blasted the room when her students left. She stacked her papers, placing them in her book sack. Then she cleaned the blackboard, swept the floor, and wrapped up to go outside to the coal bin. She had brought a pair of slacks to wear under her dress to and from school.

I'm sure glad I have my overshoes, but I'm not sure they're tall enough for this deep snow.

She opened the front door, felt the assault by frigid air, and dreaded going to the coal bin, which lay to her left beside the building. Struggling through the deeply drifted snow, she managed to pry open the icy lid, scoop coal lumps into her bucket, and head inside. She filled the coal box for the next school day, whenever that occurred, and put out the stove fire.

"I'm not going home by the road tonight. I'm taking the shortcut across the field. The snow's deeper on the drifted roads than it is in the pasture, I think," she announced to the empty room.

The distance to the Roberts' house going across the pasture was about a half mile. Normally, Emma would not go home that way, because a nasty tempered bull claimed the winter pasture as his own. But today, the bull would be huddling in the lean-to by the barn, not tempted to venture outside.

By the time Emma left, the clock said two thirty. Her chores had taken longer than she had intended, and the snow had fallen several inches deeper. Emma tossed her book sack over the south fence, stepped her overshoe into a wire slot, and tried to balance herself against the force of the north wind. Gripping the post, she managed to swing her free leg over the fence, pivot, and bring the other leg over the top. Then she stepped down—to find herself buried in over a foot of snow.

Fierce swirling wind drove snowflakes into her eyes and threatened to rip her tied-down knit hat from her head. The cold sucked air from her lungs, making it hard to breathe. For the first time, Emma felt panic growing.

She couldn't see the farmhouse through the blizzard, but she knew the north wind slammed her back. As long as she walked away from the wind and angled to her right, she would eventually run into the fence leading to the house. Staying in place would prove deadly, so she forced herself to lift her entombed boots and begin walking forward.

Emma had traveled about one third of the way when she realized her strength was failing. Each step brought painful cramps in her legs, which were sucked into the deep snow with each step. Breathing the cold air, even with her neck scarf tied over her mouth and nose, froze her lungs. The physical strain sapped her energy until she feared she could not continue. No one would be out in the blizzard, and she had taken the shortcut instead of the road, so no one knew her location if they did search for her.

She struggled onward, each step becoming shorter and more difficult. She understood stopping to rest would be fatal but wondered how long she could force her body to wade through the knee-high snowflakes.

Then she thought she saw a shape through the blinding snow, a gray form also moving slowly. She shook her head and strained to see better. Yes, something moved ahead of her.

A horse and rider trudged through deep drifts and swirling flakes. They approached her like a slow-motion movie scene.

"Emma! Emma, is that you?" yelled the man's voice.

Emma waved her arms in disbelief. "Here! Here I am!"

Turned sideways, the horse blocked the wind. The man's arm reached down to pull Emma up behind him on the saddle.

"I was hoping you were holed up at school," shouted Tom Roberts. "I never dreamed you'd be out in this storm."

Emma clung to his waistline as he turned the horse away from the blistering north wind. "The storm just got ahead of me and I waited too long to get started home," she screamed back.

They ceased any conversation attempts as the horse struggled to carry two humans through the deep snow. *He'll enjoy extra oats tonight,* thought Emma, *if we make it back safely.*

After what seemed an agonizingly long time, the fuzzy shape of the barn appeared ahead. The horse sensed shelter and added a little more effort to reach home, safety, and a warm stall. Emma had survived her first blizzard.

Ruth thawed out Emma with hot tea, a hot meal, and a warm footstone to heat her bed. She also ordered Emma to stay in bed as long as she wanted. "No idiot's goin' to school tomorrow with that much snow closing the roads."

Morning arrived as the coldest of the winter. Many telephone lines had blown down, but the Roberts' phone still worked. The party line had passed the word about a fire west of Burlington Junction, which had burned down a house, leaving the family homeless. Emma and Ruth worked on the Red Cross quilt, making blocks to be hand-sewn together in patterns.

School didn't resume until Monday, January 5, when they shoveled paths to reach the outhouses and coal bin. The next day they received their first mail in a week. It took until Friday before the county grader plowed the east-west road past the school.

Emma marked test papers, worked on entertainment ideas for the next community meeting, and read newspapers full of depressing war news. A couple of friends had carried through with their wedding on Saturday during the bitter cold left by the storm. It was the only happy news.

The war intruded into the classroom. Besides the Junior Red Cross initiatives, the United States sold World War II Defense Savings Bonds books. Emma bought ten-cent Postal Savings Plan Stamps using her own money as incentives for her students.

"Okay, Charlie, this week you did very well on your homework. You scored two 100 grades in spelling, so I'm giving you a ten-cent Defense Stamp. And here's a book to paste it in. When you get forty stamps, you can buy a Series E war bond," announced Emma.

Charlie's face lit up with happiness. He was the new kid in school, but he had done better than the long-term students.

Emma also had the children make a "Remember Pearl Harbor" poster. They drew small pictures they pasted onto the poster.

To be paid each month, Emma had to walk to Mr. Watson's house to get her teacher's warrant. Then, when she got a ride into Maryville, she would deposit the check, keeping whatever cash she needed. She paid the Roberts for her board each month. By late January, she had completed five months of teaching.

In some ways, she felt she had been doing teaching longer and, in other ways, a shorter time. Her attitude switched depending on how each day went, but she assumed all teachers felt that way. They loved their students, but some days teachers just wanted to send the children home to avoid their antics.

A new family moved in northeast of the school, and their daughter Kathy, age ten, began classes. Emma's room now had five students.

The day had been warm and the roads perfect. Throughout the winter, the roads would thaw into muddy quagmires or freeze into excellent walking paths, depending on weather temperatures.

When she arrived at the Roberts', she was surprised to find Tom seated in the kitchen. Normally, he would still be outside completing his chores before dark.

"Dang it," Tom fussed. "I twisted my ankle! I slipped on some ice, caught myself on a fence, but dang near busted my ankle. Ruth's out finishing the milking. My ankle's so swolled up I can't walk on it."

He had his foot propped on another chair. Ruth had wrapped a bag of ice around the ankle and found a cane for him to use.

"This is gonna keep me sittin' for too long, I just know it," he fumed. No farmer ever wanted to be injured so he couldn't care for his own farm.

"Well, I'll just start supper until Ruth gets in," offered Emma. She put away her books and papers, grabbed an apron off the wall hook, and stuffed some wood into the cook stove. "I better chuck some wood in the heating stove, too. It's going to be cold tonight."

Later in the evening, Ruth did dishes, watching the winter scene outside the kitchen window. Suddenly, she saw something waving in the house shadow cast by the moon. "Emma, something's wrong outside!"

Emma grabbed her coat and hat, running out the back door. Ruth followed her, with both women looking up at the house. They spotted flames shooting from the top of the chimney. The creosote had caught fire inside the kitchen stove's chimney, shooting fire, deep smoke, and soot into the air.

"Oh, good golly!" cried Ruth. "If we don't get that fire out, it can spread to the roof and burn down the house! And Tom can't climb a ladder! What're we gonna do?"

Emma was already racing for the nearby tool shed. She grabbed the ten-foot ladder and dragged it back to the house. The back porch offered the lowest roof access point, and she thought she could climb to the chimney if she was careful.

"Grab a couple of buckets and hand me one when I get on the porch roof. I'll try to drag the bucket up behind me as I shimmy up to the chimney. Get Tom to filling buckets from the kitchen pump. You'll have to climb the ladder to the porch edge so I can meet you there and get the buckets to the top."

"But you can't climb that slick roof! You'll just slide right down!"

Emma was already starting to climb the ladder. "We don't seem to have a choice! Now get me that first bucket!"

Ruth dashed into the kitchen, pumped water, yelled at Tom to fill the second bucket, and carried the first one outdoors. Luckily, there was little evening breeze to spread the flames.

Ruth carefully climbed the ladder, handing the bucket to Emma. Then Emma, carrying the bucket in her left hand, leaned her body into the gently sloping porch roof. She supported her body by pressing her right hand onto the roof. She made it to the V-shaped edge where the kitchen roof met the upstairs bedroom roof, only spilling a little of the precious water. Pressing both knees against the rough shingles, she lifted the bucket in front of her, bracing the bucket against her chest as she inched upward. Then she used her arms and legs to lift herself further up the slope.

Finally, she reached the flaming chimney top and poured the first bucket into the opening. The fire sizzled from the water and lessened its strength a little. Emma slowly slid down the V, reached the porch roof, and carefully crawled toward the ladder. Ruth was waiting with another bucket. Emma tossed the first bucket to the ground and returned to the chimney. The second bucket of water seemed to douse the fire completely, but Emma made a third trip just to be sure.

By now, Emma's legs were exhausted, and her lungs had inhaled a fair amount of smoke. She managed to safely climb down the ladder, then collapsed onto a kitchen chair.

"Oh, my dear, your knees are scratched up somethin' awful," sympathized Ruth. She hurried to get bandages and antiseptic ointment. "We'll get you washed up in no time. Now you just sit there and let me take a look at those legs."

As adrenaline slowed its pulsing through her body, Emma felt her strength fade. Gently, and privately, she reached under her skirt to unsnap her stockings from the garter belt. Carefully, she rolled the ruined hose down and pulled them off. Teachers were expected to wear a dress while teaching school, even in the coldest weather. Emma added a pair of slacks under her dress to go out at recess and to walk to and from school. She had taken off her slacks earlier but had not had time to remove her hose before the fire appeared. Now her nicest pair of hose were ruined, costing her money to replace them.

Ruth cleaned her wounds, trying not to hurt Emma any more than she had to do. Emma's knees and shins showed deep scratches, and they would hurt and stiffen more tomorrow morning. But Emma was safe, and their house had not burned down. The scorched roof shingles could be replaced.

Emma managed to teach school the next day. Her legs did hurt walking the roundtrip mile and a half to school, and for once, she taught most of the day sitting at her desk. She had the students come to her if they had questions when normally she would have gone to their desks.

Chapter 16

President Roosevelt's sixtieth birthday was Friday, January 30, 1942. Emma discussed his accomplishments with her pupils and the fact he was the first president ever to serve three terms. Everyone was present, although the temperature was one degree above zero.

Various students would be absent throughout the winter. Walking to and from school invariably caused health issues. Colds, pneumonia, and flu were common illnesses. Emma had her usual colds, which she figured she mostly caught from her students.

On Sunday, February 8, Emma managed to get to Maryville for the weekend. Edith and Emma got a ride to Melinda's parents' home where Owen's twenty-fifth birthday party was in full swing. Twenty-three friends had gathered to celebrate the birthday boy and to rib him about getting old. Owen drove Emma back to her schoolhouse early the next morning.

Lone Valley had planned a Valentine's party, so her children decorated the room and made cards to share. Between classes, students decorated a Valentine box and pasted hearts on paper cups for the party. They washed the shelves and blackboard, making the room spotless. Parents, school board members, and neighbors were invited to attend.

On Friday, February 13, Emma made a fruit salad and carried it to school. The room filled with happy people, listening to the children read a story and cipher. Then they hunted hearts and had refreshments. Everyone enjoyed a great time, feeling in the Valentine's mood of love.

That ease was shattered on February 14 when the city of Singapore fell to the Japanese. Edith and Emma listened to the radio details, feeling sorrow at the loss of life.

"You'd think they could at least take this day off," muttered Edith. "I just guess they haven't got any love in them right now, just war thoughts."

The next afternoon, they heard a gentle knock at their door. Emma opened it to find a tall young man with soft brown eyes standing with his hat in his hands.

"Excuse me, ma'am," he said. "Are you Emma Trotter, the lady who put out the chimney fire at the Roberts?"

"Why, yes, I am," Emma managed to say.

"I'm Peter Paxton. My mom sent me here with a package."

"Why not come inside out of the cold?"

The man stepped onto the kitchen door rug, carefully wiping his wet boots. Edith entered the kitchen and greeted him.

"Peter Paxton," exclaimed Edith. "I haven't seen you for such a long while. I run into your momma here and there but haven't seen you lately. You've sure grown taller! Come on in and sit yourself down."

Peter again wiped his boots on the rug and followed Edith into the living room. Edith held out her arms for his coat, which he unbuttoned and handed to her.

"What brings you out on this cold day?" Edith asked.

Peter looked uncomfortable, even shy. "Mom heard about Emma and the chimney fire." Peter almost blushed as he spoke. "She thought you was real brave. And she knows how women value such things and felt real sorry your stockings got ruint. She wanted you to have a new pair for being so brave."

Looking at Emma, he extended a package toward her. Emma opened the paper to find two pairs of new hose inside. She was truly touched.

"Well, she didn't have to do that," Emma said. "I was just at the right place when I could help some nice people. But thank her for me, will you?"

Peter nodded his head and stared at Emma until she felt like blushing. He had a warm smile and a good-looking, solid face. As tall as Owen, Peter had to be close to six feet, with a farmer's broad shoulders.

Edith and Peter talked about his parents, his younger brother Davie, and their farm until Edith had gotten all the latest news. Edith didn't believe in listening in on party lines to keep up with gossip, but she enjoyed catching up whenever she could. Edith and Janie Paxton had been friends for years, but only got to see each other occasionally. When they got telephones, they were able to talk more often. But Edith welcomed fresh news from Peter, since she would be more up to date than her other women friends.

Finally stretching his long lanky frame up from the chair, Peter cleared his throat. "Well, I better be gittin' home before dark. Got some milking to do."

Edith retrieved his coat, noted how he looked at Emma again, and said, "Now you just come by anytime, Peter. And you and your folks live outside

Pickering, so you're not so far from where Emma is staying at the Roberts'. So don't be a stranger whenever you're in the area."

Peter said his goodbyes and headed out the door. Emma watched him drive off in a black Chevrolet.

"He's a good boy," noted Edith. "His momma raised him right, and he's a hard worker. He's been helping his daddy farm since he was a boy. I guess he's about twenty-six by now. And he's smart, too."

Emma smiled at her mother, knowing how Edith would love to see her married. A lot of Emma's friends had married after high school. Many had children by now, some starting a second baby. While Emma considered herself average looking, she had never found someone who could share her dream of teaching and openness to learning. Oh, well, she would just keep looking and hoping.

For each birthday and Christmas for several years, Edith had been giving a present to add to Emma's hope chest. Edith had made a quilt, table runner, doilies, aprons, and other handmade items for Emma. She had even saved enough money for a baking dish or two. While Edith never pressed Emma, Emma knew she wanted her to be happy, whenever that might occur, and not rush into something.

Chapter 17

School continued as usual. Charlie moved to Nebraska. Miss Kimberly taught the children to twirl a baton. The students made a farm implement poster and drew a diagram of the Roberts' farm. The next unit included materials on "America Goes Abroad." Once again, the war reached into the classroom.

More of her friends were either being drafted or chose to enlist. The radio war news always seemed negative, although the United States provided extra firepower to combat the Nazis expansion.

Emma spent the weekend with Owen and Melinda. Early Monday morning, February 23, the snow lay deeply over the roads and fields.

"Come on, Emma," encouraged Owen. "I was able to drive to the Wilsons' house, but you can't walk to school. I'm gonna borrow their wagon. We're still a couple of miles from the school."

They climbed into the open wagon and started down the frozen, snow-covered dirt road.

"This wagon's not gonna make it through this snow," Owen concluded. "I'll unhitch one of the horses, and we'll go on horseback."

With Emma hugging his waist, Owen urged the horse onward through the deep snow. The horse had a lot of trouble carrying two of them and trying to plunge through drifts. After about a mile, Owen gave up.

"The roads are too deep. The wind has swept the field between here and the school pretty clean, just piling snow up on the roads and fence line."

Emma studied the quarter-mile-long field leading northwest to the school. "If I walk across the field, I can make it. The snow's less than a foot deep. I can see it already, and there's no wind today. I can make it. You go on back to the Wilsons."

"I'm gonna watch you get there safely," retorted Owen. "Only got one sister and she's not gonna be an icicle if I can help it."

"Okay, stand there and freeze while I get my exercise walking across this darn field."

When she reached the knoll crest, Emma waved to Owen. He waved back, then turned and mounted the horse.

In late afternoon, Tom Roberts arrived at the school on horseack. "I'm not risking losing our best schoolteacher to this snow. Last time was close enough. Thought you better ride home tonight."

Emma, grateful for his kindness, mounted behind him. She swung her book bag over her shoulder, and they headed for home. The wind had picked up all day, now blowing strongly from the north. More large snowflakes fell continuously, so the fields held more snow than that morning. Such occurrences were common in a Missouri winter.

The next day, a new boy named Mike, age eleven, joined Emma's class. Mary Sue and Billy did not attend due to the deep snow and bitter cold because they had too far to walk. By late afternoon, the county drag finally bladed the snow off the road.

February 5, 1942, brought sad news for the area. The first Nodaway County, Missouri, casualty of World War II occurred. John Hopple would become the first on a memorial list Emma feared would include far too many names before the war ended.

Every weekend evening, Emma and Edith listened to the radio when she was home. They tried to take their minds off the war by hearing their favorite shows. One was "Plantation Party" with its country music by the Westerners and corn pone humor. Host Whitey Ford played the Duke of Paducah, with his sidekick Louise Massey. Fun and entertainment were welcome after the distressing war news.

By March, Edith had another growth on her foot. She visited another physician, Dr. Ryan, who felt he could remove the problem, which he did on April 2. Edith went home with Owen so she wouldn't be alone, and Emma could keep teaching. He could take Edith back to her doctor's appointment to have her foot dressing changed.

The radio announced the fall of the Bataan peninsula in the Philippines on April 9. The extent of the resulting tragedy would be revealed slowly, with 75,000 Filipinos and Americans force marched sixty-five miles at huge loss of life. The event would become one of numerous war atrocities.

Emma wrote to the Social Security Administration about their new hot lunch program. An outgrowth of the Commodity Donation Program, it helped farmers and boosted the nutrition of needy children. Schools began to participate. Emma felt a hot lunch would be better than cold sandwiches for her students on winter days. It would mean more work for her, but

Emma felt the rewards would be worth the trouble. When Lone Valley was accepted, Emma used some school funds to buy dishes for the hot meals.

Two new students arrived on April 10. After the war officially began for America, families had moved more. Many farm hands left for cities and factory jobs. Farm laborers became scarce, and wages had to rise to keep good help. The men would change farms if they could get a better salary elsewhere. Farmers who decided to enlist had to give up their farms if they had no relatives to take over the work until they could return. Emma's class size fluctuated all year because of the area population shifts.

One school board member dropped by with a copy of *Grit*. Emma used the weekly newspaper, subtitled "America's Greatest Family Newspaper," to encourage her students to read. Its fourteen pages included a fiction supplement that children found interesting. The content was aimed at small town and rural families, so the material was relevant to her students.

The children passed their courses with above seventy averages. The school district tests allowed Emma to compare her students to other area one-room schools. She was proud her teaching methods worked well.

War news continued nonstop. On April 17, 1942, MacArthur was promoted to Supreme Commander of Allied forces east of Singapore in the Pacific. By May 6, the American and Filipino forces surrendered Corregidor to Japan. While Emma did not want to worry her pupils, she did use the war news the children were hearing on the radio and from their parents to teach geography. She had them find the countries on the world map. She didn't think any of her students would ever become involved in the war, since even Bud was only fourteen years old, and surely the war would be over long before he would be old enough to fight.

Miss Kimberly now taught the children rhythm band, studying songs and folk games. Her appearance each week gave the children a welcome break from having Emma teach. While Emma could play the piano a little, she never felt qualified to teach music or play for the children.

Late April found her children making Easter rabbits for art class, and Emma wrote the Easter program. Mr. Murphy brought their surplus commodities for the hot lunches. Emma made pork and beans and washed apples for their first hot meal on April 25. Another noon they had fried eggs and prunes, and later they made cooked wheat cereal and apples. The students enjoyed the new food, which meant they didn't have to tote their lunch buckets each day. Some students still brought homemade cookies or pie for their dessert or to share.

****

After Peter met Emma on February 15, he called her the next weekend. Since then, they had been on many dates.

"Remember our second date?" asked Peter as he drove Emma toward Maryville one Friday evening. "I picked you up at the Roberts', and we headed for Maryville for a movie."

"But we never got there," Emma laughed. "The bridge was out on the county road, so we tried to turn around and got stuck in the mud. You had to walk to the nearest farmhouse and get help to pull the car out. I sat in the car and froze waiting for you!"

"Yep, but it was a fine evenin' anyway, just being with you. You're a special girl," Peter said as he put his arm around Emma's shoulder, pulling her closer.

Emma snuggled, enjoying the feel of his body warmth on the chilly April night. Her mood changed, and Peter sensed the shift.

"Okay, what's wrong?"

Emma sighed. "Please pull over so we can talk."

Peter found a spot off the road under a tree. He thought he knew what was coming, but he waited for Emma to say what was on her mind. Their relationship had deepened in a short time, and Peter knew Emma was going to be his wife—someday.

"I just don't understand why you enlisted in the Army," Emma began. "Your dad needs your help to keep the farm going. The government needs all the food production it can get. We're feeding all those military people and even civilians overseas. Farmers are essential personnel and exempt from the draft. So why did you enlist?"

When the United States entered World War II, the Selective Training and Service Act was amended on December 20, 1941. All men between the ages of twenty and forty-four could serve, and all men between eighteen and sixty-four had to register for the draft. But farming was declared a necessary occupation, and farmers could apply for exemption.

Peter stared at the old Chevy's steering wheel. "I know I don't have to go, and Dad could use the help. But he's got Bill as a hired hand, and he's a good worker. He's also 4-F 'cause of his limp, so he can't be drafted and won't quit on Dad. I thought a lot about it, and I just don't want to be left behind. So many fellers are servin' and gettin' hurt, and the world's goin' crazy. I wanna do my part, whatever that is. I'm real good with machinery, so maybe I can repair stuff. I just feel like I have to go."

Emma had tried to be brave before, but now Peter was to leave on April 24. Their time together was getting too short, so she jumped into her true feelings.

"You have said you want to marry me. And I certainly want to marry you, so why don't we get married before you go? I want to be your wife and have you know I'm really waiting here for you to come home."

Peter squeezed her closer to him. "There ain't nothin' I want more than to have you as my wife. But I don't know what's gonna happen while I'm gone. I know not all the fellers that go into the Army get home, and I don't want you to be a widow. And we think we love each other enough to get hitched, but it's only been two months. I know how I feel about you, and you seem to feel the same about me. But I want you to have time to think and be really sure. 'Cause I'm just gonna get married once in my life, just like my folks. I want something permanent, so we gotta be sure."

Emma understood his logic, but something inside her said otherwise. "I don't care about maybe being a widow. I could take that, but I want you to know I'll be here for you without any doubts. If we were married, you'd know for sure. My folks only married once, too, and Mom still hasn't thought about remarrying after six years."

"But I wouldn't want you grievin' for me and not getting' remarried for years if you found someone else you loved. That's just too lonely a thought. You're too nice a gal to be a old maid forever. If we was married before I leave, you might feel obliged to wait too long to love someone again."

Peter sighed. "Besides, this way, you'll be wanting me even more when I get back. We're gonna have a grand wedding with a real chivaree! I'll have my Army pay, and we can make a big day of it. And you can plan where you want your honeymoon to be," he coaxed suggestively.

Emma just nodded her head. She wouldn't and couldn't force him to get married now if he felt so strongly. She felt let down somehow, unsure of the future. She hated it when she couldn't control fate.

Rain pounded the Chevy as they drove home after the movie. Emma didn't pay much attention to the show, just memorizing the feel of Peter sitting next to her with his arm around her shoulder. The emptiness she felt when her father died crept into her heart. Finally she had found a special guy of her own, someone she could trust, love, and believe. Peter was someone a woman knew would be there all their married life, for his strength and steadiness had been proven over two months. And Edith knew his parents were salt-of-the-earth folks.

Peter and Emma saw two movies on April 19. In Savannah, they saw *You Belong to Me,* a romantic comedy starring Barbara Stanwyck and Henry Fonda. A wealthy man met and fell in love with a beautiful doctor while on a ski trip. Then Peter and Emma drove to Maryville and saw *Ball of Fire,* starring Gary Cooper and Barbara Stanwyck, another screwball comedy about a group of professors living together in New York while writing an encyclopedia. Emma tried to enjoy the shows, but Peter was to leave for Fort Leavenworth in five days.

Monday, April 20, was the start of Emma's last four weeks of her first teaching year. Although the weather provided sunshine, Emma felt extremely dreary. Already she was dreadfully lonesome and not hungry all day. She even slept two hours after school, something she rarely did.

The next day, she felt a little better. Wild plum trees blossomed white, and purple violets nodded their tiny heads. Her students worked on a birdhouse for the school, and Emma killed a snake on the playground before it could bite anybody.

Friday, April 24, brought Emma's spirits down again. Peter left in the early morning hours for Fort Leavenworth to be examined for fitness and to be inducted into the Army. While she secretly hoped something might get him declared unfit for service, she knew his excellent health and hardworking stamina would make him an ideal candidate. He expected to be home the following week for a short time. But she resented the fact she couldn't see him leave on the bus and missed him already.

Chapter 18

Emma's routine continued to finish the school year. That Saturday, she attended a teachers' meeting concerning sugar rationing. In spring 1942, sugar was the first U.S. food rationed. America had never produced enough sugar, getting most of its supply from the Philippines. When the Japanese cut off that route, rationing became the only answer.

Rationing was inevitable because of the restricted amount of imported goods, limited transportation due to a shortage of rubber tires, and diversion of agricultural harvest to soldiers overseas. Now the Office of Price Administration set price limits and rationed food and other commodities to discourage hoarding and to ensure a fair distribution of scarce resources. Local schools became designated places where people could register for sugar ration books, so Emma and other teachers had to be trained in the process.

Emma now became directly involved in the war effort on the home front. Somehow, she felt more connected to Peter, supporting his efforts by keeping supplies heading to him and other troops. Civilians at home saw a bombardment of government advertising explaining and encouraging compliance with sugar rationing and other restrictions to come.

Even Tom Roberts had to register for the Army, which he did on April 27. He was over fifty, but still required to show up for potential service. "Only if they're desperate would they want me on the front lines" was the way he put it, trying to laugh and make light of a potentially serious situation.

The Lone Valley school board appreciated Emma's teaching efforts. They offered her $70 a month for the next school year, but she wanted time to see if she might be able to earn a better salary elsewhere. Teachers became in short supply, since some young women enlisted or worked in factories for increased wages.

On Wednesday morning, April 29, Peter came home on a ten-day furlough. That evening, he drove over and picked up Emma.

"Well, they say I'm fit for service," Peter announced. "I don't know where I'm gonna train on planes yet, but they said they'd call me about it. In the meantime, I want to spend as much time as I can with you."

They had fun at a friend's house the next evening, until they received a call that a distant relative of Peter's had been killed in a truck collision. "Well, he won't have to worry about being killed by a German," Peter said quietly.

On Friday, Peter took Emma to his high school alumni banquet in Pickering. He dressed in his best and only suit for the semi-formal occasion. When he picked up Emma, Edith remarked, "Well, don't you look handsome! You both look like you were made for each other!" Peter and Emma just laughed, but Emma still wished they would get married before Peter might be assigned overseas.

Saturday evening they saw *The Lady Has Plans* in Maryville. Starring Ray Milland and Paulette Goddard, the movie portrayed a gang of criminals who murdered a scientist, stole plans for a radio-controlled torpedo, and tattooed the plans in invisible ink on the back of a woman named Rita. Emma mostly watched the movie out of the corner of her eye, while she memorized every expression and line on Peter's face. Ten days were passing too quickly.

Emma registered local folks for sugar ration cards on Monday. Out of nine families, seven signed up that day. School had been canceled in order to handle the time needed to explain the rationing system. By Wednesday, the last family had registered.

Emma had dinner with Peter at the Roberts' house that night. He let Emma practice driving his stick-shift Chevy to Clearmont and back to the Roberts' while they talked about the future and his training possibilities.

Emma gave her students their final tests for the school year on Friday. She also packed her belongings, ready to leave the Roberts'. She would spend the summer with Edith, at her brothers' on weekends, and attend college during the week.

Peter picked her up after school. They drove to Pickering to see Myrtle Tree school where Peter had attended first through eighth grades. They drove by the Country Club and then to Edith's house.

"Well, my furlough's up. I have to leave tomorrow for Leavenworth," he sighed. "I'll sure miss seein' you regular. Don't know what I'm gonna be doin', but I hope you'll write me every day. I'll write you every day if you want me to."

Emma took his face in her hands. "Yes, I'll be writing you every day, and you better write me back! I'm gonna be lonesome without you. I've grown kinda fond of you!" she laughed, knowing that was an understatement. She loved Peter.

At three fifty p.m. on Saturday, May 9, 1942, Peter boarded the bus for Fort Leavenworth. To keep herself occupied after Peter left, Emma attended the Music Festival of rural schools at the college. Lone Valley did not participate, but she tried to enjoy the evening, knowing how hard the various teachers had worked to prepare their students for the program.

After celebrating Mother's Day with Edith, Owen and Melinda, and Jacob's family, Emma found herself back at school for the last Monday that term. Everyone was present and practiced the patriotic drill program Emma had written called "Victory for America."

Peter's first letter arrived Tuesday. He wrote about being handed a uniform that sort of fit, boots that needed breaking in to be comfortable, and other items, all green. He got his first drill instructions from a nice sergeant who "hardly raised his voice at all." Peter had written with "Ha!" after the statement. Emma missed him terribly.

Her students did well on their quarterly finals. For the next two days, they practiced the program and cleaned and decorated the schoolhouse. Thursday evening, parents attended a basket supper and closing day ceremony. Bud and Sam graduated eighth grade that night, so Emma gave each of them a one-dollar bill. Both boys beamed from the unexpected gift. Bud even told Emma he thought she "was a purdy good teacher." Emma smiled, "I hope you go on to high school, Bud. You're smart enough to do well."

The last school day was a play date. Everyone walked across a field to Bill Benton's house to join students from Prairie View. After lunch, they played baseball. Emma managed to cut her finger, the only injury of the day. Later, the Lone Valley students climbed onto a neighbor's pickup and rode over to Prairie View. Most of the parents and other siblings met the students and enjoyed a basket supper. "I'll miss all of you! You've been great students, but I'm not sure if I'll teach at Lone Valley this fall," she told them.

Emma cleaned the schoolroom Saturday morning. Owen came and loaded her belongs at school and the Roberts' house. Tom and Ruth hated to see Emma go for she felt like the daughter they never had. Then Owen drove Emma to Mr. Watson's to leave the school key and to Superintendent Burr's to complete final paperwork.

Her bank account totaled $36.38, plus she had enough money at home to pay for summer tuition. While she would miss her students and her first year of teaching, Emma was ready to attend classes toward her degree. Her studies would partially keep her mind off Peter.

On Tuesday, May 19, Emma received a letter from Peter. He was now at Jefferson Barracks at LeMay, Missouri, eleven miles south of St. Louis near the Mississippi River. Peter said it was the oldest operating military installation west of the Mississippi, founded in 1826. Now Jefferson Barracks formed a major reception center for U.S. troops doing basic training.

Finally having his address, Emma could start writing daily letters. She told him about school closing, starting back to college, and other area updates. She closed by saying how much she missed him and for him to be safe.

The first week after school, Emma stayed with Mike and Kate. She loved playing with little Tommy and got to ride Mike's two-year-old colt to see Mae Beckett. Emma and Mae talked on the phone and occasionally got together, but they had a lot of news to share. Mae was working as a cook at Gray's truck stop north of Maryville, where her cooking had soon become a favorite of local folks and long-haul truckers. Emma filled Mae with details of her romance with Peter.

Emma helped Mike and Kate with the chickens and chores, plowed potato rows, and helped Kate make soap. She babysat Tommy while Mike and Kate ran errands in town. Wednesday evening, they all went to Savannah to see *They Died with Their Boots On,* starring Errol Flynn and Olivia de Havilland. The highly fictionalized version of General George Armstrong Custer's life covered his time from West Point through the Civil War and finally his death at the Battle of the Little Bighorn.

Later in the week, she visited Gene and Janie Paxton, who gave her a picture of Peter. She told them, in general, about Peter's letters. He was also writing his parents every day, telling them about camp life.

The next week, she stayed with Edith a few days, then got a ride to Jacob and Helen's house. Emma got to play with little Alice, her six-year-old niece.

Edith turned sixty-one years old on Thursday, May 28. Her birthday was the same day as the Dionne quintuplets, who were eight that day and the biggest celebrities in Canada. They were the first quintuplets ever to have survived their infancy, and each year magazines carried a story about their lives. Edith and Emma celebrated her birthday at home with a special cake and read magazine stories about the Dionnes.

Emma received a letter from Peter on Monday, June 1. On May 29, he had been moved to Chanute Field at Rantoul, Illinois, 130 miles south of Chicago. Chanute was the second largest technical training base so far during the war. A new 15,000-man quarters had been built to house the trainees but were insufficient to accommodate the rapid influx. Many soldiers were temporarily housed in tents, but Peter had a barracks bunk.

Emma registered for the college ten-week summer term for humanities, individual art, history, speech, and physical education. Her full class load would keep her busy through the hot months. She celebrated by going up-town and buying a new dress suit and a pair of white oxfords.

Friday evening, Edith, Alice, and Emma went to see *Gone with the Wind*. The color was spectacular, but the Civil War story left Emma with fears of what might happen to Peter during World War II.

June 7 marked the six-month anniversary since Pearl Harbor's bombing. The radio shows recounted those events and updated the latest war news. On June 4 through June 6, the Battle of Midway had raged in the Pacific. The Allies won, a turning point in the war there. In late June, Germany and the Axis partners launched a new front into the Soviet Union, pushing toward Stalingrad.

All summer, Emma studied diligently. She visited her brothers and helped them with chores or planting crops, set curls and hair waves for Edith and other neighbor ladies and wrote to Peter. Her home duties included mowing grass, tending the garden, canning, washing and ironing, and helping wall-paper two rooms. At night, they listened to the radio for music or war news.

"It's been six weeks since I last saw Peter, but it seems much longer to me," Emma told Edith. "I miss him so much." Also, her nephew Doug, Bob's only child, turned ten that day, and Emma sent him a birthday card.

On Saturday evening, rain poured extremely hard with fierce winds. The 102 River on the east side of Maryville overflowed its banks. Telephone lines were down, so Emma could not reach the Paxtons to see if their farm had any damage. More rain on Sunday meant a soggy Father's Day and no out-door picnics. One year before, Emma had signed her first school contract.

Emma received another letter from Peter on June 23. He sent a pho-tograph of himself and told about his July 4th plans. His training on B-17 bomber engines seemed to be progressing well.

Emma wanted to see Peter badly. She wrote to ask if he wanted Mrs. Paxton and her to come to Rantoul for July 4th. Uptown, Emma talked to the bus depot agent and found the route to Rantoul. *A round trip ticket will cost $16.54, but I really want to do this.*

She tried four times on Monday evening to call Janie, but the phone line was still dead. At seven o'clock Tuesday morning, June 30, Emma finally got her.

"I'd be mighty pleased to go with you to Chanute, if Peter wants us to come! It just wouldn't be proper for you to go alone."

Emma quickly wrote an air mail letter to Peter to see if he could get a pass.

Finally, on Friday, July 3, Emma received a special delivery letter from Peter. He would try for a pass for July 4th, so Emma called Janie. Then Emma rushed uptown to buy a new suitcase and home to pack. Because the roads were so muddy, Janie got a neighbor to drive her in a buggy to the paved highway, where another neighbor brought her into Maryville.

Janie Paxton and Emma took an afternoon taxi at a quarter of four to St. Jo, Missouri. From there, they boarded a bus to Kansas City, where they ate dinner. At ten o'clock, they left on a Greyhound bus to St. Louis, riding all night. At a quarter of seven the next morning, the two tired women arrived at the St. Louis bus station, then left at seven o'clock for Rantoul. The bus crossed the Mississippi River at daybreak. They rode through Effingham, Champagne, and many little towns. Arriving in Rantoul, they walked to the north gate, where Peter was waiting for them. He went inside to pick up his pass, then the three left the base.

Peter had arranged a room for the two women at a little country hotel. They settled in and then ate supper. Emma was exhausted from the long trip. Excitement over getting to see Peter and people talking and jostling her on the hot stuffy bus had meant very little sleep on the long ride. As much as Janie wanted to see and talk with her son, she realized Emma and Peter needed to be alone. Finally, she excused herself. "My old bones are achin' from that long bus ride. I'm gonna let you young folks talk while I head to bed. Emma, don't be too late, now." She laughed, winking at the two of them.

The evening turned unusually chilly. Peter and Emma walked outside and along a path. The hotel had placed a small bench there, so they sat down to enjoy the quiet and be alone to talk. When the sky had finally darkened, they could see the Rantoul fireworks display.

"You'll never believe what I had to do to get my pass," began Peter, watching the brightly colored bursts light the sky. "The sergeant wouldn't give guys a pass to go see their girls. So I told him my mother and sister were coming all the way from Maryville. He's from St. Jo, so he finally gave me a pass. I didn't have any demerits, so I'd earned a trip off base. So, Sis, how do you like seeing your brother?"

Emma laughed. "So that's why you wouldn't marry me! We're really brother and sister, huh?"

"I've sure missed seeing you. I think about takin' you to the movies, or at least headin' there and maybe findin' a bridge out and we just spend the evenin' talking. This is the longest I've ever been away from home. Guess I'm a little homesick."

Emma squeezed his hand. "This is the farthest I've ever been away from home, so I can understand you being homesick. I never dreamed I'd be riding a bus clear across Missouri to see some Army private!"

They talked about his training and what Army life was like. While watching the stars, they discussed plans for their future after the war. Then they just sat and held each other until Emma's eyes refused to stay open.

"Okay, Sis, I'm taking you back so you can get some sleep. I know it's real late, and I gotta walk back to the base yet."

Peter steered a sleepy Emma to the hotel room door. Then he planted a deep kiss on her lips, inhaling her perfume and memorizing its scent.

Peter arrived at the hotel about eight o'clock on Sunday. The three ate breakfast, then sat in a nearby park all morning. The day was unusually cold, so they finally went to the hotel room to keep warm and talk.

After dinner together, Peter and Emma walked to the USO. Then they headed for a park, talking and laughing until ten thirty at night. Emma quickly picked up her suitcase, and all three strolled to the local drug store to wait for the bus. Peter had to leave at ten fifty to return on time to his barracks. It was hard for Peter and Emma to part, and Peter kissed Emma fervently, even while his mother was watching.

The ladies left at twelve thirty in the morning on the bus back to St. Louis and arrived at a quarter of seven in Kansas City, Janie and Edith hurriedly ate breakfast. Emma dashed off a quick letter to Peter, thanking him for a wonderful weekend. She bought some peaches at Union Market, then the Greyhound bus left for Kansas City at seven thirty. Both women slept, no matter how noisy the other passengers were.

By just before six, the afternoon bus arrived at the Kansas City terminal. The women disembarked, reclaimed their suitcases, and changed to the Burlington bus for St. Jo. The night taxi returned them to Maryville at nine thirty, and they crashed into bed. They had made a very long trip to see Peter, but both women knew the hassle had been worth it. No one knew when they might see Peter again.

Emma awoke exhausted but managed to walk to campus and stay awake during morning classes. By afternoon, she took a nap and wrote to Peter. "Brother" Peter had also sent letters since she had been on the road, which she eagerly read several times. She planned to keep all his letters to reread whenever she felt especially lonesome for him.

The rest of the summer passed following the same routine. Emma studied, took physical education classes, visited friends and her brothers, worked hard at farming tasks or gardening, and wrote letters to Peter every evening. At school, she wrote, practiced, and finally presented her speech on "Through History with the Automobile." She attended college assemblies, hearing speakers from all over the country who always had new information she mentally absorbed like a sponge. One guest from the Office of Price Administration spoke about the latest rationing requirements. She visited Gene and Janie Paxton as often as she could, sometimes spending the night there, since they already believed she would be their daughter-in-law. Emma celebrated birthdays and anniversaries of relatives, at least sending cards if she couldn't see them in person. Also, she sewed clothes so she would have some new outfits for teaching.

Whenever she had extra money from working odd jobs, she and her friends went to movies. She especially liked *This Above All,* a romance film set in World War II starring Tyrone Power and Joan Fontaine. A couple from different social classes fell in love in wartime England. *I wish Peter was holding my while we watched the movie.*

Emma received her new health certificate on Friday, July 24. She still did not have a teaching contract for fall.

Owen, Melinda, and Emma enjoyed a Saturday movie in Maryville. *Reap the Wild Wind* was a Cecil B. DeMille movie, his second color picture. Ray Milland, John Wayne, Paulette Goddard, Robert Preston, and Susan Hayward starred in the swashbuckling adventure set in the 1840s along the Florida coast. Crowds loved the movie, packing the theatre.

In late July, Peter wrote he had moved into a new barracks, and Emma penciled the change in her address book. Most evenings, she listened to the radio for updates about the German advance on Stalingrad and the Pacific war. Emma feared for Peter's possible involvement as wartime deaths mounted.

Peter sent three photographs of himself taken July 5 in Rantoul. His letters were always upbeat and never failed to mention how much he missed Emma. Gene Paxton left Friday, August 14, to spend the weekend with Peter, the first time he had seen his son since Peter's Fort Leavenworth furlough in May.

By mid-August, Emma got her grades. She passed all her courses and earned 11.5 college hours that summer.

In early August, Emma talked to Superintendent Burr about a fall school. She finally signed a contract to return to Lone Valley to teach her second year. Other teachers had stayed at their current schools because of being offered slightly higher salaries, so no teaching openings existed.

On August 25, Emma ordered new schoolbooks at a cost of $18.74. When they arrived, she walked uptown to claim them and carried them home in a box. That Saturday, she again attended an all-day teachers' meeting. The next day, Emma began writing lesson plans. She would again board with the Roberts and had to pay them $5.00 per week, owing $20 out of her $70 per month wages.

Chapter 19

Emma treasured all of Peter's letters, rereading her favorite sections many times to feel like he was with her. One common complaint concerned how irregular his mail delivery continued to be, with letters not coming for days and then arriving in a handful. Often, he talked about his barracks buddies Bill, Jones, and Mark. In every letter, Peter told Emma how much he missed her.

*****

Chanute Field
August 28, 1942

Dear Emma:
Friday evening and just back from Detail. Had to clean the orderly room me and 5 other boys so wont have that to do again for a while. You don't have much longer to pack and make new dress's do you?
We got our grades for last Phase to-day. Don't know just how they grade you but the daily list grade count a certain per cent, the mark you do in the shop so much and the final test so much. Will have another to-morrow and the final next Tuesday. My knees have began to knock all ready.
The boys up here are shooting paper wads with a rubber band now. We scrubbed up here to night but it don't look like it now.
The war news sure look good to night. Looks like things have een going good on all fronts.

*****

Chanute Field
August 29, 1942

Dear Sis,

No the A.W.O.L. has not showed up yet and don't look for him until after labor day. Would not be surprised if he don't wind up in the guard house.

Sunday, Aug. 30

Sunday evening and what a sleep. Just woke up or that is was woke up.

I got up about 8:30 this morning. Went to the Chaplin center. Came back and went to church at 11. From there to chow. Lay down on bunk and you can guess the rest.

I guess Bill is going home over labor day as we don't have to go to school then. There is 2 or 3 other boys here from his town and they have a car. I have been looking around for some one coming near Maryville but have not found any one yet.

Did you hear the news last night. I here Henry Ford said the war is going to be over by Christmas but of course will not be back for a while after it is over but will be there as soon as can git loose.

I see Bill has gone to sleep now. Will have some fun when I finish this letter for he is the one who woke me so I have to git even with him.

There is to be a show over to the Chaplain center to night. I think Bill, Jones, and I are going. Think they said it was something about Stone Wall Jackson.

*****

Monday, August 31, 1942, was the hottest day of the summer. Lone Valley opened at nine o'clock. Students included Wilma, first grade; Mary Sue, second; Amy and Betsy, third; Mary Rose and Billy, fourth; Kathy and Mike, sixth; and Lisa, eighth. Emma would be teaching nine students in six grades, requiring separate lesson plans for each grade. She arrived at the Roberts' house very tired her first evening.

The second day was more interesting. Wilma fell out of the swing, luckily only knocking air out of her lungs. She used them lustily when she sucked in enough oxygen, more from fear than from pain. Next, Mr. Wilson raked and hauled off the schoolyard grass, which meant students paid more attention to him than to Emma's reading and math lessons. The best news came afterward, when Mrs. Gibson brought a new set of *Compton's Pictured Encyclopedia* and a table on which to keep the books. Emma was thrilled to be able to offer her students a look into the world through the volumes.

One year before, Emma had started teaching. I *may not be an old pro yet, but at least I feel more confident in the classroom.* She used that courage to kill another mouse that afternoon, clobbering him with the coal scoop and tossing his carcass over the fence for critters to devour.

By the third day, Emma had killed another mouse. Mice were always a problem. The school sat next to grain fields, and children's food crumbs and building warmth lured field mice inside. *I need more older boy students who can be assigned the job of chief mousers.*

*****

Chanute Field
Aug 31, 1942

We got out of school at 10 a.m. Got 2 letters from the folks. Will have another mail call and think there might be a letter from Maryville 409 east 6th.

We had to put on our Class A clothes and go git paid. Of course had to stand in line for about a hour. Then had to salute.

I told the boys awhile ago that I was going to leave as Jones, Bill and another boy was going out to play ball and left there bill folds here with me and as to-day was pay day think it would have been a good time to of headed for home.

The A.W.O.L. got back last night. He told some a while ago that he felt like a million now but wait till to-morrow. So I suppose that is when he goes up before the judge. I don't think I want to be in his shoes or his socks.

*****

Chanute Field
Sept. 2, 1942

We went over to the skating rink. Jones and Bill put them on and wanted me to but I did not want them to have to put in a new floor. Think will try it some of these days.

Bill and I went down and got a malted milk. But was not so good. Not like the ones back in Mo. So remember that place where you said we could get good ones at.

113

Mom said that Davie got along fine the first day of school. How did you get along.

What was the print on the bottom of your last letter. It looked like you had been using lip stick for there was a red finger print on one page. I had to laugh when I saw it.

*****

Chanute Field
Sep. 4 1942

Well how is ever thing in Toad Hollow. I had another day of K.P. and I had to sleep fast last night to get any sleep at all as got home from school a little after one am and had to git up at 4 to go on K.P. Had to work at washing pots and pans.

They hitched me to a mop and had to work at that till after noon and was most ready to rest when I got back to the barracks.

There was another welcome letter from a Toad Hollow school teacher and think I have read it 3 times.

You spoke of the lasting intention. I guess some more have the same idea as I see a marriage licenses were given to Ronald Hylock and Virginia Main of St. Joseph. He is a brother to the boy we meet in Clearmont the night we were over there. He is only 18.

The boy that was A.W.O.L. got $15 fine and has to stay on the Post for 21 days. And another boy from up here pulled out yesterday. I would rather stay for when this is over they will have to make up all the time they were A.W.O.L. and when they turn me loose I want to be free.

You better walk over as I got a box of cookies from home to-day and we will eat a cookie and talk. I bet some ones ears would burn don't you.

There is a big game going up here to night. Heard one say he had lost all of last months pay and $5 that was mailed from home. That is about the way I would wind up if I got in the game. So guess I had better just keep on putting my spare time in writing letters.

*****

Emma's teaching ended on Fridays, but her duties did not. On Saturday,

September 5, she returned to school at nine o'clock and worked until four. She cleaned library shelves, which were always dusty from the dirt road powder blowing through the open windows. Next, she cleaned and sanitized the outhouses, concluding girls were neater about personal habits than boys. She decided to have a talk with the boys on Monday about cleanliness. While the trash burned outside in an old barrel, Emma worked on lesson plans for the next two weeks. She couldn't leave the building until the trash had burned itself out to eliminate any fire danger. Her hard work on Saturday was rewarded that night when the Roberts made ice cream.

Sunday brought more ice cream freshly frozen. Emma and Ruth washed and set their hair, eating ice cream while they waited for their curls to dry. They even had beef steak for supper. As usual, Emma wrote to Peter every evening, though no mail would leave on Monday, Labor Day.

*****

Chanute Field
Sept. 5, 1942

10:30 Sat morning and suppose you got to lay on bed till late or does Tom get you up early or does he still have the dog do it. Had the dog forgit you when you got back. But if it had will soon learn when to go meet you.

You ask about Davie. Mom said he told her the other day that he did not have to go to school ever day.

I think it a good one when you have a horse afraid to move. You must look cross. And as for you riding a horse I don't think I ever saw you. But think I heard of you riding one when the snow was to deep to go in a wagon.

We git labor day off but will have to be back on the field at 12 Sunday night and that will spoil a lot from going home. Or cause a lot to go A.W.O.L.

I suppose to-morrow will sleep till late. Go to church. Then put the rest of the day in writing letters and sleeping. That is if Bill will let me. One thing about it he goes to sleep when I don't and don't think I don't get even. Saw you once when you were about ready to go to sleep. July 4th. Ha.

*****

115

Ilene W. Devlin

Chanute Field
Sept. 6, 1942

Sunday they come in and wanted 2 to go and help move 6 fellows clothing and bedding up to the supply house that had gone A.W.O.L. A lot of the boys left last night. They told them they had to be back by 12 to-night or they would be marked A.W.O.L. Don't know what they will do if they are not here but don't look for them to do so much for there will be so many of them.

We got home from school last night about 12:30. And Bill got a chance to get a Pass at the last minute. And there were 3 other boys going to his town so he pulled out with them. I sure wish they had of been some one from Maryville that I could of went with.

How are you getting along with the mile 1/2 hike morning and night. It might be that if you would talk good to Tom he would let you ride the red mule to school as you are a good hand at catching horses. Or do you look cross enough to catch a mule. Ha.

There was a boy come in awhile ago and from the way he was walking I think he had had to much whistle (booze).

There sure is a lot of racket in this Phase. They have the engines in a large brick building and they will put a trouble in it. Then we will have to find out what is the matter. And there is 26 engines. And when they all git to running at one time if you would listen you could hear them back there.

We have to keep our eyes open when out walking around as the officers have quit wearing there bars on there sholders and are wearing them on there shirt collars. Jones was going down the street the other day and one stoped him. And ask why he did not salute. He had not noticed it being on his collar.

*****

Chanute Field
Sept. 7, 1942

Went over to the Chaplin Center to 2 picture shows last night. One was the Man Without a Country and the other was Spinning Wheels. They were both right good but don't enjoy the shows here like I did when was home.

You said for me to come over and we would run a race to Maryville. Sure

116

would like to come but leave the race out. When we used to start out was in no hurry and had no certain place to go and hope to do the same way again before so long but can not leave until after git out of school and moved to where I am going and have no idea where that will be yet.

All the boys that left Sat. night were 17 mising this morning. Don't know what they will do for suppose it is the same way all over the field.

Just another from Toad Hollow that would like to be back.

*****

On went overshoes due to rain Monday morning. Emma disliked wearing them because the weight of the shoes and the accumulated mud made her legs tired even before she got to school to stand on her feet teaching all day. Then to walk back to the Roberts' in mud meant some afternoons she wondered if she had the strength to make it all the way.

Tuesday afternoon cleared enough so Emma and her students could catch a wasp, beetle, and honeybee for Elementary Science class. She also read to her students the short story "The Man Without a Country" by Edward Everett Hale. First published in December 1863, it told of an Army lieutenant who renounced his country during his treason trial. The judge sentenced him to spend the rest of his life at sea without any news about America. Emma tried to show her students it applied just as much to World War II and how every citizen needed to support the United States to win the current terrible struggle happening overseas.

*****

Chanute Field
Sept. 8, 1942

I went to the horse show last night and it was a good one. All saddle horse's and Ponys. Had 10 classes. They had some fine horses. And I guess I have not for got my horses yet for when they would come into the ring I would guess which would be first and guessed on 8 classes and picked first on 6 and the one I picked for first on the other 2 got second.

Bill came back about 11:30 this morning and we have been talking like we had not saw each other for a long time. Guess he had a good time. Got home at 8:30 Sunday morning and left to come back at 5:30 this morning. But I think they must of drove fast.

Well Sis have been wondering if you knew what you done 4 mo. ago to-night. That was the night we started to a show and wound up by going to see a certain school house.

*****

Chanute Field
Sept. 9, 1942

It is now 1:10 p.m. and suppose you are just getting settled back to school after a hour at play.

Got up this morning at 7 a.m. Took our exerises at 8:30. The service club is the Place where we went the 4th. That is a good Place to work. They have 6 Ping Pong tables.

I got a good letter from Owen this morning with a picture of his colt. It sure looks like he has a nice colt but from the way the Picture looks don't think he had took very good care of it. It looks poor. Ha. But looks like it would look good in a horse show. Said he was breaking his saddle colt to ride. May be you can talk him out of one to ride this winter. Ha.

To-day has been rather long or seems that way. Don't know why but can't get my mind out of Mo.

This Phase is going to be a rather short one as we had one day of K.P. and did not have to go Monday. So that means we will have to do 10 days work in 8 and we might get another day of K.P. before it is over.

*****

Chanute Field
Sept. 10, 1942

This morning Bill, Jones and I went over to the Chaplin Center and I wrote a letter home. The mail had one picture of Davie ready for school and he looked like a little man. A good looking boy if I do say it my self. 2 of him and his dog and one of the three of them. They said he was getting along in school fine. Said he had started to read some.

Bill did not bother me to-day from sleeping but the flies just would not stay off my nose.

*****

Chanute Field
Sept. 11, 1942

Dear Toad Hollow Sis:

Or should I say Miss Trotter. You said that is what you was known as. It is funny that a Person is known as different names in different Places. Emma in Maryville. Miss Trotter in Toad Hollow and Sis in Ill. Ha.

In this Phase the airplane engine is set on a frame and we learn all the Parts and how they work or we are supposed to and they will Put a trouble into it some Place and we will have to start the engine and find what it is then fix it.

I wish I could walk in. We would see if the old Chevrolet would still run. Have you took any more driving lessons.

I see by the papers where it looks like they are going to ration the gas. People may have to go to using the saddle horses more.

How is your mother's foot. Does it still bother her like it did and did they git the house painted. Did you have a sign painted so we would know where to stop. Ha.

*****

The next week, Emma took her children to the bridge on a field trip for science class. They picked wild plants to mount and talked about how river floods, while damaging, restore the fields' nutrients each year.

On Saturday, September 12, Emma mailed Peter's birthday present of a shaving set, card, and a letter. She missed him terribly, and he missed her. She hoped he got his card by September 15, his birthday. *I wish I could call him and at least talk to him, but I don't have a number where he can be reached.*

*****

Chanute Field
Sept. 12, 1942

Sat. afternoon. Only the flies keeping me awake. I suppose you are in Maryville having a good time. Yes I would like to be where we could both see the same show.

I bet I could guess who the guy was helping hay. Probably was the one who drives the V8 pick up so know why you wanted to help. Ha.

I did not know the lip stick was aimed to be put on that letter. So got another good laugh when I read your letter to-night.

Got a letter from home and a package with a big cake. So walk over and I will divide with you.

Write when you can and send the lip stick if you want to for now will know its only you.

★★★★★

Chanute Field
Sept. 13, 1942

Well what are you doing. I have been to the big picnic for some. Guess it was all right but I would of rather wrote a few letters and of course took a nap or so that would not mean I was lazy would it. Ha.

Had a good dinner, fried chicken, pickles, beans, light rolls, olives, and beer to drink or that is if you wanted it. But I don't care for it. But from the way some are acting they tried to drink it all. For they had to be helped in the trucks when we started back. Bill and I and some more just set around till after dinner. Then Bill and I went across the river to a corn field to look at the corn. Came back and just set around till time to come back to the Post.

They did put on a show with a jeep. Drove it up and down banks and across the river. The water was about 3 ft. deep. They sure can go up some steep banks with them.

They were 30 trucks and some cars that took us back. Each truck had 18 or 20 men so you see there was a large group. Oh yes there was a Captain and Leautants wife there and they were drinking beer and smoking. What would Mom of thought of that.

I think in this Phase the engines are all in planes and we will have to inspect the plane. Of course they are ones that do not fly. Just go over them so will know how to check them. Have to check wires, cables, oil, fuel, bolts

120

and I don't know what all.

*****

Monday brought Emma's first absent student for the year. Mike had tonsillitis and was gone the next day also. Emma felt nearly eaten up by mosquitoes as she walked to and from school, and she also cut her knee on a fence barb. The school year illnesses and injuries were mounting early.

She enjoyed a mid-week reprieve when the Roberts took her Wednesday evening to Clearmont to see *The Haunted House,* an animated short film in the Paramount Puppetoon series. The characters Jasper and his friend and nemesis Professor Scarecrow and Blackbird were always getting into trouble. Missouri had been a Confederate state during the Civil War, but Emma could see why some criticized the film for being racist.

The end of the week wasn't much better. Clouds, wind, and sprinkles continued. The next day, Emma killed a four-foot snake and a mouse. Wilma had a nosebleed. Mike turned seven, which meant a small party at recess and eating the cookies she bought the evening before. Emma gave Mike a card and a nickel, and the students gave him comic books. On Friday afternoon, Emma walked to the west corner with six pupils, then said "Have a good weekend" as they split up to go their own roads home.

*****

Chanute Field
Sept. 14, 1942

I got off of K.P. about 4 to-night. Had to carry trays (plates to you) from the clipper back to the counter. Another boy and I carried 1760 for breakfast and 1100 for dinner. The mess hall only serves breakfast and dinner and the other one serves dinner and supper. The worst trouble with carrying trays is you git so wet as they do not dry them in the Army and we carry 8 at a time. It keeps you agoing for about 2 hr. during the meal. When it is over we have to clean up our section. Mop.

You said in your letter that I had seen a lot of sights. Yes I have but none as good as the sights of home. I like to say when I go home. I wonder if Babe Fogler will come back soon. She may do like a lot of others decide to stay near her mans Post.

As for me repairing the planes I wonder some times if they will be able to come back. It might be I should say will it be able to leave. Well all I can say I will do the best I can.

Bill and I went to the show last night but did not like it. So came back to the barracks and got one fellow up to get ready for bed as he came home and lay down with clothes on and for got his troubles. I think to much beer. There sure was some headache here to-day.

I want to thank you for your package. I each time I use the lotion will think of you.

*****

Chanute Field
Sept. 16, 1942

Jones is laying here reading to-nights mail. Don't know how many times he had already read it but awhile ago he laughed out loud so guess he had good news. I never have got caught at that but suppose if they had been looking when the letter with lip stick on it came they would have caught me.

The news just came awhile ago and sounded like they were pushing the Japs and think it said there were 5000 Germans got at one place.

I was dreaming during a nap and you could not guess where I was at. Well it is where I have set out in the car and talked till 2 a.m. in Toad Hollow.

*****

On Saturday morning, Mae and Emma drove to Burlington Junction to see *The Adventures of Martin Eden,* a black-and-white adventure film based on Jack London's novel, *Martin Eden.* Glenn Ford stared as Martin, a would-be writer who signed on as a merchant ship sailor. During a storm, the ship sank, but Martin escaped and wrote about his adventures. *I wonder how many sailors will write their stories about ships sinking in war battles. Too many,* she figured, regretting anyone having to die during a war.

*****

Chanute Field
Sept. 16, 1942

Got up at 7 AM. Took exercise at 8:30. Came back and had to go help mop the building where we git our sheets and pillow slips. Came back and Bill and I went and got a hair cut. Stoped on the way and got a milk shake. Was just ready to write you when they came up and got some of us to go help make a rock garden over at one of the churches. And have just shaved and cleaned up and ready to go to school.

Yes this Phase have to check the plane to see that it is all right. Have to make about 10 inspections. I checked the engine and got partly through with the battery last night. And the longer I go the more I find out that I don't know.

Chapter 20

Monday brought six absent students out of nine, a record high. Almost all had colds, and three had tonsillitis by Friday. The weather had been chilly and wet, and walking so far to and from school wasn't good for students' or teachers' health.

Emma managed to get her students' attention, between sniffles, enough to read part of *Colliery Jim: The Autobiography of a Mine Mule*. Jim began his life on a farm in the American West, was later sold and sent to a Pennsylvania mine. Jim described how livestock were shipped and told vividly about working the coal digs. The students thought it was interesting a mule could talk about his life. Emma discussed the harsh conditions mining required and how much the world needed coal for various uses. She was able to combine reading, history, and science together from the perspective of one mule.

*****

Chanute Field
Sept. 18, 1942

Well how is ever thing in Toad Hollow.

I think I have some good news. The Captain said this morning we could not get a furlough while in school but would get one when shipped to our permanent base.

Yes I got another letter from you. And do you know what the sign is when you git hung up on the fence climbing over it (getting old). Ha. And of course the 7 hours in the class room there is no work to that.

I hope you have a big turn out at your community meeting and ever one will git in and help as that is what it takes to make one go. Would like to be there my self. You said you thought you could write 10 pages when you git started. Well when you have time go ahead as I enjoy reading them very much.

I was sorry to hear one of your scholars had to be absent as when they miss they lose interest and makes the teachers report look bad.

Well I see the letter this morning from you had no lip stick but had a X. And then kind I miss the lip sticks or the X. Ha.

*****

Chanute Field
Sept. 19, 1942

They let us sleep later this morning. Think it was close to 8 when I got up. Had no exercise.

There was a boy up here that was barracks guard and he wanted to go to the show so I took his place. It is a good job for they can not take you on detail cutting grass, shoveling dirt or something else. Might have had to go help move some barracks bags as some of the boys that were shipping out.

That is one thing you don't want to do is stay around the barracks until about 2 p.m. Don't like to do that way but all the rest do. And if you do stay you can do all the work. I don't mind doing my part but don't like to do it all.

Well there was a good joke played on one of the boys here last night. There was a boy that worked on K.P. yesterday and he never had worked on K.P. before and guess he was tired last night. So when we came home about 1:30 and he had forgot all of his troubles. So 4 of the boys picked his bed and moved it to the other end of the barracks and he never knew anything about it. He moved back about 4 this morning. Don't know what he thought for he won't say much about it. He is one of these kind that can't take a joke very well. But that is one thing a person can't do is get sore in the Army for if one does the more he will get it.

Well I guess it is a good thing you were not here to-day for there has been no sun and you would have froze. In fact I had a wool blanket doubled and over me most of the time. And Bill is setting here writing a letter with a blanket over his sholders now.

Your letter came this morning. The fellow will hold the letters in hand while calling them off and I have got so I can spot that Toad Hollow school teachers writing ½ way down in the pile and am always glad when I see it.

I got a letter last night saying that dad was coming back out next week end. I wrote them last night and told them about getting a furlough so don't know for sure weather he will come or not. Would like to have him come but if I get to come home soon would not be much use. For I can come on ½ price that he can but I am not sure that I will get to come. But here is hoping.

*****

Chanute Field
Sept. 20, 1942

Got up early this morning about 9 a.m. Went over to the breakfast club and had some coffee and cake. Then went to church. Did a little work on my lessons. Dug out some of my old letters and read them. Tore them up and threw them in the trash.

I did try on my winter clothes this morning as we have to change back to them Oct. 1 and if I can not trade mine for some large ones will have to have some tailor work done. But think I can turn them in at the supply as I have hardly wore my winter clothes. I wish things would turn out so would not need them as I think I could get along with the ones at home if the war ends soon.

Are you taking any driving lessons now. Have you drove any since I left. If you have not we will have to try it over again when I get back. That is if we can get the gas.

We will have no test this Phase but will have a test on all we have had at the end of next Phase. So will know then how much I have remembered or learned.

I had to take time out to refill my pen so washed my pen out with warm water. I have been thinking I would do that for a long time but never took time.

Do they have your house finished painting. I have to keep up on how things look for might git back some day as far as Toad Hollow. I think I could go any where up there with my eyes shut.

Well how is the scar you got in the fence. Hope you are not still lame for if you have to walk 1 ½ mile a day you need 2 good legs. One thing about it if you get tired walking you can always run. Try it some time when the mud is deep. Ha. Or you might git to ride in the V8 pick up. How would that be.

*****

Chanute Field
Sept. 21, 1942

I got 2 letters from you this morning.

Yes I think you had enough for one day the day you found the snake. And as for your troubles first write any thing you want to for if you are like me when you git the blues makes you feel better when you can tell some one.

Bill and I went to the show last night. It was a right good one but the machine broke and they did not git to finish it.

I don't know how many programs I was to at Monkey Run school but enjoyed them all. Would like to know I would be able to go to as many this year.

I had to go on detail this morning. Had one load of blankets and a load of barracks bags with the boys laundry in to take down to the laundry. Well it sure is a wonder how they keep it straight.

You ask where Bill was from. He is from Unionville, MO. We have a lot of fun together. He is laying here now covered up like it was zero and I reach over and pull the blanket off about the time he goes to seep. That is not mean is it.

Just another from Toad Hollow

P.S. I hope this letter don't take as long a road as the one did a week ago Sat. I don't know what was the matter unless they don't know where Toad Hollow is at. Ha.

*****

Chanute Field
Sept. 22, 1942

Think we are going to do some moving around here to-day or tomorrow as the boys are on different shifts. And it makes it bad for the ones that go to school at noon and get out at 6 p.m. for us to come in at mid-night and wake them up. So they are going to try to git the ones on the same shift in any barracks and I think that will be better.

My pen just went dry and Bill was laying here by me asleep so I stole his for I was to lazy to git up and refill mine. That is getting bad don't you think.

Oh yes I did a big washing this morning. 3 pair of socks. I took the rest of my clothes to the laundry but don't like to send my socks for they git them mixed some times.

I guess I did not make any thing by getting Bills pen as it went dry. So had to fill them both. But that is the way I do try to git out of work and git in to 2 times as much.

Well Emma I have come to believe that our minds run together some of the time. For I will write or I ask you something and before you have time to git the letter I will git the answer. For I wrote you the other day and ask if you had drove after I left and the next morning here come the answer.

*****

Chanute Field
Sept. 23, 1942

Got home from school at about 1 and had to git up at 2:30 a.m. and go on K. P. And my eyes feel like they would like to close and my pen don't always go to the way it should. And still have my daily chore to do. Shave. Think when I git back will let them grow.

10:10 a.m. Friday morning. Had our exerise. Came back and changed my sheets and pillow slip. Then came over to the Chaplin Center as there was no fire in the barracks. And when we got over here all the tables were full so guess there is no fire any place except here. There was a large frost last night. The roofs were white this morning.

I got another letter from you and think you set a bad example for the children. For they are trying to do like you but you were late for school. Ha.

You are not the only one that send lip stick for I looked over last night and Jones had a letter and it had lip stick on it. I kidded him about it. I thought how I would git it if he knew what was on mine. But he don't and no one else. Only you. For I thought that was no ones business but ours.

I got a letter from home last night and dad had decided not to come this week end. Said he would wait a few days and see what turns up.

The letter I got last night made me hungry. You telling what you had for dinner Sunday. We have good eats and plenty of it but it don't taste like that you git at home. Don't know why unless there is so much cooked at one time.

I most forgot to tell you what my job was on K.P. yesterday. Well I run the clipper. Some job. I put 270 racks with 8 trays to the rack for breakfast. That is not counting the forks, knives, spoons, bowls and cups. How would you like to wash them your self. Did not have so many for dinner. Only had 142 racks.

*****

Chanute Field
Sept. 25, 1942

Friday morning. It was a lot better in the barracks last night as they had a fire. It sure did feel good.

We had a moving in our barracks last night. They were trying to git it so the different shifts would be in the same barracks. Jones, Bill and I got to stay but Siegel had to move. I have not been with him very much lately as he goes out to be with his wife and he goes to school at noon and gits out at 6 p.m.

Bill and I are together as much as always. One fellow said the other day that where he saw one he would see us both. He is a nice fellow and can have a good time with him. And he don't drink or have bad habits and that is a lot.

I guess I had better tell you the joke that was played on me last night. I was sound asleep when all of once I woke up. And there was a spring clothes pin on my nose. I never said a thing but took it off with some pain. And I knew who did it. So this morning I ask what the big idea was. And the fellow said I had to stop you from snoring some way. I don't think I was snoring for I layed awake one night to see and I never snored a bit. But that is all right. I will git even some way.

*****

Chanute Field
Sept. 26, 1942

10:30 Sat. morning. Inspection over. This was the first inspection of locker and personal items. I worked most of the day yesterday getting mine in shape. It had old letters, old books and gum wrappers and I could not tell you what all. Then this morning had to put on best clothes. He did not say any thing so guess everthing was all right.

Several of the boys are leaving to-day and I wonder if I will be the next. Just got through saying good bye to a boy that was in Chanute with me but he got sick and lost out on school. And as they are turning this into a specialist school they are sending him to Neb. to finish.

★★★★★

Chanute Field
Sept. 27, 1942

8:30 Sunday evening. I got up just in time to go over to the Chaplin Center to the breakfast club. Then to church. Then Bill and I came down to Champaign and we have walked 100 miles more or less. But from the way I feel it is more. Went to a show about 5 and have just got to the U.S.O. now.

This is a lot nicer U.S.O. than the one you saw the 4th of July, as this is all brick. There is a dance up stairs.

We walked all over the Campus and there sure is a lot of nice buildings. The school here is a lot larger than the one up to Maryville.

We walked down by one Place where they had some riding horses that they hire out. Must have had a 100 but from the looks of them don't think they would have been worth over a $100. I would not of traded my saddle horse for the hole bunch. I don't suppose they could have a good horse to hire out to the school students for saw some ride and they did not act like they ever saw a horse before. I never saw any girls riding. And if you could not do better than some of the boys I saw I would not claim you as Sis. Ha.

Think Bill and I will watch them dance a while but that is all I can do. How about a lesson in dancing as well as ping-pong or is that to much to get free. Ping pong, dancing lesson and a hair wave set.

★★★★★

Chanute Field
Sept. 28, 1942

I have been wondering how you were getting around yesterday with your sore leg and today after riding horse back.

Bill and I got home last night at 10:30. Don't have to git up until 9 of a morning. Take our excrise from 10 till 11. Changed my blankets for clean ones just before noon. Then Bill and I took a few pictures of the Chaplin Center, 2 of the Chaplin and got some of a group of us that have been together for a while. We had a borrowed Kodak.

I bet I could guess why you were going down to see the clerk. Did you have to do like me when you git paided stand in line and salute.

I was sorry to hear your sister-in-law was sick and I hope she is better by now. Wich one was it. I think I have your brothers all pretty well straighten out. Any way I can tell they are all brothers for I think you all look some alike.

What did you tell the children when they said I was your brother. I did not think we would ever git to be brother and sister in Mo. even though we were in Ill.

I saw a boy and girl coming in to the Post the other day. He was as tall as I and she was rather short. And I wondered if she was his Sis. I had to laugh for I thought we could come nearer passing than them for we were both tall and I wondered if he forgot when he was telling her name.

It was real cool here yesterday and last night. I wore my wool clothes and they did not feel bad. Saw several with their overcoats.

*****

On September 29, Emma hosted the PTA meeting. Four sets of parents attended, reviewing the school's progress and discussing needs. Emma updated them on the commodities' pricing changes from the letter she had received earlier in the month.

*****

Chanute Field
Sept. 29, 1942

Tuesday afternoon. I am waiting on Bill to get the films out of the Kodak. Then we will take this weeks laundry off and up to the P.X. to have the pictures finished. Got up this morning at the time you take up school. For our excrise we had to go through the obsticle course. That is where we go over ditches, high walls, through tunnels and what not.

131

Bill went over to see the Captain about a few days off when he gits through school. Said he talked like he would git a few days but there were a lot trying and he was turning a lot down. I had thought I would go see him to-day but if that is the case may wait till to-morrow. And the chances look slim.

You said every one in school had colds. Well most ever one in this barracks have and think I will be lucky if I don't.

Bill is just starting to write probably to his girl. I notice ever day he has a letter to some one by the name of Mary and usually gits one with the return of Mary on it. Neither one of us got any letters today. He said I hope you do get some letters to-night for if we don't we won't be able to live with you. I did not think I was that bad.

*****

Chanute Field
Sept. 30 1942

Well this is a big day here to-day as it is Pay day. Got up at 8. Went and bought a hair cut. Came back and shaved. Put on good clothes and went and got my months pay. Of course had to salute. Suppose there will be a high old time here the rest of the day as some have already gone to town.

You said you had not heard when Smiths wife went home. Well she did not stay but a few days. She had to git back so the children could start to school. And Jones wife is still here and is working on the Post at one of the restaurants. I think Tom said she got $16 a week and meals and uniform. Looks like that is right good pay.

Had a right good dinner. Bread, butter, roast ham, butter rolls, ice cream, milk, turnips, rassins, and coffee, mashed potatoes.

You are mistaken if you think I would run if I came up when you did not have your hair curled unless Tom got after me with a shot gun and I will risk that.

You said the china clipper was a good job. Well I don't care to git on the clipper. Just as soon work at the counter. As for the jokes we hear yes we hear a lot of them and some would not do to repeat.

As for the people getting an idea of the people in Mo. from I and ill ever one seems to know Mo. They will say that is where all the mules come from.

You said the teacher had to study harder than the kids. I wonder what they would say to that.

You ask if I could stay in the 35 mile per hour limit. I think I could unless us and Marks were going to the show and were late. You remember Mark thought we were going a little to fast one night and there is one other time that we was fast. If I had the Chevrolet here and they would say you can go home I might see how far that foot feed was from the floor board and hope for the cop to be out of sight.

Chapter 21

Chanute Field
Oct. 1, 1942

They moved us to another barracks but will go back some time to morrow. Some of the boys had found some pets in there beds (bed bugs). I have never found any. Guess they did not like to chew on me.

Surely you don't come down stairs after your mail real fast. I stay up stairs and that is about the way I go down when they hallow mail call.

You ask about the furlough. Ever time I plan to go see the Captain something turns up. Yesterday Pay day. The day before to busy and to-day nothing to wear except my coveralls and we have to dress up to see him.

Well don't think I have not even do some dreaming some times. Had one the other night. I was in Toad Hollow setting in front of a certain place listening to a radio and you might guess who was with me.

You ask if this furlough would be 10 days. Yes I think 10 days is the most I can git if I git that. Unless I git a long ways off. Then they give you a few days more some times.

You ask about the lip stick. Yes I saw it but did not know but what it was lip stick. Good judge don't you think. I do like you say you do. Read, reread and when miss a day reread. And when I git about so many will git a can and start reading and tearing them up and throwing away.

From what Tom said about your eyes I guess he has not stoped teasing. One thing about it that helps keep the blues away. You can better git your lessons for to-morrow and not be cross. Ha.

*****

At midnight Monday, Edith's uncle Owen died. Edith took the train from Maryville to Savannah to be with the family. Emma got permission from the school board to dismiss school Friday so she could attend the funeral in Savannah and the burial in Bolckow. All the Trotter family attended except the three children. Edith's three sisters and one of their husbands also made the trip. Emma would have liked to spend more time with Edith to console her for missing her favorite uncle, after whom she had named her son Owen.

Being in Maryville on Saturday, however, gave Emma a chance to buy a sweater and Halloween decorations. She also paid down her latest bank note and returned $5.00 she had borrowed from Edith. She worked on her school lessons on Sunday, getting a ride back to the Roberts' in the evening.

*****

Chanute Field
Oct. 2, 1942

Got up at 9 this morning. Took 30 min. excrise and 30 min. of drill. Got the pictures. They were right good. Have some made and will send you one of a Toad Hollow Farmer if you would like one. It would do to keep the mice and snakes away.

I got your letter this morning. Was sorry you did not have no more at the meeting than you did. And as for something going on at Pickering there is always something there when I git there. I think you are trying to make fun of a good town.

You said that you could stay up as long as I and talk. That might be but just how cross would you be the next day. It would be all right with me for I am getting to be a good hand at staying up since I started to school of a night.

Tonight is the big test over the entire course and I don't know how I will make it.

Don't know if it was finger nail polish, lip stick or barn paint but any way I got it.

*****

Chanute Field
Oct. 3, 1942

Well just finished moving back to the barracks 294 and have it all moped and cleaned up except making my bed. Think I will wait till after noon and let it air out. For it still smells of the bug spray.

The list is up for the ones that stay for the extray 40 days of school but I do not git to stay. Will probably be moving about the last of next week but don't know where. Most all of the boys thinks that the ones that don't stay are better off. For they say the ones that take the 40 days will be expected to know all about it and will go right on as soon as get out. But that is all talk and you can hear any thing when in the Army.

The talk is that the ones that don't stay will be shipped to some base or factory. Then they will find out what you are the best suited for and will send you from there to a factory. About all the boys I run with git to stay. Bill, Jones, and Smith all stay. I suppose I will git a furlough as soon as I am moved or that is what they say so things might turn out so I could be to the next Monkey Run school meeting.

I got your letter this morning and was glad to git it. But was sure sorry to hear about your uncle and you folks have my sympathy.

You said your work kept you late at school. Why don't you leave school before 6 and what you don't git done will be there the next day.

You said you would have to catch a ride back Sunday and I think I know what you were wishing a guy in a V8 pickup would come along. Ha.

Well Sis keep right on writing to the same address and if I am moved they will send it on to me. And I will write you just as soon as I can after I git a new address. And I hope to see you before so long.

*****

Chanute Field
Oct. 4, 1942

8:30 p.m. Just back from K.P. I dished up gravy for dinner and forked up cheese for supper. And when the meals were over had to clean up the counter where I worked or should say three other boys and I. The counters are of stainless steel and there can not be any streaks when the big shots come around to inspect. If there is we have to do it all over. Had to wash with soap and water, clear water, then had to go all over it with vinegar. One thing did not have to run the mop.

Bill got a five day furlough yesterday at noon. I don't know how he did it. Guess he just put up a good talk. I went over yesterday to see if I could git one. Did not git to talk to the Captain as he was not there but talked to the first sergeant. Have to talk to him before you can the Captain and he said that the only way I could git a furlough from here was in emergency. He said if I thought it was absolutely necessary to go over and see the red cross and they would git in touch with the red cross up there and if they found it necessary then I would git it now. Did not go for could not think of a excuse that I thought would work. He said that I would git one as soon as I got to my base.

Well Sis I wish you was here for we could have a talk right here in the barracks to-night as I am the only one up stairs. Some gone for the week and some gone to town, some to the show, and three just left for the P.X. for beer.

Would like to be there so could take you back to Toad Hollow to night. I bet we would not be through talking this early for it is going to take some time to git caught up.

*****

Chanute Field
Oct. 5, 1942

I got up a little before 9. I made my bed, moped and had to shave the first thing for did not yesterday. Usual shave of a night but after working on K.P., making 3 reports after 8 was ready to turn in. Got a letter from you. Just about got one page read when had to go for excrise and don't think that was not a long hour not able to read it. Had 30 min. of excrise and 30 min. playing volley ball.

I don't know weather I will know where to stop when I git back or not. You painting your house and I hear the folks are doing some work on ours. Are doing some work on the front porch and building one on the west and think they will do some painting. You said you would of liked to of ciphered with me and might some time. I don't know if that would be best or not for you all ready know what a poor writer I am and if you know what a poor one I am at ciphering don't know what you would think. So I believe it would be better to just talk.

Yes I think it would be all right to git extray supply of gas. We might need it for we never knew where we were going when we started out.

I think you are hearing to much about my having fun when pitching hay and learning people to be windy. I am to well known in Toad Hollow. Ha. Who do people blame for things that happen back there now.

How do you make it at school being up 3 nights in a row and writing letters after you get back.

You should be here now as there is a ping pong game going. It might be I could have a lesson when they git through.

I guess we had a vistor in the barracks the night after Paid day for some of the boys bill folds were gone the next morning. Don't see why they leave them in there coveralls. I would hate to be the one if any one woke up and caught them. I expect the whole barracks would be on to them but might be surprised if knew who it was. It probably was some one that had lost his money in a game. They found one bill fold in another Squadron but no money and one they took a $20 bill and left 2 ones. Guess they did not want to leave him broke.

*****

Chanute Field
Oct. 6, 1942

Tuesday afternoon. Had to go through the obsticle course 2 times for our excrise.

I had to turn my I.D. card in awhile ago. That is the card with that good picture on it. Said there was a shipping order coming out to-night. Said if I was not on it they would give it back but I think I will be on it.

Well to-night will wind up my school days at Chanute field. Have to go at 7:30 in the morning to git my diploma.

To-day is the day I send the laundry off but I am not going to send any for if I got shipped might have trouble getting it and if any of our clothes are lost we have to pay for them and don't want that to happen for that would cut down on the malted milks back in Mo.

*****

Chanute Field
Oct. 6, 1942

We got our shipping order about 5 this evening and is now most 9 and I have been awful busy. Had to pack my clothes. Will have to turn my bedding in early in the morning but no telling what time I will leave. I don't know just where but have got some talk and if it is true will be quite a long ride.

Bill is supposed to ship but he will not be back until to-morrow night. I wish he was here so we could go together but I know some more of the boys and will just have to git a new pal.

Well Emma you will not need to write any more until you hear from me. I hope I git the mail in the morning before I leave for I know there will be one from Toad Hollow.

*****

Emma added to her school duties by organizing the Junior Army scrap iron drive on Monday. The War Production Board launched a nationwide campaign for metals. Emma sent letters home with her students asking them to comb their farms for metals to be melted down for war materiel. She and the teacher from Prairie View agreed to a competition to get people enthused to see which school's students could collect the most metal. Also, Emma wrote to her relatives and friends about the competition, enlisting their aid.

The Wilsons brought their scrap iron to the schoolhouse Friday afternoon. Emma decided to pile it along the back fence. She explained, "It'll be away from the children's playground. I don't want cut fingers, arms, or legs from students trying to climb on the metal." She arranged with school board members to have a pickup come as needed, maybe with a flatbed trailer, to haul away the scrap when a sufficient pile had accumulated.

On Saturday night, October 7, Emma attended a chivaree for two newlyweds. So many of her friends were getting married sooner rather than later due to their concerns of their men possibly being drafted. With many local men enlisting, farmers who applied for exemptions got them, because farm labor was badly needed. Food provided sustenance for military personnel, and farmers were planting every inch of land they could to meet crop production demands.

Emma got a ride into Maryville on Saturday. She bought a new green dress for $3.98. Then she visited with her mom and three aunts and bought some cider to enjoy with the Roberts.

Mae picked her up and drove to Burlington Junction to see *Ride 'Em Cowboy,* starring Abbott and Costello. The two rodeo peanut vendors got involved in the adventures of a western novelist. Emma felt like all the movies were either serious adventure stories about winning some kind of conflict in various time periods as analogies to World War II, or comedies to take everyone's mind off the war. That night she needed comedy to keep her distracted over where Peter might be posted after leaving Chanute Field.

*****

Oct. 8, 1942

Well Sis I hope you don't have much to do the day you git this for it will be some job to read it. I can't git the swing of the train. It is zig zaging and I zig when I should zag.

I left Rantoul yesterday at 1:15. Ate breakfast at Omaha and ate dinner a little while ago. We have just come into Kansas. Came through Lincoln Neb. at 11:30.

We eat and sleep on train. They said awhile ago that we would hit the mountains about night. I got your letter just before I left. Have all ready read it 2 times and may have to reread it several times before I git another.

I did not git much rest last night. Had a good bed but the swing of the train bothered me.

I am going to ask you to do me a favor. When you git this call Mom and tell her I am on the road and all right.

I think we are taking a round about way to where we are going. I think I will be on the train till some time Sat. and think I am going to a factory but don't know.

*****

Whenever Janie or Emma received a letter from Peter, they called each other with updates. Of course, Emma kept the more personal notes from Peter to herself, but she let Janie know if Peter was okay.

*****

Oct. 9, 1942

Just got back on the train. They lit us off for a little walk and don't think it did not help. We are at Green River Wyoming. We came through Denver Col. last night about 9 but I was tired and was asleep. Rested good until about 2 this morning and from then on would just nap a few min. at a time.

We were in Wyo. when we got up at 7 this morning. We have saw a lot of Jack rabbits, lots of Pheasants, some wolves and some of the boys said they saw 5 deer about day break this morning. We ate breakfast at Rawlings Wyoming. Think we are about ready to eat dinner. It is now 1:25 p.m.

We got to git off the train last night at Goodland Kansas. The boys are just like a colt that has been shut in the barn for a while. We will run jump around when we git off.

Well Sis, you think you saw some hills in Toad Hollow. Well there is no hills there to what there is here. About all we can see is hills and rocks and a few weeds and all that could git to them would be a goat and it would have to be shod.

Had a good dinner, roast beef, gravey, potatoes, soup, salad, coffe or milk to drink. I don't know what time we will eat supper but think it will be late for the car I am in ate first at noon so we will have to eat last to-night.

I don't know if I should tell you my weight or not for I am getting to heavy. I got weight just a few nights before I left Chanute Field and weight 203. And if I stay on this train much longer think I will be still heaver for all I do is eat and sleep and git no excerise. I did one thing yesterday that I never did before. Shaved while traveling.

We have had a better track to-day is not as hard to write but bad enough. Was afraid to use a pen for fear I would spoil the point. This would be a poor place to run out of gas for the houses are few and far between and most of the roads just take out across the country. Looks more to me like a cow path. See a good highway once in a while but not often.

Saw two or three covered wagons with a bunch of sheep to-day. Have not saw many cattle. Well we are going along a right good looking highway now but sure looks funny for there is no fences not even along the rail road. Just passed a herd of cattle. They were all fat but I don't see what they live on.

We don't see many buildings and what we do see looks like they are about ready to fall down.

*****

Emma's school days were never boring. Scrap metal could arrive at any time by various vehicles, including horse-drawn wagons. The event would interrupt lessons while the students watched items being unloaded. Emma had to write the fall play, and students practiced in any spare time. She never knew if the children who were rehearsing would be healthy on the play's performance date and worried about how to fill a part if someone was absent. She also tried to review the latest ration coupon values and pass along the information to area families. *When did all these extra duties appear in my job description?* she wondered.

*****

Oct. 10, 1942

Still going and have a rather rough track. Just heard the major say we were going to git to where we were going to git to at 11:15 to night. Just came through Haines Idaho. I am going the right direction this morning. I was turned around in my seat about all day yesterday.

We are seeing some better looking country this morning but still have mountains on both sides. But is a good sized valley where we are going through.

We have not been off the train since yesterday noon at Green River. I suppose if we stop for any length of time they will let us off some time today. We came through Pocatello last night about 8 p.m. and the U.S.O. gave us some cookies.

We are seeing some better looking towns in Idaho than in Wyoming and better buildings. I don't know what the people in Wyo will do when they ration the gas unless they go to town one week and stay till the next week and git the next ration and come home for I don't think one ration would take them to town and back.

I have saw a lot of country since I left Rantoul last Wed. but none that looked as good to me as Toad Hollow.

We had to turn our bedding in at 4:30 Wed. morning then go for a talk of what to do and don't. Mostly don't. Then they told us to go down and they might give us our diploma. So that is what we did.

Chapter 22

Seattle Washington
Oct. 11, 1942

Dearest Sis:

Sunday morning. I can tell you now where I am at. They did not aim to let us go to bed on the train. But after we were going to be so late they made our beds about 10:30 and they side tracked us till morning. Got up at 6 and there were trucks there to meet us. Came out here about 7. Had breakfast and I have just finished a letter home. I have not unpacked yet.

The barracks are different from the ones at Chanute. All one story. Have a folding cot for a bed. Have a new mattress and pillow. Have not got the blankets or sheets yet. There is 35 to the barracks.

Have just got back from getting sheets, pillow case and blankets. Got all new ones. Have my bed made and swept out and unpacked and my clothes hung up.

I saw a lot of sights coming through Orgen. Lots of pine trees and mountains. Would be going along and look out one side of the car and could look straight down and look out the other side and would have to look straight up. Saw several streams of water coming down the mountain side.

I think they said we came through 10 states. I will try and git a map some day and mark how we came.

Yes I am still going to have to go to school to the Boeing Aircraft Co. They build the B17 plane. Don't know if you know what that means or not but it is the same in a plane as Ford, Chevrolet, Buick or another make of a car. It is a large 4 engine Bombing Plane. I think from what I can find out the course will be about a month and will be moved then to some air base where they have all B.17 planes and that means that I git no furlough untill I git out of here.

There is no use of me trying to tell you all I saw on the trip. Will try and remember most of it and then we can have something to keep us going until 2 a.m. Ha.

I have been wondering if you got the letters I wrote while on the train or if they kept them until we got to Seattle. The Sargent that brought us would take them up but I suppose I will hear before long for am looking for a letter to start from Toad Hollow as soon as this one gits there.

Just back from dinner. Had beef, gravey, mashed potatoes, green beans, corn, apricots, milk and coffee. And another good thing. They say we don't have K.P. here.

Pvt. Peter K. Paxton
Flight B-36 A.A.F.T.D.
Boeing Aircraft Factory
6600 Ellis Ave.
Seattle Washington

*****

Seattle Washington
Oct. 12, 1942

Have to be to school at 9:30. Will be assigned to our classes to-day. Some of the boys say this course is rather hard and we have a lot of writing to do. Some say we will be in the class room 4 days and in the shop 2 days a week.

I guess things are sure high here. A lot of boys went to town yesterday and had to pay $.85 for a very small meal and it costs $.75 for a haircut and $.50 for a shave down to town. We git our hair cut here on the Post for $.40 but they do no shaving. May be you should come out here and go into the wave setting business.

I sure did rest good last night. Went to bed about 9 and did not know any more untill 5 this morning and once when had to pull another blanket up over me. I did not even know when one boy came in and we sleep next to one another.

Back from school. Gave us a lot of books and books to fill out. It looks like they are going to put a lot at us but I don't know if I will be able to catch it or not.

We go to school at 8 in the morning and git out at 4. Have a hour off for noon.

*****

Seattle Washington
Oct. 13, 1942

Tuesday evening. I got through another day of school. Had the electrical system this afternoon and we had instruments this morning. And my head is all in a whirl.

Well we did not have mail call last night for they did not have it all sorted. Your letter was the last I got while in Chanute a week ago.

We came back from school and one of the boys put a 5 gal. bucket of coal in the stove and it is sure putting out a lot of heat.

It looks like we may git some rain. I think some would be all right for the dust here is about a foot deep.

They still play some jokes on one and another. Some of the boys give another one a hot foot and another one they short sheeted. I don't know if you know how they give a hot foot or not. They will catch some one asleep and put matches along the sole of his shoe then light them and run. And to short sheet a bed is to fold a sheet and when you go to get into bed you can only use 1/2 of your bed. I did not teach that to the boys even if I do git the blame back there.

Have to put on my Class A clothes to eat supper. Reading my mail and I feel a lot better for had 4 letters from Chanute. One from you, 2 from home, and one from a cousin in New York.

Yes I will send you a picture when I git it but Bill took them home with him and said he would have some made while there. I left some money with Jones and told him to have Bill send them to me. So will send it when I git them.

*****

Seattle Washington
Oct. 14, 1942

Wednesday evening. They came and told us we had to go to the study hall for 2 hr. a night and 2 nights a week. Will be in the hanger in the after noon till 6 p.m. Will have some work on the plane.

Rained off and on till noon. Suppose there will be a big fog in the morning for have been here 4 days and have had 4 fogs.

What is ever one doing. I don't know why but my mind has been a long way from here to-day. Have thought of most ever one back there. It has even been in Toad Hollow. Part of the time about hauling hay, going to see some school house. You said my parking space was reserved for me. Well I sure would like to park there again.

I have my diploma in a book stuck down in suit case. And don't know if I like a air plane enough to have it framed or not.

Well how did you make it picking up iron. I bet I know where there is a V8 you might got. Of course you would have to have a driver. Ha. He might even give you a lesson at driving or are you going to make me do that in exchange for a hair wave set, lesson in ping pong and I believe there was a dancing lesson if I could stand you walking on my feet. And I think I could for I feel sometimes like would be willing to let some one stand on them if that would only git me back.

A lot of the boys go into Seattle ever night. Sometimes I think I want to go and when the time comes I don't care. Will just git some one you can call your friend and they will split you up and you have to be so careful who you make friends with in here. So many gamble and drink here. Would rather stay at the barracks and write letters than to be out with that kind of a bunch. There is a boy from Iowa and Neb. that seam like fine boys and we have been to-gether a lot on road out and while we have been here. But you see so many that seam like good fellows and are but when they git to where they can git whistle drink just can't leave it alone that a person is afraid to leave the Post with most any one.

The one from Iowa told me the other day that he would have been married now if it had not been for the Army. The one from Neb. don't say much but he writes a lot of letters.

It sure seems funny out here. It rained all night and you could go right out this morning and not even git your shoes muddy. I bet you would like to have that kind of soil to walk to school with. I think of you most ever rain wading to school in mud and going through wire fences and wondering if you have to feet left.

*****

Seattle Washington
Oct. 15, 1942

7:50 p.m. Had to go to study hall this morning till about 10. Then they had us go over to where they had been doing some building and break up some boards and bring back to the barracks to build fires with. Had to pick up paper, sticks and things around the barracks. Then after noon we had to go to the hanger and had some of the parts of the plane explained and took some apart and put back to gether.

Last night the boy from Iowa and the one from neb. and I went up to the P.X. and got a malted milk and candy bar. The malted milks are O.K. and don't cost but a dime. But have not found any that came up to the ones in Mo.

We had a good teacher to-day and you can't guess why. He was from Mo. Ha. Think he said he was from Independence but said he had been to Maryville. Never thought to ask him if he knew where Toad Hollow was but if he is from Mo. he has heard of that place.

I sure do miss the Chaplin Center out here. No place to write. Write part of the time on my knee. Am laying on bunk now (can you tell that. Just had to refill my pen.) There is a sargent just moving in to this barracks bout 4:30 this evening. Came from Colo. From the way he talks I don't think he thinks much of this place. But it is not so bad a place. My worse trouble is that I git so sleepie. The teacher said to-day that was the way he was when he came out here. Said it is the low altitude that does it. We are only 11 ft. above sea level here. Some times in class I think I will have to prop my eyes open for they sure do git heavy most as bad as they were July 6th.

Do you have any trouble getting gum back there. I hear it is hard to git. Will only let us have 2 package at a time.

Saw one boy come in the other day and wanted 2 cartons of cigarettes and they would only let him have one but can go back as often as we like.

It is most time to go shave for the lights go out at 9 and I might not do such a good job in the dark.

*****

October 15 and 16 found Emma at the teachers' meeting. She ate lunch there, which was a treat after eating government hot lunches at school.

Afterward, Rosalie and Emma saw a double feature at the Maryville The-ater. *My Gal Sal* featured Rita Hayworth and Victor Mature in a musical about 1890s composer and songwriter Paul Dresser and singer Sally Elliot. *Fly-by-Night* was a thriller screwball comedy with Richard Carlson and Nancy Kelly. The young doctor tracked down a Nazi spy ring in order to clear his name after being charged with murdering a scientist. From comedies to war films, nothing in-between seemed to be made anymore.

*****

Seattle Washington
Oct. 16 1942

Friday evening. I suppose you have just finished another week of school so your troubles are over. Have been wondering if you was in Maryville or Toad Hollow.

Got up a little after 5. Ate breakfast at 6. Then went for the class room. Some days we are in one then the next we are in another. Was about a ½ mile from the barracks to-day. Have it handy some days for one class room is just across the alley from the barracks.

One of the boys ask awhile ago what I was working on. He is doing the same getting a lesson back in Iowa. Think he said she taught school. So I suppose he will git a good grade for he has a tablet and doing some writing and don't see any books around.

We can leave any night at 6 and be in bed by 11. And on Sat. we can leave at 6 and stay till 12 midnight Sunday. But I guess that means to be back for some of the boys went to Seattle and one boy was 2 min. late and he had to do 3 hr. labor the next night.

I am afraid we are going to have poor mail service here. I wonder if you have got the letters I wrote while on the road out here. I know Mom is most wild if she has not heard regular but I guess all I can do is just wait and see if a letter gits back.

We had to wash the windows and git gas masks. Don't know why but they gave us all one. Of course had to stand in line awhile but that is the way. Hurry to git there then stand in line for awhile and that is as tiresome as working.

Well are you having to git up early now. I suppose Tom is about ready to start picking corn and I suppose he will want to git up early. Saw several gathering in Ill. and Iowa on the road but here saw several fields that they were getting ready to use a picker. I would like to be back to pick some. Got a letter from Glynn the other day and they were talking of paying 10¢ and 12¢ a hour up there to help pick. I believe I could make enough in a week for a show and a malted milk at least once a week if I could work steady at that price. We never see any corn out here. Don't suppose some would know what corn is.

*****

Seattle Washington
Oct. 18, 1942

Was busy when we came home. Had to shave and clean up. Put on Class A clothes for inspection that was at 5 p.m. When that was over had to go sign Pay roll and had to stand in line from 5:30 till a little after 7. Started to write you and the Neb. and Iowa boys wanted to go to town. So quit and went with them.

We just walked around as we had no places to go. Did not git to Seattle or that is the main part. The part down here by the Post they call George Town. Saw some nice homes. Did some window shopping. Saw several that was taking a wide walk and was not only the men. Would walk by a window and the men and women would be setting in there smoking and drinking. When a person does go out and see things like that it makes you think you don't care weather you leave the Post or not. After we had walked around for awhile we had a big drink (malted milk) and came back to the barracks about 10.

Went to breakfast a little before 8. Did a little washing, some socks and handkerchiefs. Went to church at 11. For dinner had beef steak, mashed spuds, gravy, spinish, bread, butter, peanut butter, black berry jam, coffee and milk.

The mail delays make you feel like you are a long ways from home and as near as I can figure it is some over 2000 mile from home.

2 of the boys in this barracks have radios. Don't seam to git so much music. Don't know if the boys don't tune into them or if they don't give out so much out here. Most of the songs that we git are Western songs. Have not even heard Sitting Under the Apple Tree since I came out here. We would

hear that about ever night in Chanute.

*****

Seattle Washington
Oct. 19, 1942

Only about 20 min. till the lights go out and have to shave yet. Don't know wich is worse to have to shave each day or to have to roll your hair ever night.

Got 9 letters to-day. 3 letters from the folks that came from Chanute. One from Maryville wanting me to send for a absentee ballot but don't think I will for would have to go before the Captain and a lot of red tape.

Tuesday morning and have about 1 ½ hr before school. Went to study hall yesterday morning about 1 hour when they came and got us to tear out some old board fences. Had to tear it out and break the boards up to have to build fires with. Cut down some old dead grass and weeds. Dig some holes. They are going to build a obsticle course. Have things to jump, walls to climb and what not. They let us off that at 11. Cleaned up and went to dinner and layed around till about 20 till one. Then went to the hanger to work. Stayed there till 6 and had to go right to supper. Had to change sheets and pillow case and git the laundry that I took off last week. And think it is plenty high. Had 5 lb. and it cost 63¢ and it don't take many clothes to weigh 5 lb. wet again. When I got that all did it was most time to turn in for the night.

I went to town Sunday afternoon. The fellow from Iowa and I had some letters to mail and went to the show.

This is some town to git turned around in. None of the places looked the same to me Sunday and was only there Sat. night. And I know what you are going to say and that is not it at all for I was sober. Ha. I think what makes it so hard to keep things straight is that the streets run in ever direction. May be 2 or 3 streets leaving one at one place. They just wind around through the hills.

Well you said something about seeing the Chevrolet drive up. Will soon be 6 mo. since I have drove. May have to have some lessons myself.

You ask if I knew where I was going before I got here. I did after we got started but they told us not to write. And if I had and they had opened it might of caused me some trouble. So just had to wait till I got here.

*****

Seattle Washington
Oct. 20, 1942

Tuesday morning. Over to the study hall working on lessons awful hard. It will be all right for there will be a teacher grade this one but if I can't think of more to write don't know how the grade will be. I don't know why but sometimes it is hard to think of any thing to write and other times have 2 pages full in just a little while. Ha

Yes I think 250 bu. of spuds would be very near enough to last till the next crop. I don't know if I would want any more or not if I had to pick them all up by my self.

I see in the Seattle paper where they have turned out some of the schools to help in picking the apple crop. So I guess it is out here like ever where else. Help is hard to git.

Had my first drill to-night from 4:30 till 5:30 p.m. We are supposed to march to and from school in formation. And some of them had got so they were like a bunch of hogs. All try to go at one time and after we had got through the Captain said we would have to march until we had improved the formation going to and from school. That is the way it goes. Some people don't know when they have a good thing.

They have also shut our passes off for a few days. They caught a bunch leaving the other night before they should at 6. And one fellow went to town and the cops picked him up. Another came in with his face black and blue. He said he fell out of a car. I think the way some of the boys have been doing is why we are all shut in.

I have not saw much of the town but have saw enough to know there is some tough places and places I would not want to go down by my self. And would not want it to be known that I had any money. May be I am wrong but when you go through places you can tell about what kind of places it is.

I suppose there is some nice places. Am up town but guess it is hard place to git any where in on account of the streets run at a angle, in curves and ever other way. Awful easy to git lost. They have a lot of good cars out here and large ones. But some of them are sure jammed up the fenders and bodys all smashed up. Don't look like they take a bit of care of them. It is funny how different it is in different places. They take no care of there cars here of a rule. And we came through places on the road out here where the building would look like they were about to fall down and up by the side of a old house where when you are off a ways you would think no one was living there but when you would git up close you could see curtains up to the windows there would be a big fine car all polished and not a scratch on it.

Even had it shined up better than I used to keep the Chevrolet. Ha. You know that was not the best.

Chapter 23

The school weeks flew along, occupied by program practice, lessons, scrap metal, and weather. Students were present or absent, depending on the latest area illnesses. On weekends, Emma visited relatives and friends whenever she could get a ride. As the war news increased, the need for fun escalated. A sense of do-it-now-or-lose-it permeated the region. Everyone lived the daily routine with the stress of war news always present. Diversions of whatever kind were welcomed.

*****

Seattle Washington
Oct. 21, 1942

You said that the people in Toad Hollow only saw the sun during the summer. Well I think the people out here git to see it but one day a year and then are lucky for might not shine but a few min. I even wonder sometimes if they don't have to ask what it is when it does shine.

Bill and I had a lot of fun about our letters. When one of us would miss a day how the other one would give it to him. I would tell him Mary has gone back on you. Tell him how bad he looked. And you can guess about when I would fail to git your letters I would git it in return. He got about 3 one day from Mary. I told him that was bad and ask him about being best man. Just kidding and he took me up. Said we git back I am going to hold you to that. And I will be the same for you. I told him I was just going to be a old bachalar and he said I have a picture of you doing that the letters you git. Any way we had a lot of fun.

Yes had another hour of drill to-night but they let the boys go out to-night but said we will do the same thing again as soon as you fail to obey orders about getting back. And I expect it will be longer the next time. Would not be so bad if they would just keep the ones in that don't do as they should.

A lot have gone to town to-night. Some have gone to bed. Some writing.

The fellow from Iowa is writing to a school teacher. He does about as bad as I. Writes each night. He has been writing all evening.

Bill mailed me the pictures so will send that pictures. I will send that one to keep the snakes and mice away.

*****

Seattle Washington
Oct. 22, 1942

We went to study hall till about 10. Then they came after us and took us over to a old building here on the Post that looked like it had been a barn at one time and had been a catch all for some time. Had old boards, tin cans and what not in it. Said they want to git it cleaned up so they could store some things in it.

Quit a little after 11. Had to go to the hanger this after noon. Left there at 6 to supper. From there to the barber shop. Will go to study hall at 7:30 p.m. till 9:30. And we will have to stand personal inspection at 5 p.m. Sat. and I did not want to git called down on account of long hair. Think I would have been all right if Sis could have been where she could of put a few waves in it. Would not of looked quite so long.

A lot of the boys came back from town about 11 p.m. and woke us all up. Were feeling good or acted like they were. And I think a lot better than they did this morning for I think some of them were feeling bad when time came to git up.

*****

Seattle Washington
Oct. 23, 1942

Friday evening. Got to see the sun to-day so can say I saw the sun while in Washington.

To-night I got one letter from the folks but none from Toad Hollow. Have been wondering if I made you mad just because I told you where you could git some one to help you gather up the metal. Well I did not mean it. Ha.

Have been wondering what you were doing to-night. I suppose you are working on the program for a week from to-night. I thought may be when I left Chanute I might be able to be back so I could go. Thought I could stand in the back and laugh at you when you were making the opening speech and your knees were knocking or have you got over that.

Lucille said in there letter that Davie wanted them to drive around a while Sunday. Said may be they would find me. I sure would like to see him. It seams like it has been a long time since we had a romp.

There is about 35 in study hall. And I think just two are working on there lessons and the rest writing letters. I don't know what good they think it does for us to come over here for there is no instructor. And could not study if wanted to for every one talking.

The Captain told us some good news to-night. Said there would be no personal inspection to-morrow but told us to all have our hair cut before Monday. I have heard some talk that there was to be some great general here to inspect this camp.

Well do you know where you were 6 mo. to-night. I don't remember the date but think that was the night we went to the big town of Pickering to the play.

I will soon be in the Army 6 mo. Sometimes it don't seam long and again it seams like years.

Mark said that he was going to try to git 2 load of corn the next day after he wrote. So I suppose if he has started Owen has and I suppose those two are running a race to see wich one can git to the field first. Then the one that gits there first will laugh at the other one.

I wish you could walk in this week end. We would sure put the time in talking but think it would be better still if could park the old gray Chevrolet at a certain spot in Toad Hollow.

*****

Seattle Washington
Oct. 24, 1942

There was 2 letter from you in mail call at noon. Was sure glad you folks went down to my home. You are welcome any time and it does them a lot of good for some one to come. Helps them pass the time away and I know

155

they git lonesome.

We can see a mountain from here. Don't look so far away but looks like quite a ways on the map. It is Mt. Rainier. The top was all covered with snow. Don't look like it could be so warm here and yet see snow.

Most of the boys have gone to town to-night. Think the 2 old farmers will walk down after a while. The one from Iowa is making out his report now and the other is setting here waiting for us to finnish. He don't have a report to make each night. I guess there is not a school teacher caught up with him. Ha.

You spoke of the button polisher. No I don't have one. Have been thinking I would git one for have been listening for them to say go polish them. You said you had one. How about you coming and showing me how to use it. Ha.

*****

Seattle Washington
Oct. 25, 1942

I feel now like if you had of walked as far as I and we would of went the right way we could of met. The Iowa boy and I went down to town this morning. He had a address that he wanted to look up. We ask several where it was at but no one knew so we went down to the Police station to find it for they have a map of the town there. I was most afraid to go in for fear they would lock the door. We found it was about 5 mile out so we loafed around for a while then came back. After dinner we decided to go for a walk. I guess we went north west of here but looked to me like we went South east. It would not be safe for me to git out of throwing distance for if I did I would be lost.

This morning was like all others a big fog. All the trees and bushes were covered with water and was not safe to walk under a limb with some one for they would hit the limb and you know what would happen.

The three old farmers went down to town last night. Had a malted milk and came back and talked for a long time. We did not have to git up till most seven this morning.

You said in your letter that you did not know if I could read it or not for you was writing 50 mile a hour. Well don't worry about me reading it for I will git it read. You must be getting to be a run around going places 5 nights in a row.

You said for me not to do to much studying. I don't think any one in the Army will hurt there self at work after they have been in for awhile. I wonder sometimes if I will even amount to as much when I git out as did when I came in. And most everone knows that was bad enough. I told a fellow the other day we would not amount to a thing when we got out for would see some work to be done and would go off some where and hide so they could not find us.

As for me making it back to celebrate your birthday with you I sure would like to. May be moving some place about that time. Will be through here the 12th of Nov. And for getting in at 2 I don't know if might be all-right if there were enough nights till 3. But know one would not be enough. What do you think.

You said you liked to hear about my work. Well there is some things we are not supposed to tell of. Course you can put 2 and 2 to-gether sometimes.

Have been thinking I would get a map but the oil stations all close early and are all closed on Sunday. From the way the cars go out here they must fill them full the night before.

There was another large bunch of boys come in yesterday from Texas. They said this was real food to what they got down there. That is one thing we can not kick about here for it is good and plenty of it. Of course not like home but can't expect that.

*****

Seattle Washington
Oct. 26, 1942

Went to study hall till about 10:30. Then had to go pick up some pieces of old boards. Worked till about 11:20. Time to go to the hanger at one. Stayed there till 6 p.m. and must of been 6:30 when we got to supper.

I bet you are getting cross with the children staying up 6 nights in a row.

You said I should be hurrying toward Missouri. Well all they have to do is to say the word and I will be on the road and not losing any time. You ask how Seattle was supplied with girls. Well I think there is plenty but a lot that I don't think you would want people at home to see you with. So I think I will just run around with the other 2 old farmers till I git back to Mo. Do you recon there will be any left back there.

You ask how close we were to town. Well this camp is just at the edge. It is quite a ways up to the main town but can catch a bus 2 blocks from the gate.

As for getting up to Toad Hollow when I git back on a furlough I will try and make it if there is still a parking place.

You ask if your letters were censored. No they are not. I have wondered about mine.

*****

Seattle Wash.
Oct. 27, 1942

Had two tests. They were either hard or I had not been studying hard enough. I got through one all right but don't know how I made it on the other one.

We had to clean up around the barracks some to-night for that general finally came and he is going to make the inspection in the morning.

Was just ready to go to supper and they came and got 6 of us and had to go move a picture machine. They were showing the Battle of Midway here on the camp. When we got it all sit up the fellow run the picture through for us and to git the sound set. Was right good.

Went from there to supper. From there to sign for ration money and of course had to stand in line for awhile. Then came back and one boy had some pictures we looked at.

Wed. morning. Breakfast over, bed made, floor sweep but might have to shave before I go to school. This is the coldest morning we have had sence we came. Lots of frost.

*****

Emma got a ride into Maryville on Monday evening, October 26, and heard Wendell Lewis Willkie speak on his world tour. The 1940 Republican presidential nominee against the winning Roosevelt had made two wartime foreign trips as Roosevelt's informal envoy. Roosevelt had urged Willkie to see W. Averell Harriman and Harry Hopkins, both on London missions from Roosevelt, and had given Willkie a letter to hand-deliver to Prime Minister Churchill. During World War II, it was unusual for politicians to travel abroad. Emma found his speech fascinating.

On October 28, Emma and her students carved two jack-o-lanterns for the Halloween party. Miss Kimberly taught music class. For two hours, Mrs. Johnson visited school, and Mr. Horn left some items for the holiday. Students hung decorations and practiced the play. Emma got herself ready to substitute for Kathy in the play, since Kathy had been ill several days. Emma had an upset stomach but managed to keep moving.

*****

Seattle Wash.
Oct. 28, 1942

If I git something wrote down that don't sound right think nothing about it. For there is a fellow here hitting my arm, blowing smoke in my face and don't have room to tell it all. But don't think I won't git even for he trys to write sometimes.

I am at study hall. Supposed to be getting my lessons but this is a much better place to write than on bunk. I try several different positions be fore I git my letters wrote and I wonder some times how any one ever reads them.

Well how did corn shucking go. I would like to strap a hook on and see if I could shuck a load my self. I guess it would be no trouble to git a job if was back.

That chicken sure does sound good for chicken and dumplings are my favorite.

Why do I always git the blame for one in Toad Hollow being windy. I have wondered sometimes who taught it to me.

You said you were planning on gitting a blanket at the carnival. Well I hear you were disappointed. Well that is the way I always was when I took a chance. And as for it coming in handy some night about 2 a.m. yes it would be all right for we could not run the heater with the gas ration. Would have to save to go and then we might have to coast down hills if you could find any hills in Toad Hollow. Ha.

Mom said in her letter that Davie won two tablets at the school house Fri. night. I ask Lucille who he was going to write to and said to me so I guess he still knows who taught him to be windy.

*****

Seattle Wash.
Oct. 29, 1942

Here I am laying on my bunk with your letter laying in front of me. I usually write your letters with your letter where I can read a ways and then write a few lines.

Sat. you said you went to the corn field early. How did they ever git you to wake up. And you told of all the things you had the matter with you Sat night. I think you thought it was corn shucking. I will tell you what it was. Old age. Ha.

Don't you think the midnight show kept you up to late. Should always git home early as we used to at 2 a.m.

You said the leaves were most all gone there. Ever thing here is as green as in summer. When I was out Sunday saw some lawns that had just been mowed just like spring.

As for me studying to hard on lessons or the pretty girls I don't think any one needs to worry. For put most of my time in writing letters.

*****

Seattle Wash.
Oct. 30, 1942

8:30 p.m. Am over to study hall. Have worked the past hour on school lessons. Seams like my mind keeps wanting to wonder back to Mo. I suppose the Haloween party is under way. Would sure like to be there.

I would not be surprised that there is not a high time here to-morrow night for to-morrow is pay day and being Halloween to except some of the boys will celebrate some.

We had a A.W.O.L. in our barracks. He left last Sat. evening and no one knew anything about him. We were laying around at noon and here he come walking in and you should have saw him. A big cut on the head, a cut on the lip that they had taken 3 stitches in.

When he came in some of the boys ask him where he had been. He said on a furlough. I sure hope I don't look like him when I git back from mine if I git one and here is hopeing.

Some of the boys ask him what was the matter and he said he did not know. That he went to town Sat. night and got drunk. And when he came to he was at another camp in a hospital. That was Sunday noon. Had been there until to-day and don't look or act like he feels any to good now. I would not be surprised that he and some more got together and drinking Whistle and it ended up in a big fight and he came out looser.

It rained all day. We did not have to take excrise or drill to-night and a good thing for I am so sore I can hardly move for yesterday was the first excrise I have had while here. They put you through all kinds of movements and if you don't take them for awhile then when I start again for the first 2 or 3 days ever muscle in my body is sore. Yes I know what you are going to say. Old age.

I have been wondering if you were not holding out on me for I hear that D. Worth had a dance awhile back and I know you were there for he would not think of having it unless you could come. Ha.

Sat. morning 7:15. Have had breakfast, the floor swept, and bed made. I suppose you are in Maryville now and ready to go to the teacher's meeting for 7:15 here means 9:15 there.

I am sure I will have guard duty. It will be two hour and might be 4 if I am lucky enough to git the 11 to one shift. Will only have 2 hours but if I have it any other shift would be on guard 2 hours then off 4 and back for 2. Will just have to walk around and watch with club in hand.

*****

Rosalie gave Emma a ride to Maryville on Saturday, October 31, to see *Across the Pacific*. The American spy film was set during America's entry into World War II and starred Humphrey Bogart, Mary Astor, and Sydney Greenstreet. Emma wasn't sure if she liked seeing war movies or not. *I enjoy seeing how our military and counter-espionage units fight the Nazis, but I worry more afterward about where Peter might be sent.*

*****

Ilene W. Devlin

Seattle Wash.
Oct. 31, 1942

I am not on guard to night so guess I can fill out a report.

It sure does seam odd to me for has rained most 2 days and one night and no mud. So much sand. I sure don't like the climate. They say it is rather nice here in summer but awful bad in fall and winter on the account of being so damp.

You said that the dog Curly was sitting there watching you write. I bet you have to write your letters right after supper so the dishes will be through when you finish. Ha.

You spoke of having a lot to do gitting things ready for Thursday night. It don't look like the teacher would have any thing to do for the children have the program to put on. As for things coming out okay I will bet on that.

Yes the picture was taken at Champaign. As for it being good I would not say that.

It sure is quiet here to night as all are gone but Iowa and I and another fellow. The one from Neb. has been most sick with a cold.

Yes we got paided to day. Had to line up at 1 p.m. and was 3 when I got my money. Had to come back and go to school for a hour. There has been a big game going about all the time since. Would not be surprised that some are not broke by morning. For what they did not loose in the game they will spend for pop to-night. I guess one fellow thought he might spend his down town to-night for he gave me $40 to hold for him to night. Said he was going to town and might loose it. I would hate to think I could not take care of it my self wouldn't you but some can not stay away when there is gambling or liquor around.

Chapter 24

Seattle Wash.
Nov. 1, 1942

5:30 Sunday evening. I suppose you have the wood carried in, hogs fed, milking done and about ready for bed.

Sun shinning about all day. I got up this morning and had a busting headache. No it is not what you are going to say (hang over after pay day). I don't know what was the cause but don't think standing out in rain for 2 hours to git paid yesterday did me any good. One side of my throat is sore. Have been using Listirine all day. Think I will go up in a little while and git me a malted milk and go to bed.

The boys came in Sat. night all hours and some taking a wide walk. One came in and I think he fell over ever bed from the door to his bed and hit the floor before he got there. Thought at first I would git up and try and git him in bed. Then thought if he knew no more than that he would have to sleep on the floor. He finally got on his bed. Clothes, glasses and all. Some one came in finaly and took his shoes and glasses off and covered him up and he never got up until noon.

*****

Seattle Wash.
Nov. 2, 1942

I am feeling some better to-night. My head still hurts some and throat still some sore. Had to go to study hall this morning but my head was just busting and did not git much done. Went to the doctor at noon. Had some fever and he told me to come on back to the barracks and lay around this evening and come back in the morning at 8 a.m. He painted my throat and I suppose he will again in the morning.

Yes the button polisher came through fine and thanks a lot. And as for thinking of a Missourian I do that most ever day. Some times I will be trying to study and my mind will just keep going back to Mo. Will be glad when I can go with it.

Will say thanks for the polisher again.

*****

On Tuesday evening, November 3, the fall play went well. Three sets of parents enjoyed themselves, and everyone loved the refreshments. The students remembered their lines, making Emma proud of them.

*****

Seattle Washington
Nov. 3, 1942

Tuesday afternoon. Went back to the doctor this morning. He painted my throat again and gave me some more capsules and said I had better stay at the barracks again to-day. But I had no fever this morning. It is sure some job to lay around the barracks all by your self. I would try to read some. Did have a fair nap.

Yes we have another A.W.O.L. He left for town last night and has never come back. He drinks some so no telling where he is. May be has got into some trouble and is locked up and may be like the fellow that came back last week.

I think Owen thinks he has some job gitting his corn shucked. So may be you can git another job doing it.

How is Tom gitting along gathering corn. Does he send the dog up early to wake you.

The dice game is still going. It has been going all the time since we got our pay Sat. I would think they would git tired.

*****

By Thursday, Emma had learned her student Mary Sue had recovered from an attack of appendicitis. At school, Wilma had not felt well. Illnesses kept mounting as fall progressed.

The Roberts and Emma listened to Bing Crosby and Rudy Vallée on the radio. Vallée was the most prominent and first of the new crooner singing style. Strong voices by early singers had to project to fill theaters before electric microphones were developed. Vallée's soft crooner voice was well suited to the intimacy of radio and inspired Bing Crosby and others. *I just love closing my eyes, listening to Vallée sing, and pretending Peter is holding me in his arms,* thought Emma.

*****

Seattle Washington
Nov. 4, 1942

I got another Toad Hollow letter to-day. I think you have a time having a school meeting. Seams like there is always something rain, sickness, or something going on at Pickering.

You said you did not want to go to college classes because they tease you so much. I know them when I see them. They always acted like they thought they were just a little smarter than any one else but may be I just thought that.

You said you had some questions to ask. Well don't think I don't have some to ask my self. And hopeing that it won't be long until we can have a good long talk.

You spoke of Tom having a team and dray wagon. Well that might be all right for we could go to the mid night show and could have a long talk for would take along time to go home.

I don't know why you don't git a letter ever day. Some here taking care of the mail don't care if we git mail or not. They have a strip on there arm and it has all gone to there head.

I went back to the doctor this morning. Had no fever so went on back to school. He did give me a excuse so I would not have to take excrise the rest of this week. My throat is a little sore yet but not bad. I think a few days in Mo. would cure that.

I hear they are having a time with Davie. He trades pencils at school and gits the worst end of the trade. I guess he does not tell a thing that takes place at school. Mom says they can not find out a thing that goes on at school from him but said he was gitting along fine.

****

Seattle Washington
Nov. 5, 1942

What are you doing. I suppose turned in for the night for it is gitting close to 9 and that means 11 there.

Had to go at 8 and help break up some boards for kindling. Worked till 10. Then went to study hall and stayed till 11:30. Worked on a engine some till 6. Don't seam like I have done my days work until I have wrote a little home and a little to Toad Hollow.

Yes I am back on full feed again. Feeling good to-day.

Iowa and Neb. have gone to mail the letters. They have came and brought ice cream and a Hersheys candy bar.

Friday morning 7:10 a.m. Floor swept and shaved. Am ready to go to school at 8. Yes it is raining again and we have inspection so that means we will be out most all day.

I will have to tell you a joke they played on a boy in here the other night. He was gone and they nailed his shoes to the floor. They are all the time playing some kind of a joke on some of the boys and they did not learn it all from me.

*****

Seattle Washington
Nov. 6, 1942

I think you and Mary Jane had some time Sat. night going to show then going home and going to bed. Then gitting up at 2:45 and going again. It sounds to me like we are not the only ones that stay up late or may be I should say early in the morning.

You talk about gitting teased most ever where you go. Think nothing about that for we all do. I don't so much here but I would git plenty if I was back there and sure would like to be there and teasing. Does not hurt when it is all in fun.

Yes the Chevrolet should be rested up by now and if it is not it will just have to git tired. That is if we can git the gas and I have heard we can git gas when on a furlough.

I will try and remember all about the mountains so I can tell you and if you would like to see them I hope you git to some time but hope you are not forced to as I was.

You spoke of not leaving your letter around. Well don't worry for no one gits them but me. And if there is any thing talked about like you mean I usually leave in my packet till read a few times. Then put in stove or tear up so small no one could put them together.

I have been working on a plane all day. Was inside the plane while it was raining.

Had to sign my ration check over to-night. $51.00. That is what the people git for feeding me while I am here. That was a seperate check from our pay check so you see the food bill is no little thing here.

We had a little excitement a little while ago. One fellow came in and said there was a barracks on fire up the street. So we all tore out up there but when we got there it was only a flue burning out.

*****

On Saturday, November 7, in Maryville Emma bought Peter's Christmas gift and shopped for other relatives. She even bought herself a new dress for $2.29, some hose, and supplies. *How wonderful to have a paycheck coming in each month!*

*****

Seattle Washington
Nov. 7, 1942

I am going to George Town to-night. But would be a much better time to go to Maryville to show. But suppose I would want to go to Toad Hollow or 409 east sixth first then might start and fail to ever git to a show.

We will take our final examination next Tuesday. I don't know how I will make it for they sure have give us a lot to learn for the short time I have been here.

Think I may hear how you make it at the meeting but I already know that you did fine. I hope you had a good crowd. I think it is easyer to git up before a large crowd than just a few. For you can't see just who all are looking at you.

I suppose corn shucking is in full swing back there now. Everone trying to git all they can shucked before bad weather. We see no corn here. Here where we are it just a valley and hills all around. I don't know if you would call them mountains or not for they are not so high.

There is several that don't feel good in the barracks I am in. They are all like I was the first of the week sore throat and headache. I don't know if I gave it to them or not. They just as well blame me for it as not for git the blame for ever thing that go wrong back there so guess I can take it here.

Worked at starting and stoping plane this after noon for that will be partly our job is to start it and see that everthing is ok. and that everthing is working.

*****

Seattle Washington
Nov. 8, 1942

Sunday so walk over and we will go to the show. I would not say how much of the show we would see but we would sure have a talk.

Got up at 7. Swept around my bunk. Inspection at 9. Then did some washing. I thought when I was doing it how you would laugh at me if you could see me for I don't think I am any to good a hand at the job.

The three old farmers all went down town last night. Just mailed our letters, had a malted milk and came back. Was wake up several times during the night for some of the boys came in and they had had stronger malted milks than we did so as they would come in they would wake ever one up and ask them some foolish question.

I had to laugh at some of the boys this morning. They were picked up down town some where and was taken out to dinner. Not supper but dinner. At night (we always eat dinner at noon in Missouri don't we). Well when they got out there guess they had the dinner but was served in courses served by maid. Eat one thing then she would bring something else and had a silver spoon, fork, and knife for each thing. Said they did not know what to pick up to eat with. I don't think I would like that way of eating eather. Would rather first be a old Missouri farmer and use my fingers.

Was talking to the people that run the drug store while we were drinking our malted milks and they said that the news sure did sound good last night. Ever one seamed to think that ever thing was going good and that the Germans would not last so much longer. And here is hopeing they know.

I told you the other day that I saw Mt. Rainer but did not know how far it was to it. Well a fellow told us the other day that it was about 60 mile. I guess there is another mountain about 90 mile north of here or it seams north to me but I have forgot what he called it. Said you see it of a clear day. It sure does seam funny to be standing here and not be cold and look at the mountain and it be covered with snow.

*****

Seattle Wash.
Nov. 9, 1942

Hear I am at study hall. You said that you forgot your rabbit foot is the reason you did not git the blanket down to Sunrise. Well I know now why I never won any thing for never had the rabbit foot. Ha.

Well you said you wished you could slip in while I was on guard duty. Well I have not had it yet. It looks like they have skiped me and that sure makes me sore but if you could slip in I would not mind it a bit. Don't know how much guarding I would git done unless it would be guarding you to keep the other boys from taking you away from me. Ha.

You said I was thought of more often than you. I would not say that for I know you are thought of often. I bet your ears burn a plenty when you git to filling out the gas ration cards.

Yes the flowers are still blooming here and they are sure pretty.

You ask if I was not glad I was not coming up on account of you eating onions. I think some times I could stand a lot more than onions just to be able to talk and tell what I would like to but am afraid to write some thing for fear it might be opened.

Mom said there were 2 boys back on a furlough from Pickering. It makes me think that the Army air force is the wrong thing to be in for all the boys that came in when I did and after I did have all been home on a furlough.

On detail this morning Ricky and me had to build a fire in the furnace at the shower room. Don't think the ashes had been cleaned out for a month.

I hear we git a party next Thursday night and a dance for each class when they git through. So you better git over here and give me that lesson or I may not do so good. Guess I will have to be a wall flower.

*****

Seattle Wash.
Nov. 10, 1942

You spoke of spending the rest of the evening listening to the radio. Sure would like to be there so could join you.

A notice up on the bulliten board to-night says to have ever thing packed and up in front of building 111 Thursday by 10 a.m. I don't much look to leave till some time Thursday evening. Will probably know where before I leave here but don't know if I will be able to write it or not.

A lot of the boys have gone to town to night. And I would not be surprised that some don't come in feeling pretty good.

I guess all that is in this barracks except 2 or 3 go in one group so I guess the 3 old farmers will get to stay together for a little longer.

This letter says that you have a birthday before long and I don't have a thing and don't know if I will get where I am going in time to get it there by the 20th or not. So it may be a little late. May be I will just get to bring it back, for I am going to try for a furlough as soon as I get a chance.

All they have to say is the word and I will be on the road. Would like to get back before they ration the gas for would like to break in the Chevrolet again. Don't know if I could drive it or not for has been most 7 mos. since I had ahold of the wheel.

*****

A teachers' meeting was called for Wednesday, November 11. Emma picked up supplies to register for gas rationing beginning the next week. Mandatory gasoline rationing had started in the eastern United States in May 1942, but a nationwide voluntary program failed. America had plenty of fuel, but civilians had to eliminate nonessential driving to conserve tire wear, and thus, rubber. Almost a year after Pearl Harbor, gasoline rationing made it difficult to use cars.

President Roosevelt declared rationing would begin December 1, 1942, and last for the duration of the war. Five classifications were created:

- Class A drivers were allowed only three gallons of gasoline per week.
- Class B drivers (factory workers, traveling salesmen) received eight gallons per week.
- Class C drivers included essential war workers, police, doctors, and letter carriers.
- Class T included all truck drivers.
- Class X was reserved for politicians and other "important people."

Classes C, T, and X were not subject to restrictions.

To receive a gasoline ration card, a person had to certify a need for gasoline and ownership of no more than five tires. The government confiscated any tires over five. The national speed limit became thirty-five miles per hour. All automobile racing—including the Indianapolis 500—and sightseeing driving were banned.

Emma had to know the rules to educate and to register people who lived around her school for gasoline rationing cards. Emma laughed and said to Rosalie. "I must have missed that day in college when they described all these extras I'm required to handle as a teacher." But she understood and accepted the new roles as part of her war effort on the home front.

*****

Seattle Wash.
Nov. 11, 1942

Will start my report as I am rushed for time for we are supposed to be up to building 102 at 7:30 and it is now 7:20. Ever one packing. I hope to git the mail before I leave. The last I got from you was wrote a week ago to-night.

They had a little party for us last night. Had ice cream, candy and cookies. Sang a few songs. Have a copy wich I will send to you if I don't for git it.

*****

Seattle Wash.
Nov. 12, 1942

Had to git up at 6. Went to breakfast. Came back and shaved. Then packed and turned in my bedding. Then took my barracks bags up so they could be loaded out. Then had mail call about 10. Had a letter from you.

We have to go up and git our diplomas at 2 p.m. Will git 2 here. One from the Boeing Plant and one from the Army.

I went and got a hair cut after dinner. Did not have so much cut off so you can still give that wave set and I hope it is soon.

*****

Seattle Wash.
Nov. 13, 1942

Will try and write a few lines. I am on the train and on a rough track.

We are in Oregon in the mountains seeing some snow. A lot of timber mostly all fir and of course a lot of rock. In a tunnel now.

We left camp last night about 5:30 p.m. and left Seattle a little after 7.

We are going over some of the same road that came out on but some of it I don't remember. Think it must have been night when we came through.

We are now going through Meacham Oregon. Don't know if you will be able to find it on a map or not for think it is a small place.

We did not have breakfast till about 10. Only had one dinning car and a small crew and we were the last car to eat. Ate supper last night at 4 so we were all about ready for eats when they came.

We should have dinner first at noon. It is now 12:40 and they have not started feeding us yet. We picked up the dinning car at Portland Oregon last night about midnight. Some one said that we would git into Boise Idaho some time this evening.

The portar just came through and said that we would all git off at the next town in about 20 min. We have been going awful slow but any way I am getting back a little closer to Mo.

Yes the three old farmers are all together. Me and the same one had to sleep together last night that did on the way out here. And I hope we git to stay together.

Chapter 25

Salt Lake City Utah
Nov. 14, 1942

We got here a little after noon. Had dinner around one and after dinner we just stood around waiting for orders. They brought us up to the barracks about 4. We have a right nice barracks, a lot better than the one at Seattle. Most like the one at Chanute if any thing a little better.

Yes saw a lot of sights coming through the mountains. We would be going one way and would turn around and go right back. One place I don't think it was ¼ of a mile across from where we had just come and we had turned around and was going back. Saw a lot of mountains that were covered with snow but none to speak of down where we were at.

Ricky, Bill, and I are all in this barracks. Our beds are double one over the other. Bill and I have one and I am on the bottom so will be all right if he don't fall through. And if I was on top I might fall and would have to far to fall.

I don't look to be here only a short time. Some say from 2 to 6 days.

In the morning they will reclassify us and will be assigned to some squadron then be shipped to some base but have no idea where. I was talking to one fellow that said they shipped to 10 states as far east as Kanas City Mo.

I look for it to be a hard day to-morrow for they will ask us all kinds of questions. And expect to-morrow will be when the three old farmers git split up.

It is level right around here where this camp is. But there is mountains all around here. Came through some places where the ground looked like it was nothing but salt.

*****

In mid-November, Emma spent a weekend in bed with a bad head cold. "At least being in bed gives me time to write more letters to Peter, when I can get my mind clear enough to finish complete sentences," she hoarsely told Ruth. Emma made it to school on Monday, but most of her pupils also had colds.

*****

Salt Lake City Utah
Nov. 15, 1942

They got us up at 6 this morning. Ate breakfast and cleaned up the barracks. Then they took us down to the hanger where we were supposed to be classified. Stayed around there till a little after 10 and they told us to come back to the barracks and wait.

But they did never call for us and when we came back after supper they told us that we had just as well go back and git our blankets for would not go back till some time to-morrow. They said our service records did not git here as they should.

Clouded up and rained rather hard for awhile. Then turned to snow about 10 and it sure did snow about as large a flakes as I nearly ever saw. The mountains look pretty from here for they are all covered with snow.

*****

Salt Lake City Utah
Nov. 16, 1942

What have you been doing. I think I know. Busy at school. I have not done a thing only lay around, sleep and think of Mo.

Sure has been a long day. Got up at 6 and went to breakfast. Cleaned barracks up. We thought we were going to the hanger to be classified but they have never called yet. But we can not leave the barracks only to go eat. Can't even go to the P.X.

You said the reason I was sick was because I had ate or drink to much. Well it must have been eating for can see enough drinking to do me. You ask if I had saw Mt. Riner any more. I think I saw it 3 times while I was at Seattle.

The mountains on the east are about 8 or 9 mile and those on the west about 30 mile. But it looks like you could walk over to the foot of them in just a little bit.

Yes Harold is making his report to the Iowa teacher. Ricky just runs around like a chicken with his head off.

*****

Salt Lake City Utah
Nov. 17, 1942

We final got classified to day but has been tiresome. So much setting around. Got up at 6. Then cleaned up the barracks and went to the hanger at 7:30. Then they took us for a physical examation. Guess I was O.K. except teeth. Said I should have them fixed so guess I will go down some time to-morrow and have some work done.

Had to sign pay roll while there. Got ½ months pay. Then they gave us a big talk about going to the gunner school. Would be 5 weeks but I did not think I wanted any of that for would have to fly and I want to keep at least one foot on the ground. So when they ask me if I wanted to take it I said no. So they classified me as a spelist on a B-17F, so I guess I will be one of the ground mechanics.

A fellow said he did not know how long we would be here. Would depend on how soon a order came in for some mechanics.

I have been hitting the Nellis camps. This is a new place here where we are the first bunch to move in. Of course there is a old Post where we were just across the road.

I think you will be having a birthday about the time you git this letter. Heres hopeing you a happy birthday and many more. I suppose you feel big now being your own boss. Ha. I will tell you one thing. The next 10 yr. will go a lot faster than the last 10 years have. I sent a little package last night. Was not just what I wanted to send but could not git off the Post so had to git what I could at the P.X.

Yes the three old farmers got split up to-day. Bill and Ricky are in a different barracks but there is a fellow here in the bed next to me that was with me at Chanute. Think he is a good fellow but never got to running around with him.

They still say we will git a furlough when we git to our base. But I suppose I will have to ask for it then wait till my turn comes up.

Ilene W. Devlin

Well Sis will say happy birthday and good night.

As always.
Pvt. Peter K. Paxton
C.R.P. Sq G-A.A.B.
Bks. 5
Salt lake City Utah

*****

Peter's letters told that Fort Douglas was established in 1862. Now it was an Army Air Field and home to the 7th Bombardment Group of B-17s. Fearing a Japanese attack on the U.S. mainland, the Army had moved the 9th Service Command headquarters from the Presidio in San Francisco to Salt Lake City in January 1942. Now the Nellis camp held German POWs and expanded housing for the incoming Army forces being trained on B-17s.

*****

Salt Lake City Utah
Nov. 18, 1942

I have been to the dentist to day. Had three teeth pulled. Is that because I am getting old. It was not as bad as I thought it would be. I was afraid these army dentist would be rather rough but they were as careful as they could be. They sure was a lot that had teeth pulled today. Think there was seven in this barracks. One had 5 pulled and has to have 10 more taken out. So I guess I was not as bad off as some.

These barracks are one story buildings and 35 to the barracks and is heated by 3 stoves.

Some of the boys have gone to Salt Lake to night. We are given 7 passes to the barracks each night. Have to take your turn. I think my turn will come about Sat. night. Think I will take a pass if it is so Bill can git his the same nightThis is the first night that any of us have been able to leave the Post.

They all had to go drill for a while this after-noon but said those that had been to the dentist did not have to go. We had better stay in the barracks and not git cold in where we had our teeth taken out.

I was laying here the other night and my mind was back in Toad Hollow.

176

Remembered of you telling in a letter about spilling powder on my picture ever time you were getting ready to go. Well you have nothing on me for I have your picture in my bill fold and think I told you where I keep it so I can sleep with my head on your picture each night.

Will be a week to-morrow since I got your last letter.

*****

On November 19, 1942, a day before her birthday, Emma began gasoline rationing registration for her area, and everyone signed up that day. Emma had distributed the first food ration books in May. Most people grumbled about the books, but they didn't hold her responsible.

Emma received several birthday cards that week. The students gave her one pat on her back for each year, with some pats being a little harder than others. The Roberts gave her a card, a potholder, and a necklace. Peter sent a letter and a makeup compact with wings on top. She wrote to his new address in Salt Lake City and was proud that he was going to be a Flying Fortress mechanic. Since it was Friday, Emma got to relax and enjoy her birthday evening.

*****

Salt Lake City Utah
Nov. 19, 1942

I suppose you made some more tracks in mud to-day if it was there like here. Sleeting when we got up this morning and turned to snow about 8 but melted as fast as it fell. And we have no side walks around here and the mud is getting rather deep.

They called us all out right after breakfast and marched us up to the orderly room and had a shipping list. I think they called most all the boys that came here with me except the ones that had teeth pulled and those that are taking the gunner course.

A lot of the ones that wanted to take the gunner course took there exam to day and they were a lot turned down. I think most of them on account of there eyes.

They divided the shipping list in 4 bunches. About all the boys I knew were in one group. I was hateing it because I was getting split up from the rest of the gang. Told them to all be in front of the orderly room at 1:15 that they were shiping out. And when the time came for them to go they just went about a block from here to a different squadron. I am hopeing that I git moved to the same squadron.

They did call us to go down and clean up a new barracks. When I got down there I said I had some teeth pulled yesterday and he said you had better go back to the barracks for this is not a fit day for you to be out. Of course I did not wait for him to tell me the second time.

*****

Salt Lake City Utah
Nov. 20, 1942

All packed up and ready to move again. They called us out this morning and had another shipping list and my name was on it.

I have been moved about a block. But did not know where I was going till I got here. Had everything packed like I was going to along ways. Looks like they could tell us when we are just being moved to another squadron.

I moved to the barracks next to Bill and Ricky. But I don't know if we will ship out of here to-gether or not. Just git to knowing some one then will be moved in with another bunch.

As always
Pvt. Peter K. Paxton
Prov. Squad. M – Bks 1505
Army Air Base
Salt Lake City Utah

*****

By Saturday night, the Maryville area had its first snow, with more light snow and wind the next day. Emma studied, read, wrote letters, listened to the radio, and cleaned her room.

*****

Salt Lake City Utah
Nov. 21, 1942

Sat. evening. I got a letter from you. The last letter I got from home was wrote 2 weeks ago to-day but think they surely are allright or they would of got me word some way.

Yes it would be fine if we could talk over the telephone ever day. And lets hope that it won't be long until we can.

I sure hope the gas is not rationed when I git back. But may be I can buy some and if I can't I still have a good saddle horse and I think I could still ride her.

You said that you knew two girls hearts were happy by getting my letters you and Mom.

I could of got a pass to go to town to-night but turned it down. For I did not know any one that was going. You have no idea how you have to watch who you run with here for so many here does things that I don't care about.

I have been on detail all day. Had me on the handle of a shovel. Went to work at 9. Worked till 11. Then back to work at 1 and worked till 3:30. And there was 12 to the truck. All we had to do was load the truck then lean on the shovel while the truck driver went and unloaded. Had quite a rest between loads. If the folks back there had of saw me they would of said I was working on the W.P.A. and I think my shovel handle was out of shape to-night and it was not from work. Ha.

*****

Salt Lake City Utah
Nov. 22, 1942

Sunday evening and I don't know just what I would give to be back to Toad Hollow.

This camp is different from any that I have been at for it is 7 days a week. Sunday the same as any other. Can git off to go to church but did not know it in time or would of went.

They got us up at 5:30 this morning. Had to go sign the pay roll. Had to all go up to the orderly room at 8 and I was picked for detail.

Another fellow and me had to clean up a barracks. Did not take long and we got to lay around till 11. Then had to go back at 1 and they put 8 of us to putting up beds. Think we set up about 100 beds and swept out.

I don't think I told you we can see Salt Lake City from here. It sure is pretty of a night. So many lights. The town is right at the foot of a large mountain covered with snow.

The fellow that was over us on detail name was Trotter. I ask him if he had any folks back in Mo. Thought may be I could find out about some folks by that name I know. But he said he did not so I was out of luck. And I don't think he did for did not look anything like the ones I know and they all look some alike.

How is Owen getting along gathering corn. Have you had to go back and help any more.

*****

Christmas Seals sales opened Monday. Students would again raise money to fight tuberculosis, an ongoing national health crisis.

Emma also learned two of her friends had been poisoned by bad wieners. They would recover but had been very ill for several days. Then Peter's letter stated he had had three teeth pulled. Emma was thankful she just had a cold, for she disliked going to the dentist.

*****

Salt Lake City Utah
Nov. 23, 1942

I am feeling better to night for got to letters from home but did not hear from Toad Hollow. I got a box of candy from our mail carrier. It was mailed Nov. 13 and had went to Seattle.

I had to go drill this morning then they took us to play some games. I played volley ball. Some played basket ball and some foot ball. We played till about 11 then had to go on detail afternoon. Had to help with some new lumber. Worked at that till 4 and got paid at 4.

*****

Emma's November program on Tuesday evening was canceled due to icy roads. Also, she learned two more friends had left for the Army. By Wednesday, the roads were still bad, with a light dusting of snow in the afternoon. She let out school for the two-day Thanksgiving holiday.

*****

Salt Lake City Utah
Nov. 24, 1942

Have been on detail all day. Went to work at 8 at the hanger. Had to sweep out 2 rooms where the boys are reclassified. Then had to go and clean up a small P.X. that is in the hanger. They just sell small things like gum, candy, cigarettes, razor blades and Pop. My job was to keep things filled up and keep the pop cooler full. And when I was caught up on that had to wait on people. It would keep the 3 of us rather busy at times. Worked till 12. Then went back at 1:15 and worked till 5.

Bill and Ricky have gone to town again to-night. I could of got a pass but did not want it. Am glad now that I did not since it is raining rather hard.

It looked funny here to night. Was most dark here and we could look at the mountains east of here and could see the sun shining against the top of them.

As always,
The Mo. farmer
P.K.P. xxx

*****

Salt Lake City Utah
Nov. 25, 1942

All fore noon worked down to the hanger in the P.X. I was a drug store cow boy selling Coca-Cola. At noon they had a shipping list out and I was on it. About all I know are going except the ones that are taking the gunner course.

This afternoon turned in my bedding and packed my barracks bag. Just waiting for orders. May not go far but am very near sure I am going quite a ways and if it is where I think will not be quite as close home as here. But not quite as far as when I was at Seattle.

*****

By the weekend, Emma got to Maryville for some serious Christmas shopping for school gifts and candy for her pupils. For herself, she splurged on a new box coat for $20.52, which took a large amount of her monthly teacher's check, but she needed a warmer coat for the walk to and from school. She also got Ruth Roberts an end table, since she had been so accommodating to Emma while she boarded there.

Emma spent Saturday night and Sunday with Owen and Melinda. She helped them finish chores early so they could go to Hopkins to see *They All Kissed the Bride*. The screwball comedy starred Joan Crawford, with Melvyn Douglas as a trucking firm executive who fell in love with her. Crawford had taken over the lead role after Clark Gable's wife, Carole Lombard, died in a plane crash in early 1942. Emma told them, "I read Crawford donated her entire movie pay to the American Red Cross. Even big stars are supporting the war and relief efforts."

Peter's next letters came from Geiger Field, Spokane, Washington. Known as Sunset Field before 1941, the War Department bought the airport, renaming it Geiger Field after Major Harold Geiger, an Army aviation pioneer killed in a 1927 crash. Now a major group training base for the Second Air Force for B-17 Flying Fortress heavy bombardment units, the field also served as an aircraft maintenance and supply depot. Peter would continue his mechanic's training there.

*****

Spokane Wash.
Nov. 28, 1942

We left Salt Lake last Wed. evening. Left camp about 7 and they took us to the station in trucks. It was about 11 when we pulled out. I went to sleep in Utah and woke up in Orgen.

We did not git to see so many sights on this trip. For it snowed all day the 26th and could not see far but far enough to see a lot of mountains and rock. Saw one place where I don't think a person could ride a horse through for the rock and they were large ones. We came through a lot of tunnels and some were quite long.

We did not git much to eat yesterday. We were supposed to git here at 6 yesterday morning. So after supper the 26th they took the dinning cars off and in the night they had some trouble with one of the cars. Had to take the men out of it and put in another car and that made us late. Got into a small place about noon and they let some of the boys go get stuff to eat and I think they about bought the town out.

We got into Spokane about 3 yesterday afternoon and they had trucks there to meet us. I think there was about 350 came with me. Most all that I have been with for awhile came.

Spokane was sure some sight yesterday. It is awful hillie and there is a lot of pine trees covered with snow.

It snowed on us all day Thur. and some places it was getting rather deep. We rode for a while and I went to sleep and most broke my neck. When I woke up we were back in more snow and there is quite a lot here but it is not so very cold.

I have been rather disappointed for they told us all through school that we would git a furlough when we got to our base. But now they say there will be no furloughs while here. I don't know why they kept telling us that if they did not aim for us to have one. I would of rather they would of said no right from the start.

I think I will like this camp a lot better than the one at Salt Lake. And the food is better or at least I think it is.

Did you git to eat turkey Thursday. If you did I bet you are sick to-day from eating to much. Ha.

We had turkey for supper. They say they sure had a feed here.

I am begining to wonder how things are in Toad Hollow. The last letter I got was wrote Nov. 13. It had gone to Seattle. I know there is some on the road some where.

They have had us over and ask us a few questions. Don't know just what my job will be but guess it is mostly watching filling with gas and such on the start until I learn a little more and I have plenty to learn if I ever know any thing.

I understand we will be here till about January. Then will be moved to some other state so we will git used to all climates.

Pvt. Peter K. Paxton
336th Bomb. Squad.
95th Bomb. group
Geiger Field
Spokane Washington

*****

Geiger Field
Nov. 29, 1942

Sunday evening. We were supposed to git assigned to crews to day. They took us to a building this morning. Waited around till about 10:30. Then they told us come back to the barracks and come back at 15 till one. Then they took us over to get some more clothes. Got some gloves, sheep lined coat and trousers and over shoes. Will git a wool sweater a little later but they did not have my size to day. You would sure laugh if you could see me all dressed up in this out fit.

I have another tax token for you. It is from Utah. Will send it when I find out if these letters are coming through O.K.

I don't know yet the hours I will have to work. Some goes to work at 6 a.m. and work till 6 p.m. Then there is another shift that goes to work at 6 p.m. and work till 6 a.m. They will work that way for a week then change. And we get a 24 hour pass once a week.

I wish it was so I could spend that 24 hour in Toad Hollow. May be we could git partly caught up on talk.

The barracks here about the same as the ones were at Chanute. All the beds are one over the other. I have a top one so if you hear a big crash some night you just think I have fell out of bed. Ha.

*****

Geiger Field
Nov. 30, 1942

At 6:15 had to take about 15 min. excrise. Cleaned up the barracks. Another fellow and I had to clean up the bath room this morning so did not have to report for work until 1 p.m. It was about a 30 min job and we had all fore noon to do it.

After noon a bunch of us had to check a plane for loose parts. They were supposed to take it up but I guess the weather was not right for they did not go up. Just started it up and run for awhile. Then we had to refill with gas, check oil, then cover it all up for the night.

Wednesday will be my day off. You better walk over and we will have a talk. Might go into Spokane and have a malted milk and see a show.

Well to-morrow is when the gas ration goes into effect. How is Tom getting along with the coffee. Does he use both his and your ration card.

*****

On November 29, 1942, coffee joined the U.S. ration list. Despite record coffee production in South America, shipping was needed for other items. Also, butter supplies were reserved for military breakfasts, plus sugar and milk supplies became limited. Nearly one-third of all foods commonly consumed by civilians would become rationed at least once during the war.

Santa Claus day in Maryville was Monday evening, November 30. Emma saw a free film, sang carols around town, and window shopped. She and several friends enjoyed dinner together. "Let's go for one last fun ride!" said Rosalie. "After all, gas rationing begins at midnight, and who knows when we can cruise around again?"

The next day, the northwest wind and cold temperatures made the school day feel like winter had arrived. Everyone was present to watch the afternoon snow fall. They worked on Red Cross projects, studied, and made Christmas gifts for their mothers.

Chapter 26

Geiger Field
Dec. 1, 1942

Tuesday evening and if it is back there like here you will be able to make those tracks 4 inches deep in the morning. It started snowing about noon. The snow is getting rather deep. It is not blowing and the trucks keep it packed down.

I have a good one to tell about Washington. The snow gits so deep out here that air planes git stuck in the snow banks. There was a plane getting ready to go up and got off the run way into where they had shoved the snow with a snow plow. Had to shovel out in front of the wheels.

I bet there were more car gas tanks the nearest full they were ever before last night. They said over the radio this morning that all the filling stations were sure busy last night. Told of one woman that went into a filling station and said to fill the tank full and all they could git into the tank was 4¢ worth so I guess she wanted it to be full.

It won't be long now till Xmas. I suppose you have begain to be good and not getting into any mischief now. Well if I git to see Santa I will give him the facts about a certain Toad Hollow school teacher. But don't suppose it would do any good for she would say I taught it to her. Am I right?

I have another chore to git done to-morrow. My suit to the cleaners to be cleaned and pressed. Drop in to see the barber for my hair is getting rather long again and have a little washing to do. Drop over if you want a job.

*****

Geiger Field
Dec. 2, 1942

I am feeling a lot better to-night for I got 8 letters, 4 from you. And one from you to night.

The one that was mailed Nov. 14 they had just about run out of any place to put a address. It had went to Seattle. From there to Squadron G at Salt Lake. Then to Squadron M. Then on up here.

Yes the Life Saver came through o.k. and thanks for I ate it while laying on my bunk reading my letters.

You said the kids took time out to pounded you on your birthday. If I had of been there you would of got a good one.

I can't tell you much about Salt Lake for did not leave the camp while there. And as for the pretty girls don't think you need to worry for from what I have saw would rather stick to Toad Hollow. As for you joining the WAAC's take my advice and stay a cross school teacher. I sure hope your friend is right about the war being over by Xmas.

I disagree with you about joy riding in the air. Would rather just take the old 38 Chevrolet and strike out like we have before.

I might have had to rode Old Beauty while it was snowing but I still can do that. But I am not saying just how I would feel the next day as it has been 7 mo. now since I have rode a horse.

Well I have guard duty Dec. 4. Will be in all night. Will have to guard a plane. It will be awful tiresome just standing around.

I suppose Tom is feeling good having his corn all in the crib.

I hope your cold is better by now. Do take care of your self and don't git sick. For a cold can sure make a person feel bad.

*****

Geiger Field
Dec. 3, 1942

Got us up at 4:30 this morning. They had got a order for a plane to go up and we had to git it ready. Had to take the frost off, fill with gas and oil. We had it ready about 7:30. It has not come back yet. Don't know just where it went to or when it will be back.

We may be called out in the middle of the night to go check it over when it comes in. After it left we just sit around a building till about 10. Then came back over to the old barracks and moved down here. Have a nice barracks just across the street from the mess hall wich is a new one. Each Squadron has its own mess hall.

I don't know what I will do when I get out of here. Will just lay around and wait for some one to tell me to do something. Then may wait for the other fellow to do it. No one gits in a hurry to git any thing done here.

You sure have to wach your step here for there had been quite a little snow and the trucks and people have it packed down till it is most ice. I have not fell down yet but don't think I did not do some danceing yesterday to keep from hitting the ground. Think my feet was higher than my head at times but finaly landed on my feet.

How is your cold. I suppose you will say I gave it to you. You know they say a cold is catching and there has been some lip stick so you know what that means. But I don't think you caught it from them. Ha.

How does it seam to be your own boss. I don't know about you but I could not see much difference when I got to 21 only the years go faster than they did before.

*****

Dec. 4, 1942

Put the day in mostly standing around. Had no work to do on a plane. Had to shovel a little snow off the run way and help move a little building. I think I could of moved it in 30 min. my self and a team. And there was 25 of us with a big tractor and it took us all fore noon so you see we worked hard.

I have to laugh some times when talking to some of the boys here. We meet all kinds and ones that have done all different types of work. There is one that sleeps by me that don't know a thing about a farm and of the questions that he can ask but I expect I would ask just as funny questions to him about his work.

Yours truly
The Missouri farmer

*****

With Peter's new address, Emma mailed his Christmas present insured on December 5. Then she wrapped presents and sacked candy for her pupils. By the next day, snow covered everything.

*****

Dec. 5, 1942

Got us up at 6 this morning. Went to work but when I got over there there was nothing to do so (time out to re-fill my pen) just layed around in a warm building till noon. Then done the same work after noon. Even got up on a table and had a nap.

It has been snowing here about all day. The ground was all ready covered with snow and ice. I was not quite so lucky this morning as I was the other day for steped out in the porch and did not keep my feet under me and it was a rather hard seat.

A letter from you and one from the folks and one from Mark. Mark was doing a lot of kidding about a certain Toad Hollow person. Can you guess who. Said he had saw you in Maryville the day Santa was there. Said you were rather busy keeping your bunch to-gether. He said that Davie marched with the group. I bet he thought he was as big as any one there.

How are you keeping Tom out of mischief now since he is through gathering corn. I suppose he has made time to tease you about your mail. How did him and Uncle Theo git along with there long green chewing while he was helping shuck corn. He sure did make Uncle Theo happy last Xmas when he gave him that sack of long green.

You never did say how that dance was over to Dennis Smiths. No use of you trying to hold out on me for I know you was there. Ha.

*****

Geiger Field
Dec. 6, 1942

Here I am over here waiting for orders to do something and there was another boy here that had this writing material. So I begged 2 sheets and a envelope so will write you a letter on Uncle Sam's time.

There is a card game going on that I suppose I could git in on until my money run out. But that wouldn't take long so guess I will just scribble a few lines instead and try to save a little for a malted milk some day. Think I would git more enjoyment out of it.

We are short on planes now and what we do have are not here. They left a few days ago and the storm has hit them and they are grounded some where. And it has been so snowie and fogie may be I should say hazie that it has not been safe for them to try to come back. They say we will git some new planes before long.

Yes I know you are busy at school for this time of a year is always a busy time. Of course it is not work for the teacher. I suppose you know that by now.

You said that you all went to a free show and the kids all got a orange. Was you counted as one. Ha.

Yes I saw some places where there would have been some nice scenes for a picture. But I did not git any and I guess they won't let us take pictures here on this Post. I thought the other day that would try and git one with this leather suit on but guess I won't git to for won't have them on when I am off the Post.

Yes the Xmas mail has started to come. You ask about the packages. We will git them as fast as they come and they git them sorted up. There will be no tree.

Yes I think I like it here as well as any place I have been out side of being so far from home.

You want to be careful and not fall in any snow drifts this winter.

Do you know where we were 7 mo. ago to-night. If I am not mistaken that was the night we went to Clearmont and what changes have been made since that time.

*****

Monday, December 7, 1942, marked the one-year anniversary of the Pearl Harbor attack. Emma got two letters from Peter and could not help being angry at the Japanese for starting that mess of a war. "How can they think they can take over the entire Pacific and all the countries there? What egotists!" expounded Emma, pounding her pillow with her fist. "Now they've put so many lives in danger and killed thousands! And Peter may be sent who knows where soon!"

*****

Dec. 7, 1942

Here I am and just heard that I was leaving here about to-morrow evening.

I have not done a great lot to-day only guard some stuff for about 2 ½ hours.

Had a package at noon from Uncle Jimmies a box of stationary and a diary, and a letter from you.

I have no idea where or which way we are going. But look for it to be warmer. Don't look for a letter to soon for would not be surprised if we are on the train several days.

I have not got a thing for you for Xmas. To-morrow was my day off. Thought might go down to town but won't git to now.

With best wishes
Peter xxx

*****

Geiger Field Wash.
Dec. 8, 1942

Have a bad cold and you know how one feels when they have a bad cold. Have a bad cough. Haven been eating cough drops all day.

You should here some of the tales that is told when we are just laying around. Heard a good one to day. The different ones were telling about what a good state he was from. And one told one then this one said that is nothing. Me and my brother was shucking corn and I saw him go to the house. When I got up where he was he was back and had the log chain. He had found a ear of corn he could not git in the wagon. Said we had to put all 4 horses on that one ear. Said we pulled it up to the hog lot and 500 head of hogs ate on that one ear of corn all winter. What do you think of that one. And you couldn't guess what state he was from. Tarkio Missouri (I didn't learn that to him either).

*****

Emma had a bad day on Wednesday. She walked the mile and a quarter roundtrip to school, then stood on her feet teaching all day. The mild sleet in the afternoon melted, making the roads muddy to walk home. Then Emma discovered she had left the key at the schoolhouse. She had to walk back to the school to lock it securely, then walk home one more time. "I've walked a over three miles today, not counting the distance I've crisscrossed the schoolroom teaching. Oh, my aching legs!" she moaned to Ruth.

*****

Dec. 9, 1942

To-day has been my day off. Did go up to git a hair cut. Looked around the P.X. some and the rest of the time when I was not to chow or mail call put the time in laying on my bunk.

To write I have a wooden box for a desk. Am sitting on the bed with one foot on each side like I was riding a horse and have the desk in between my legs.

No I don't think you would of went to bed at 9:30 if I had of been in Toad Hollow. Would not say you would not went to sleep for I saw you once (July 4) when it took a lot of effort for you to keep those eyes from going shut.

The folks got a letter the other day from Theo. He sure did talk favorable about the war. He had said it would be over by Xmas and did not think now that he was far wrong. Said he told his mother the other day that he would be home to plow corn next summer.

No your package did not come to-day. Well Sis you will never know how your letters have helped me pass the time away. And I sure do enjoy them and I hope I can help you in some way.

I heard a good one the other day and guess it was true. There was a fellow that went A.W.O.L. When he got back of course he had to go see one of the higher officers. The officer ask him where he had been and the fellow said home. The officer ask what his excuse was and he said well it is this way. I wrote a letter to my wife and to another girl one night and got them mixed up and put in the wrong envelope. And I had to beat that letter home.

I don't know what punishment he did but I would say he should of got plenty for I think if a man has a wife she should know it if he is writing to some other woman. It would make no difference with my letters for you. Uncles, aunts, cousins, and some of the neighbors is my list and if I did git yours mixed up would not make much difference. The only thing they wonder what some of the signs are. But I expect they would know what the red was on your letter even if it was not always lip stick. Ha.

*****

Geiger Field Wash.
Dec. 10, 1942

This has been about the best day we have had since I come and I don't think I ever saw the snow settle so fast in my life.

Sure makes good snow balls and they sure have been flying aroud here. Was not safe unless you had your back up against a building. It was nothing to look out and see two down in the snow and each one trying to wash the other ones face in snow. And about the time they were going good some one or maybe I should say a bunch would run up and go to pileing snow on them both. And some looked most like snow balls when they got up.

They say there is a personal inspection in the morning at 8. I think I had better ring off, go shave and brush my shoes up a little.

*****

Geiger Field
Dec. 11, 1942

Your package came O.K. to-day and thanks a lot. I sure think it is nice.

To-day is another damp, fogie day. The weather in Washington is so damp I think most ever one here has a cold.

Well we had inspection this morning. Guess I got by ok for he did not say anything.

I am packed and most ready to pull out. Look to go some time to-morrow. They told us where we were going. Would like to tell you but don't think it best to write it for we aren't suppose to tell where or when.

I had a map awhile go and it is going to throw me a lot closer home. The map shows about 800 mile from K.C. and think Maryville is some closer than that. I thought we would go to a warmer climate but guess it gets colder there than here but not so damp.

How is school going now. Busy I know. Getting ready for Xmas and all. It don't seam like it should be Xmas.

Well Emma I will say thanks a lot for that package. You will git one but it may be a little late for we can't go to town when we want to and I think you will under stand how it is but will send something as soon as I can.

*****

Geiger Field Wash.
Dec. 12, 1942

Sat. after noon. Don't look to move until some time to-morrow. Just have to be ready to go when the orders come.

I sure am proud of your package. I take it and open up and look at it for little while then pack up and put back in barracks bag and have it ready to be shipped.

Last night at mail call I had 4 letters and a Xmas card. A letter from you, the folks, Mark's brother, and a Xmas card from the mail carrier. I spent the evening just read them and reread. Then packed them away.

I suppose you are working to-day getting ready for Xmas and getting the school work around to start another week.

Yes it would have been fine if you could have been here the day I had the 24 hours off. I bit one thing and that is I would not of stayed at the barracks all day if you had of been in Spokane. We could at least of got partly caught up on talking. That is if you had not went to sleep on me. Ha.

*****

On Saturday, Emma received a letter from Peter that included a sales tax token from Utah. In 1937, Utah Governor Henry Blood had signed a sales tax bill requiring aluminum tokens to pay fractions of tax on sales under fifty cents. Regular pennies were used for a fifty-cent and higher sale. Shoppers had to carry aluminum tokens as well as pennies, which angered the public. Citizens quickly nicknamed them "Blood money," after the governor. By June 1942, aluminum was a scarce war material, so Utah switched to the newly created composition called plastic. Emma mused, *I'm glad Missouri never created tokens. What a hassle to have to carry coins, tokens, and ration books around for shopping!*

*****

Geiger Field Wash.
Dec. 13, 1942

I am still in Washington but will leave to-ward night. This is some job just laying around waiting and nothing to do.

I think if it is so I can I will call the folks as soon as I git to where I am going and I expect Mom will call you if it is so she can git through. I look to be on the road several days as these troop trains go so slow and they take a round about way to git there. About as bad as we used to when we would start to Maryville. Ha.

Chapter 27

Maryville had an evening test blackout on December 14, 1942. Although located in the center of America, constant fears remained of either the Nazis or Japanese attacking the mainland. Emma felt people always seemed on edge, concerned about loved ones serving in the military, the war's effect on food and consumer supplies, or a foreign attack. While everyone tried to continue daily routines, the undercurrent of tension pulsed through all adults.

By mid-December, a friend arrived home on leave before being assigned to Dutch Harbor on Amaknak Island in Unalaska, Alaska. Emma marveled to her students, "What strange-sounding geographic places our local men are now assigned to. We'll have to look up Dutch Harbor on the map, if we can find it." In June 1942, the Battle of Dutch Harbor was one of the few sites, besides Pearl Harbor, in American territory that would be bombed by the Japanese during World War II.

*****

Rapid City S.D.
Dec. 16, 1942

I am at Rapid City South Dakota or that is at a Army air base about 12 mile out of Rapid City northeast I think. I would not say for sure for the sun came up in the west to me this morning.

We left Geiger Field Sunday evening about 8. Have been on the train ever since. Got into Rapid City early this morning but they switched us around a lot and gave us our breakfast before we came on out here.

I thought all the time that Dakota was a dry state but the mud is sure deep here now.

I saw a lot of sights on this trip. Came across the mountains on the northern route. We came through Montana and Wyoming. Came through Great Falls and Billings Montana. There is a lot more smaller towns but don't suppose you could find them on a map.

Came through one little town called Crow Agency and all the people there were Indains. I think they said they were all Crow Indains. It was close to where there had been a big Indain battle in the early days. There were little Indains kids running everwhere.

We saw a lot of timber. Most all fir. Came through one place where there had been a forest fire. Trees laying ever where. Some were still standing but had been killed by the fire. Came through one place where there were nothing but rocks and I think you would of enjoyed seeing them for they were of all sizes and colors. I can't tell you much about this camp yet for have just got off the trucks and came into the barracks.

They split the 95th Group up in 3 Groups to come out here. One bunch that left awhile before we did have not got here. I guess they must of took a longer route. The bunch that left on Sat. night got here about one yesterday.

Pvt. Peter K. Paxton
336th Bomb. Squadron
95th Bomb. Group
Army Air Base
Rapid City South Dakota

*****

Rapid City S.D.
Dec. 17, 1942

I think this camp is going to be about the same as the others. Have good eats, a good barracks. The bad part is we have poor water. The fountains run all the time and it is still warm. Taste more like water back there that has sit in a warm room for a long time.

I worked at the hanger all day. Helped fix the brakes before noon and packed the wheels with grease and this after noon have just washed grease off the plane with gas. You would never know there was a gas ration on around a Army camp.

Yes I called home last night. Sure did seam good to hear Moms voice again. I was sure suprised for thought it would take quite a while to git a call through but I don't think it was 5 min. from the time I started the call through till I was talking to Mom. And after I got through I thought of a thousand things I wanted to ask about. And I know it would be the same way if I got back there but they don't talk like we will git a furlough for a while yet. But I am still hopeing.

A bunch that left Geiger field a little while before we did Sunday evening just got here a little bit ago and had been on the train all the time.

We never saw so much wild game on the road out here only pheasant and we sure did see a lot of them. One boy said he thought he saw a deer standing back in some timber but I think there was a lot of wild game in places where we came through for we come along a river for a long ways and would see paths in the snow coming down out of the hills and we thought it was where the deer would come to water. And talk about the mountain streams. I think you said once that you thought one would be pretty. Well I saw some on this trip that had froze where they had come over some large rock and there would be ice cycles that looked to be 5 or 6 foot through and water running over them. Sure was some sights.

Sun was bright all day and it was not a bit cold. Did not need a coat if you were working. Of course I suppose you would of froze.

*****

As December progressed, Emma had five students out with colds. Others who did attend suffered fits of bad coughing. Emma tried to avoid catching their illness but finally had a mild cold.

At ten Friday evening, Emma rode with Owen to Barnard. A party in honor of a hometown soldier friend kept Emma dancing until three Saturday morning. Later that day, a cold northeast wind brought snow and sleet while Emma visited her mother in Maryville. Emma turned in a scrapbook the students had made to the Army and $2.13 for Christmas Seals to Mr. Burr. Emma caught a ride with friends back to the Roberts' Sunday evening, still with her mild cold, but she managed to catch enough sleep to face the school day ahead.

*****

Rapid City S.D.
Dec. 18, 1942

Friday evening. What are you doing. Would like to be there so could take you back to town.

To-day has been a real winter day here. Has been trying to snow all day and the wind just goes clear through you. And even I froze. After noon I put on my sheep lined suit and got along good.

To-day I sat around down to the hanger. Did have to cover up some of the planes to keep some of the snow and frost off. They gave us all some more shots after noon to-day. Gave us one in each arm. One was for some kind of fever. The other some big name. I think they said there would be 5 of them all to-gether. They did not hurt so much at the time but my right arm is real sore to-night. The shot in my left arm did make it ache for awhile.

I go to work now at 6. Have to git up at 5. Git about a hour off at noon and git off at 6 in the evening. After awhile will have to take my turn at working of a night. Will go to work at 6 p.m. and work till 6 a.m. and I bet 2 a.m. don't come as soon as it has a few times when we were talking. And I think if I could git back now would just have to stop the watch. Do you think you could keep your eyes open. Ha.

*****

Rapid City S.D.
Dec. 19, 1942

Came back from the hanger at noon and had 6 letters. Tonight had no packages but 6 more letters, 3 from you that had all gone to Geiger.

Helped cover up and uncover some planes. Help take some snow and ice off the planes. I had never thought about why the planes did not take off until I read one of your letters. Would not be surprised if you were right about me working on the plane was the reason for it staying on the ground.

They have the mess hall all decorated up for Xmas about the same as they always fix the school houses.

You can tell Roberts that I got there card. It sure does help to know that people back home think of you.

I git next Monday off. Wish I could drop in at a certain Mo. school house and just see what kind of a teacher they have. May be I could put some mischief in the kids head. What do you think.

*****

Ilene W. Devlin

Rapid City S.D.
Dec. 20, 1942

I got two more letters from you to-day. Both had gone to Seattle. In one of them you said if the stamps were tore they were no good. Do I git them cut out right. If I don't just say so. For you know that is what the teacher is supposed to do. If you don't do it right they make you do it over. Ha.

I worked down to the hanger all day or should say was down there. Did not do much work. Will be a little work now for one of the engines on one plane has to be changed.

I went over to mail call to-night and the moon and stars were so bright and you can't guess what I thought. I thought Sunday night and such a nice night. I wonder just where I would be if I was back at Pickering Mo. but not much use of wondering for I think I would be in Toad Hollow. Might be about 2 a.m. in the morning that is if I did not git run off before.

I moved again to-day but just to another barracks. They moved all the supposed to be machenics to-gether.

Well walk over. A boy just gave me a candy bar and I will give you a bit if you will promice not to take to big a one.

With best wishes
Farmer Paxton

*****

The week began with cold, rain, and ice covering everything. Tom cut a cedar Christmas tree for the schoolhouse and brought Emma and the tree Monday morning. Her students had fun decorating it with homemade paper chains and snowflakes. All week, they practiced for the winter play, decorated the tree and room, and finished homework for the semester break. The Watsons brought some presents for the students. Tom returned from town with the five dozen oranges and two pounds of candy Emma had ordered for her pupils.

*****

Rapid City S.D.
Dec. 21, 1942

6:30 Monday evening. To day has been my day off and I have been to lazy to even eat. Had to go down this morning and get a package and come back by the P.X. and got some candy bars. We sure git candy cheap here. Any kind of a bar for 3¢ each and they sure sell a lot of them.

You ask how I would like to spend a day on the farm working 12 hours or longer. Nothing would suit me better. Unless it would be more than one day and if I wanted to do some work. Just travel back to Toad Hollow north side. Do you suppose I could work if I did git back there for it would take quite a while to get caught up on talk.

That is a good one when you forget the key and have to run back after it. No I don't want to contest you for a five mile hike.

Got to diging around in my barracks bag and found some old letters. I took the stamps off of 30 and then tore the letters up and threw in the trash can. Now the fire man can have something to start a fire in the morning with.

I don't know if you will git this letter before your do a package or not. Don't know just how you will like it. I tried to git a roll of films but they did not have them but said they were not hard to git. That you could git them any where and the instructions are in the box. Be sure and set front for the distance. It is fixed for a time exposure. When you try it out tell me how you git along. And if you can't git the films tell me and I will git you some and send.

Guess had better wish you merry Xmas and a happy new year and will say good night.

*****

Rapid City S.D.
Dec. 22, 1942

Tuesday evening. So to morrow is your last day of school till Monday and I bet you are sick again then after eating all that dinner Friday. But I suppose you will go to bed early Thursday night so to be asleep when Santa gets there. Ha.

How is the colds by now. I hope all are better and back in school and be careful and don't git sick your self.

I went to the hanger this morning. Worked for awhile. Then they called down and wanted 3 men. So the crew chief said for me to go and if it was a bad detail he would see that I did not have to go on the next one. So when I got up there they put us on the fireman job. I will not have to work any unless one of the others git sick or go A.W.O.L. Then I will have to take there place. It will be that way until next Monday.

It is run on 3 eight hour shifts. Will work from 8 a.m. till 4 pm. Then the next week from 4 p.m. till mid night. The next week from mid night till 8 in the morning. Or that is the way the shifts go so I will just have to lay around the barracks till Monday if I stay on.

Went back down to the hanger after noon and told my crew chief what they had put me on and they said I would be on it while I was here. And the crew chief very near blue up for them taking me and having so many that had never went to school and were not mechanics and were just laying around.

Then to-night my crew chief that is my boss and the flight chief have been having it round and round. And the flight chief told me awhile ago that I would not be on only a few days. It would be a easer job but would rather work down there for would learn a lot more and would learn what I have already studied about at school.

I did right well on my mail again to-day. Had 3 Xmas cards and two letters and a package of candy, apples, cookies, and grapes from the folks. It was all in fine shape except the grapes and they had been on the road to long and were spoiled.

The letters were one from you and one from the folks. A Xmas card was from a boy that we met in Clearmont one night. The folks say he had to leave for the Army to-day.

*****

By December 23, the roads had thawed. Deep mud prevented the Watsons from coming to the winter program. Emma and her students exchanged presents, ate popcorn and some of the candy and oranges, and happily left school to enjoy the Christmas break. Tom even picked up Emma in the wagon so she would not have to carry her gifts and food home. "I'm really grateful you gave me a ride. This mud gets unbearable sometimes, especially if I have to carry anything," Emma said.

She had received two boxes of stationary, two makeup sets, a picture, and a handkerchief from her students. Her heart felt touched by their generosity, knowing their families had little money to spare.

The Roberts surprised Emma with a box of chocolates, a pair of pillowcases, and a dish towel. They even gave her and her mother some homemade butter and a canned chicken. Emma had come to love the Roberts. Best of all, Emma received two letters from Peter.

On Christmas Eve, Owen arrived to drive Emma to Maryville. They picked up groceries, cleaned Edith's house, wrapped gifts, and helped get supper. The other three brothers and their families arrived by evening to enjoy roast duck, stuffing, ice cream, and cookies. Emma had to wash all the dishes, but her sisters-in-law helped dry them. They spent the evening talking, laughing, and telling stories before finally going to bed about two in the morning. Emma shared a bed with her mother. Two couples took the extra bedrooms, with other adults and children sleeping on floor pallets. The packed house was filled with family and loving feelings.

The children were up early Christmas morning, to the groans of adults who got to bed so late. Everyone had fun taking turns unwrapping thoughtful gifts. Emma received a portfolio, two makeup sets, a slip, a pitcher and glasses set, photograph album, fountain pen and pencil, powder puffs, towel and wash cloth, bookends, and a sugar and cream set. Most items would go directly into Emma's hope chest, as the family expected Peter and Emma to marry as soon as the war ended.

Emma's heart was so grateful for her supportive family. She was saddened, however, by the thought of thousands of people worldwide who had died during the past year and the military personnel spending Christmas away from their families. She found such conflicting emotions becoming more a part of each day the war lasted. Sometimes she felt her head spinning from the common daily life she led and the world events swirling around her.

*****

Rapid City S.D.
Dec. 23, 1942

It has been affine day here. Been clear most all day and warm for the time of year. Of course I suppose you would git cold for it is colder than it was on July 5. Ha.

Stayed in bed till about 7:30. Cleaned up, swept and mopped around my bunk. Went down to the hanger about 10. Thought I might be able to look on and learn something. Stayed there about 1½ hour. Then went for mail call and had quite a pile of it. And as you said some was from some Toad Hollow girls.

Letters were from friends and families I know. Two were girls I went to high school with. One from Mrs. Trotter. I think you have saw it for checked the hand writing and it compared with some I have saw before that is on the envelopes. Sure was nice, a card and letter to-gether from Bill at Terrant Field, Ft. Worth Texas.

Be sides the Xmas cards I got a letter and card from you.

You ask about my mouth. Well I would never know that I had any teeth pulled. Only there seams to be quite a hole in my teeth there. Don't know how I can fix that unless I go to chewing tobacco and keep a big chew there all the time. What do you think about that. Bet I can guess. Ha.

The letter I got from the folks the other day there were telling of things that Davie had said. He got up the other morning and said Dad I tell you what we will do. I will help you haul out your hay then you can take me to school. So that is the way they did it. He sure can think up some good ones.

I suppose by now that you are off untill next Monday. I hope you have a good time over Xmas and I know you will.

*****

Rapid City S.D.
Dec. 25, 1942

They say we are going to have a big Christmas dinner. And this morning sure is a fine one. The sun so bright.

It don't seam one bit like Christmas to me but I sure have got a lot of cards and presents. And the longer I wait the more I would like to be at home to-day. This is the first time I have missed being there on Xmas.

I had 8 letters and cards yesterday. Most of the cards they had wrote a little and had a package from Ruth with candy, gum, a fruit cake and a puzzle. A 2 ½ lb. box of candy from Rhonda.

I did not git up until late this morning. No you did not guess. It was 10. Finaly got up and shaved and cleaned up. And some of the boys said that there had been some more mail came in late last night and we could git it if we went over. So that is what I did.

Had 11 cards and letters. Mostly neighbors and friends around home. I had 2 letters from you yesterday. One had went to Geiger.

I also had a package this morning from Uncle Theos. It was candy, nuts, and gum. I sure have a lot of candy. I expect I have more right here in the barracks to eat than a lot of people will have to-day.

Well Sis it is most eleven and I suppose you are getting a big dinner ready. I wish it was so we could be to-gether to-day. Don't think now I would care if had any thing to eat or not. Would just like to talk.

We have to put on our Class A to eat dinner to-day. So I guess I had better begin to git ready. Will write a little more this after noon. Or that is if I can for they say they are going to have beer. So if the next addition is worse than this you will know what is the matter. Ha.

Well here I am back from chow and if my hand is steady enough will scribble down a few more lines. I thought I would write what we had but I got a chance to git another menu so I think it will be easer to just send it. They did not put the beer, Coca Cola on there. They had orange pop to and I drank a bottle and thought of you.

There was only one thing that was wrong with the meal and that was we could not eat it at home where we would all of liked to.

Have to write to several and thank for packages.

With best wishes
Peter. x.x.x.

*****

Bob and his family took Edith and Emma to see Grandma Bailey in the afternoon of December 25. While Edith stayed for a few days, Emma went with Bob to the movies to see *Gentleman Jim* and *In Old California*. In *Gentleman Jim*, Errol Flynn starred as heavyweight boxing champion James J. Corbett and the movie was based on Corbett's autobiography, *The Roar of the Crowd*. The second film starred John Wayne as a Boston pharmacist who relocated to Sacramento during the Gold Rush. Emma appreciated the escape from her world's reality, at least for an evening.

Emma went with Melinda the next day to see *Panama Hattie*. Red Skelton starred, and Ann Sothern played Hattie Maloney, a saloon owner in Panama where various characters assembled, frequently singing and dancing Cole Porter's songs. The theater provided a great way to spend a rainy day.

*****

Rapid City S.D.
Dec. 26, 1942

The day after Xmas and I have been wondering if you were able to be up or if they had to have the doctor. For I know you had a big dinner and of course you would not eat to much. Ha.

Had a little snow last night and it was cold this morning and the wind blowing about 90 mile a hour. And up here there is not any hills or trees for a long ways to break it. It looked for a while like it was going to be a real old blizzard but about noon the wind quit blowing so hard and the sun came out.

Worked in side all day. For we are about throwing distance from the mess hall and about ½ mile from the hanger where I have to go to work. But they took us and brought us back in a truck.

I had a letter from the folks and 3 Xmas cards to-day.

I had 2 papers in the mail to-day. Saw one letter to Santa from Davie. Looked over them and thought I might see yours for I know all kids like to send him a letter. Ha.

*****

Rapid City S.D.
Dec. 27, 1942

Just worked down to the hanger all day. Lay around and wait for a plane to come in. Then would have to go out and check it over to see that ever thing was all right. Of course I would just help fill with gas and oil. If I had what gas I helped put in the planes would at least have enough to take us to Maryville to a show. Helped fill 2 and put 800 gal. in each one so you see that would take the old Chevrolet quite a ways. Might even git to go over some Toad Hollow hills for a change.

I suppose you are ready to start school in the morning. I bet some of them have some big tales to tell you about what they got. Mom said that Davie talked to Dad and said that old Santa was comin to the school house the night before but had run out of gas and had to walk the rest of the ways. And he told them that it was not the real Santa over to Pickering that he was just playing like he was and that it looked like Martin Beckett and sure enough that is who it was.

To-day had one letter from you and one from the folks. A nice box of candy from Marks. I don't know if I will be able to eat it all or not but divide with some of the boys here. And they divide with me. Was figuring a while ago and had got a little over 8 lbs besides what Mom sent and it was a 2 lb. graham cracker box of home made so don't you think that had ought to last for a while. Walk over and I will let you look at it and see how good it is. Might turn my head and you could sneak out a little to taste. Ha.

*****

On December 28 all but one student was back in school. The pupils took down the tree, carefully removing the decorations to keep.

Emma got a package from Peter with a camera and a letter. "Oh, Peter," Emma said aloud in her bedroom, "This is the first camera I've ever owned. And I've always wanted one. If only I could have had one when Dad was alive. I've only got a few pictures of him. Now I can send photos to you."

*****

Rapid City S.D.
Dec. 29, 1942

I have your letter here on one knee and my writing on the other. Say that supper makes me hungary. And I sure wish that I could of walked in and joined you at the big party.

I wonder why Alice and Doug woke up early. Don't suppose you ever did that on Xmas morning. Ha.

The two shows sound good. Have just bent to 3 shows since you and I went. Guess will just wait till I git back to Missouri.

I enjoy hearing what you have been doing. Any thing is worthy reading in the Army when it comes from close home. I would of enjoyed helping you with the dishes but would we of got any thing done for talking.

You ask about K.P. Yes we git it here and for 3 days at a time when we do. But I have been lucky enough not to have it since I left Chanute. May be I should hit on wood for luck so will hit my head.

Mo. Bomb on my address don't mean that I am a bombardier or at least I hope it don't. For the bombardier is the one that ride in the plane and drops the bombs. And I don't think I would suit for that.

I guess where the bomb comes from is because the plane I work on is a large bomber. But in this Group there is ever thing. Supposed to be mechanics like my self, mechanics that is over us, truck drivers, cooks, doctors, general duty men which are men that work ever where, pilots, gunners, navagators and I don't know if that is all or not.

Yes I think there is something wrong about the furloughs. They keep saying we will git one a little later but I have heard that so long I have begain to wonder. But I of course still hoping. It seams like all the boys that came in when I did and later have all been home.

I was like you. I got up the way town folks do about 6 this morning. Swept and moped around my bunk. Then layed back down and that is the last I knew till after 10. Then shaved and cleaned up. On down to the P.X. and got some more stationary. Back and wrote 3 letters.

Oh yes. I did my washing this after noon. Would not say how good a job I did but went through the motion.

I suppose the way you talk that you had to go back to Toad Hollow with the saddle horse.

I thought of you to-day for when I was down to the P.X. I had a malted milk. And as you did not like them I wished you were here so could tease you by watching me drink mine. Ha.

*****

Rapid City S.D.
Dec. 30, 1942

Had to git up this morning, have my floor swept and moped and breakfast over and to the hanger by 6 a.m. and ready for work. But it sure gits tiresome. You stay down there for 12 hours. Had to clean up the hanger, help check the planes and refill with gas and oil. Then lay around and wait for another one to come in. We have a volley ball and basket ball and play some of both when the planes are all flying and that helps pass the time away.

We got off work at 6. They told us we had to scrub the barracks. Mop was after 8 when we got through.

Well had some more Xmas cards again to day. Had 2 cards and a letter from Marks that had all went to Geiger and another from Marks that was telling all about Xmas.

I have been wondering how you were making it back and forth to school. Be careful and don't git stuck in a drift again.

Well Sis if you can read this you are doing good. For I think I have wrote faster than the B 17 will fly.

*****

Rapid City, S.D.
Dec. 31, 1942

All cleaned up. Moped and everthing looking fine. I have not had to work down to the hanger to day for me and another boy was room orderly. So it was our job to sweep and mop the center of the barracks and clean the bath room. Had it all cleaned up this morning and the first sargent came through to inspect and said it looked good. So I thought ever thing was O.K.

But about a hour ago the barracks chief come in and said for ever one to git in and help. There had been some mud tracked in and he said ever thing wanted to be cleaned up in good shape for the captain. Said that if every thing was not cleaned up good in about a hour when he come through there would be no passes over New Years. But if it was he thought he would let us off to-morrow and don't think everyone that was around here did not dig in and help.

Had three letters at noon. One from you and one from the folks and one from Harold.

It looks like you have plenty of make up sets. I suppose I will git all kinds of lip stick, ruge, finger nail polish and what other kind is there on your letters. Ha.

I bet you did dread to start back to school. All kids do when they have been out for a few days.

You said come on down and we could visit. That there was some time left after you got your hair rolled. Well don't think I would not like to and it would make no difference to me if your hair was rolled or not. For we could talk either way don't you think.

And as for talking good to my boss I am doing my part. But don't know if I will get a furlough in January or not. I do know one thing. It will be welcome and they won't have to tell me the second time that I can leave. And I don't suppose the train would run fast enough when I got started. And if I had a car and gas expect would break the speed limit.

We got paid right after dinner. Of course had to stand in lines for a while. Went from there and stand in line and got 2 more shots. One in each arm. Have to go back a week from to-day and git one more and that will finish them all up. They did not hurt much but my arms have begain to git a little sore now.

I see some pictures awhile ago that a boy had got down to the P.X. Think I will git some the next time I go down. May be you will enjoy looking at them.

*****

As 1942 closed, the newspapers and radios stations kept describing the Soviet counterattack against the Nazis. Soviet troops broke through Hungarian and Romanian lines northwest and southwest of Stalingrad, trapping the German Sixth Army inside the city. Hitler demanded no retreat, so the Germans dug in for a siege.

Time to Emma flashed by in school yet stood still while waiting for word from Peter. When would he be home again?

Chapter 28

On Monday, January 4, 1943, the weather became so cold the old stove failed to warm the entire schoolroom. All students were present to begin the third quarter. Emma lost a filling out of her front tooth the next day, but she couldn't get it fixed until Saturday. Thus, the year began with good and bad news.

Tom Roberts pulled a car out of the mud that week. The roads continued extremely muddy until Friday, when they finally froze. By Saturday, they thawed again.

Emma got a ride to Edith's on Friday night. The next morning, Emma bought a pair of black slippers, exchanged a dress, and bought film for her camera, Peter's Christmas gift to her. She also had Edith's radio fixed for $2.25 so Edith could listen to the Grand Ole Opry Saturday evening.

On Sunday, Emma got a ride to Peter's parents. "You both just stand on your front porch and smile! I'm taking this picture to send to Peter as a surprise." Gene and Janie thought of how proud they were of Peter and smiled the best they could, even if a little self-consciously.

School continued amid the thaws and freezes of January. The pupils took tests, which Emma graded in the evenings, and Emma began to teach from Unit III from the Missouri State Course of Study. Her students studied well, and she was proud of their efforts. She gave Kathy a card and a nickel for her seventh birthday on January 15.

"Okay, kids, we're going outside so I can take your picture! I know it's cold, but the light's better there. I want to see all your smiling faces in my teaching scrapbook." Some children had never had their photograph taken, so they were eager to see how they looked after Emma got the film developed.

Jacob's and Mike's families joined Edith at Owen's home that weekend. They helped Owen do chores, then everyone went to Hopkins to see *West of the Tombstone*. Charles Starrett starred as Marshal Steve Langdon, who investigated a rumor Billy the Kid was still alive. Emma loved Western movies, since her folks had lived in Oklahoma when Indians still lived in the area.

Monday, January 18, was the coldest day so far. A strong northwest wind blew snow almost all day. Emma burned her arm on the stove as she banked the fire for the night. To make matters worse, she nearly got frostbite on her face while going home. Tom had headed out to meet Emma to ensure she got back safely, so she rode in his wagon part of the way.

The wind died the next day, but frigid cold iced the land. Only three children were present to study the solar system. Emma was taking cold, so no one was greatly interested in learning. She did read *Martha of California,* by James Otis, to her pupils. Martha was a twelve-year-old-girl living on a Missouri plantation. Her father heard stories of California, so he sold their home and moved the family. The book highlighted the American westward expansion with life in a covered wagon and the trip's obstacles. Since a lot of local families still had wagons, her students could relate to traveling across country in them.

Emma thrilled to a letter from Peter on January 21. He might get a furlough in February. She felt her heart beat faster at the possibility of seeing him again after such a long time. She even bought a twenty-five cent Defense Stamp, making $9.25 she had accumulated so far to support the war effort.

Emma reread Peter's letters each evening. *I can hear his voice in my mind as if he was here talking to me. I can't help envying my friends who got married and had their men stay home to farm instead of enlisting! I wish Peter had stayed put. He's being moved all over the country and not allowed a furlough like most of the guys seem to be getting. Why?* At least her anger over being separated helped warm her body in her chilly bedroom.

Emma had ordered a college algebra book and course. That weekend, she mailed in her first lesson to earn more college credits before summer school.

A surprise greeted Emma on Monday with a letter from Peter. His leave was coming sooner, and he arrived Tuesday evening, January 26, 1943. When Peter drove his old Chevy into the farmyard at six o'clock, Emma ran from the house and jumped into his arms. He hugged her so tightly Emma felt her ribs would surely break.

"You're really here! And how you've gotten taller!" she exclaimed.

Peter kept staring at her as if she would disappear if he blinked. "I've been waitin' to see you for so long, you just don' seem real. And you look even prettier than I remembered! Even more than your photos you sent."

Emma felt her cheeks warm. Peter was so sincere and such an honest guy. She was lucky to his love, and she appreciated it.

"Everyone's waitin' for us for dinner. We better get goin' and talk some on the way," he finally announced, letting her step out of his arms.

They drove to the Paxtons' home where Owen and Melinda joined them for dinner. The group talked and asked Peter questions so late Emma got to bed at four fifteen in the morning.

She thought Peter looked wonderful. His Army work had added even more maturity beyond what he had already accomplished with farming. He presented her with a pair of bronze miniature cowboy boots welded together at the inside heels as a souvenir of his time out West.

"Peter, thank you," she said, her eyes shining with happiness. "I'll keep them to remember I want your boots under my bed as soon as this war is over! You just look forward to that and get home as soon as you can!"

"I want that, too," said Peter. "And I better not find any other guy's coat hangin' on the hall rack when I surprise you some day when I sneak home unexpected!"

They both laughed, knowing they were already committed to each other, whether or not they had been to the altar.

Wednesday went slowly for Emma. Finally, Peter arrived to take her to Pickering and Maryville after school. They ate dinner at a local restaurant, then visited until nearly four in the morning. Emma's second night without much sleep affected her only a little for her excitement at having him home kept her going each day.

Peter again picked her up for a meeting at Prairie View on Thursday. More good conversations until midnight followed dinner with his folks. Peter excused them so he could take Emma back to the Roberts', but they managed to talk in the car until nearly two in the morning despite the cold. Peter gave Emma a match souvenir and some precious memories of talks about their relationship and hopes for the future.

Unfortunately, Peter had to leave Friday afternoon at one fifteen, so Emma could not see him off. She was so disappointed and lonely that her heart, for once, wasn't in teaching. Peter rode a bus to St. Jo, then caught a train to Omaha. There he was scheduled to catch a train to Rapid City sometime on Saturday.

The Rapid City Army Air Base, a training location for Flying Fortress units established by the U.S. War Department on January 2, 1942, had been completed in October, with five hangars finished late that year. The airfield had three concrete runways for the 17th Bombardment Training Wing, II Bomber Command. The 88th Bombardment Group was reassigned to the base in October 1942 as the Operational Training Unit. Peter was excited about learning to maintain and repair the B-17s, and Emma had to be content knowing he was stateside, not in danger overseas.

At school, Emma read *Five Little Peppers & How They Grew*. The book series by Margaret Sidney had been published from 1881 to 1916. Covering the lives of the five children of Mamsie and the late Mister Pepper, they related how the family was born into poverty in a rural house but rescued by a wealthy gentleman. Most of Emma's students came from simple farm families, so they could understand the Peppers' trials.

Emma got weekend rides to see her mom and brothers as often as she could. She loved the chance to visit, help with farm tasks, go to the movies, and just be a family again. They enjoyed parties, chivarees, and having meals with friends. While a little envious of her female friends having weddings and babies, she sincerely wished them the best. Also, she often visited the Paxtons. Having Emma come was as close as the Paxtons could get to having part of Peter home.

Peter's February 8 letter contained a pair of silver wings. Peter had been promoted to corporal on February 5. The day was extra special since Owen turned twenty-six years old.

The next day, rationing began on shoes. Each citizen was allowed only three pairs yearly. A person could buy one pair between February 9 and June 15, 1943. Designated stamps in War Ration Book One were required to buy shoes, with only six shades of leather being produced. Men's rubber boots and rubber work shoes had been rationed since September 30, 1942. To obtain new pairs, men had to apply to the local ration board, prove they needed the shoes for essential industry, and turn in the old pair. Galoshes and overshoes escaped rationing because they were made of less crude rubber. No one could foresee that by March 20, 1944, the ration would be reduced to two pairs of leather shoes per year.

Emma and her students exchanged valentines on Friday, February 12. At an evening community meeting, one family sang accompanied a guitar. Everyone had a great time, forgetting the war news for a few hours.

Wednesday was warmer and clear. Only Betsy and Lisa attended because everyone else had illnesses.

"Since we have the school to ourselves," Emma told the girls, "we'll do something different today. There's no use trying to learn new lessons when so many students are gone. We'll just have to work even harder when they all return."

They spent the day erasing marks in books and mending torn pages and covers. The Lone Valley limited book budget meant reading material had to be tended carefully.

Emma received her $68.80 monthly teaching check with the Victory tax of $1.20 deducted first. The United States Revenue Act of 1942 added a five percent Victory tax on all individual incomes over $624. *I don't have any control over my take home money, but I've sure got more than when I cleaned houses and worked as a maid.*

Peter was promoted to sergeant on Tuesday, February 16. Emma called the Paxtons, who were thrilled for him.

"Peter's always been a hard worker!" exclaimed Janie. "It's nice to see the Army recognizes him as a level-headed guy other guys like."

On Saturday, Emma attended a meeting about canned goods rationing. With the Japanese controlling seventy percent of the world's tin supply, the U.S. military needed the metal for ration tins, ammunition boxes, plasma containers, and morphine Syrettes.

Beginning March 1, 1943, 300 more items would become rationed, including canned, bottled, or frozen fruits and vegetables; canned or bottled juices and soups; and dried fruits. Fresh fruits and vegetables, pickles, relishes, and Jell-O were exempt. Each rationed item received a point value, which changed monthly due to supply, demand, and region. War Ration Book Two had blue stamps to provide forty-eight points worth of processed foods each month. That equaled thirty-three pounds of canned goods per person per year, which was thirteen pounds less than pre-war usage. Since no change was given, shoppers had to be careful to use the exact number of points.

Emma registered twenty-six people for the canned goods program on February 25. Many were frustrated with the constantly changing points system.

"Land sakes," exclaimed one neighbor. "I no more than git Book One remembered than they go 'n change the dang points for Book Two. How's a body suppose' to keep up with all the new rules?"

Others felt the canned goods rationing would not affect them too much. They grew and canned their own garden- and farm-produced food and meat in glass jars they reused year to year.

"We're farm families," replied Emma. "and do our own canning. But city folks are most hurt by the changes. They really have to be careful about how they use their points each week. We're actually pretty lucky."

Emma went with Owen and Melinda to see Immortal Sergeant on Saturday. Set in the World War II North African desert, Henry Fonda starred as a corporal lacking in confidence for his war service and love life with girlfriend Maureen O'Hara. Emma loved Maureen O'Hara as an actress and wished she had as much courage as Maureen always portrayed.

That same day, Emma had her eyes examined. She needed glasses.

"I'll check my account," she told the doctor. "I think I can order them after I get paid." She tried to keep as much money in the bank as possible to pay for summer college classes.

Winter illnesses grew as February closed. Janie Paxton had the flu. Emma's sister-in-law Kate had pneumonia. Emma again felt a cold arriving and dragged herself to school on Tuesday wishing she could stay in bed. Several students also suffered with various ailments.

On Saturday, March 6, 1943, Emma marked the fourth anniversary of her mother's move to Maryville. How their lives had changed with the easier ability to walk on paved sidewalks and streets and having grocery stores nearby. Emma also worried less about her mother since she had neighbors with whom to chat and gossip.

The third quarter ended, and Emma gave her students four tests. A new health unit arrived that Emma studied each night. Three Newman family children joined her room, totaling seven pupils.

Each evening, Emma relaxed with the Roberts by playing cards, talking, listening to war updates on the radio, and writing letters. On March 10, Emma mailed an $11 check for income tax for 1942. Ruth gave her three photos to paste in her album. Emma also graded papers, studied her algebra, and read.

When Miss Kimberly came to teach music for two periods, Emma had a chance to relax. Sometimes she worked on the school's library, cleaned shelves, or brought in coal so she could leave earlier after school.

"It's so nice the days you come," Emma said to Miss Kimberly. "I get to talk to an adult for a change. I love my students, but sometimes I just need someone older around!"

Emma got her glasses on Saturday, March 13. From her $68.80 teaching check, her spectacles cost $14. She also had to pay board of $20 per month to the Roberts. Still, she considered herself lucky to be working regularly. No war production plants had been located in Maryville, so she would have had to move to Kansas City or elsewhere for higher wages. She didn't want to leave her mother to live so far from home.

A few months after the war began, Emma had thought about becoming a WAAC, a member of the Women's Army Auxiliary Corp. Emma again discussed her idea with Mae.

"I could train at Fort Des Moines. It's only 144 miles from Maryville! I could go by train and come home on leave to see Mom."

"Might as well be 200," replied Mae. "That's a mighty long ways to be away from home for the first time for any long time."

"But I've always wanted to travel," Emma retorted. "Look at Peter. He's been clear to the west coast and across the mountains twice now. He's gotten to see so much of this country! How I envy that part of his trips."

"But he's also homesick," Mae reasoned. "The food ain't as good as here, and he can't even leave the post when he wants. Can you imagine trying to sleep in a barracks with all those guys snorin' each night? My pa snores enough to shake the house apart sometimes. What if there were thirty-five of them at once?"

Emma had to laugh. "I know I've never been far from home. My trip to Rantoul was the farthest I've ever been. I just would feel like I was working to get Peter home sooner if I could enlist in the WAACs."

A few local women had enlisted. Emma felt maybe she wasn't doing enough for the war effort. Then her conscience would bother her, reminding her she was the main person responsible for her widowed mother and how could she consider leaving Edith alone? Once again, Emma concluded her job as a teacher and being in charge of war efforts like the scrap metal drives, Christmas Seals, Red Cross work, and rationing programs were good patriotic contributions. She gave up the dream of travel to live her life in the local world she knew best, at least for the war's duration.

Mike Trotter turned twenty-seven on St. Patrick's Day. Emma had sent him a card and called to wish him well. Some friends had a chivaree in the evening, but the Roberts' car wouldn't start so they couldn't attend. Tom had bought a new black mule that day. "That durn mule'll never have the problems that car can have!" exclaimed Tom in frustration.

The next day, nearly six inches of snow fell by evening followed by a northeast wind. Mrs. Newman brought her three children their overshoes so they could walk home and keep their feet drier. She stayed awhile at school listening to the lessons.

The following day found deep snow everywhere. Emma and the children played fox and geese at recess. They dragged their overshoes around the school yard, making a large wagon wheel shape.

"Now everyone stamp down a four-foot circle in the center of the wagon wheel as a safe zone for the geese," instructed Emma.

One student became the fox and chased the student geese until he tagged one, who became the new fox. Everyone had to stay on the trails, with no jumping from one spoke to another. The geese could rest briefly in the home circle safe from the fox. All were laughing, tired, and happy by the time recess ended. They got some good exercise even on a snowy winter day.

By late March, the playground became too muddy to use at recess. The students had to play games inside.

Owen, Jacob, their wives, and Emma went to see *Hitler's Children* on Saturday. The American black and white propaganda film portrayed the brutalities associated with the Hitler Youth. One line from the movement's song was featured: "For Hitler we will live and for Hitler we will die." Emma could never imagine her students being brain-washed. *How can any country teach their children so much hatred for other people? I feel sorry for the German children under Hitler's rule.*

Peter mailed Emma a photo of himself at Mt. Rushmore. Emma envied him for getting to see so much of America. She also missed him every day, wishing she could be closer to where he was stationed.

Chapter 29

School work continued. In early April 1943, Emma gave geography, history, and civics tests. Her pupils seemed to pay special attention to geography, since many knew someone stationed overseas and wondered where all those strange-sounding names appeared on the map.

Emma went with friends to Clearmont for the class play *No Bride for the Groom,* a 1939 farce in three acts. The students did well, and the audience applauded their appreciation. Everyone welcomed any distraction from war news.

Buffeted by a very strong wind, Emma shopped in Maryville on Saturday. She bought hose, shorts, and school supplies. Janie Roberts had an appointment with the doctor, and Emma hoped everything went well.

By Monday, Emma received five more photos of Peter at Mt. Rushmore. He looked so handsome, and she could see his new sergeant stripes on his uniform. *I just want to hug him and completely wrinkle his uniform.*

Emma took a photograph of her Lone Valley school building on Tuesday, April 6, and a local election was held for school board directors and county superintendent. Mr. Watson and Mr. Pool became directors. Mr. Burr won reelection as superintendent, beating out two contenders. Ten voters cast ballots.

April 7 marked one month until Emma would move back to Maryville. She would miss her students, but her college work meant an eventual degree, which she truly desired. She also sent a roll of film to be developed so she could send Peter more photos.

Emma bought a pair of white oxfords, using some of her ration stamps on Saturday. She deposited her warrant and paid the Roberts in cash for her board. Each month, her pride grew as she watched her bank balance slowly increase. She didn't need a lot of possessions, so most of what she considered her spending money went to see movies for ten or fifteen cents or an occasional meal out.

Peter mailed Emma a pillowcase from Rapid City. She loved his thoughtfulness. *I'll add it to my hope chest collection. We're going to need those things soon to set up a home. I just know this war can't last too much longer.*

Emma had been having trouble with her sore throat, which seemed to linger too long. Finally, she saw the doctor, who painted her throat and gave her some gargle. Then she went to a Saturday matinee of *Yankee Doodle Dandy*. James Cagney portrayed George M. Cohan, known as "The Man Who Owned Broadway." The film covered his life from a youngster in vaudeville to the leading star of Broadway musicals, especially those with a patriotic theme. Emma left feeling even more pride in America than she had already possessed.

Two board members came to the school on April 15.

"Emma, you're a good teacher," they began. "We appreciate your success at getting the students good marks. Plus we know how hard you work on the war drive and rationing programs. No one could have done better. And the parents have told us how glad they are you're teaching here!"

Emma smiled. "Thank you. I've tried to do my best. I know I'm new at teaching, but I do love my students."

"We're offering you a raise to $80 a month. We hope to have a little more to offer in salary after the state aid meeting is held," they continued.

Emma hesitated, "I appreciate your trust in me, but I want time to think about the offer." She knew other one-room schoolhouse teachers earned higher wages. She had heard some rumors the school board at Prairie View might offer her their teaching spot.

Later, she talked to Mae. "Today, April 17, is one year from my date with Peter when we went to a play in Pickering, then talked for a long time afterward."

It was also seven years since Emma's father had died, and she missed him daily.

A third sad event occurred when a sister of her father died the same day. Emma, all her brothers and their families, Edith, and Grandma Bailey attended the funeral. Owen, Mike, and Bob joined three friends as pallbearers. Emma contributed fifty cents toward the family flower arrangement for her aunt's funeral. The cycle of life and death continued on the home front, as did the daily reports about war fatalities.

Emma's Easter card to Peter now routed through the Postmaster, N.Y. No 3917 APO Serial 37199201, 336th Bomb. Squad, 95th Bomb. Group. She had never been completely clear what all the designations meant, but only cared that her mail successfully reached Peter. In her address book, she penciled in his latest mailing address. Peter left Rapid City on April 21, 1943, and Janie Paxton thought he might be headed overseas. They would have to wait for details in Peter's future letters.

On Friday, April 23, Emma and her students held an Easter egg hunt. She gave each pupil a candy rabbit and eggs, plus a card. Two students presented her with a little basket of goodies. They were good children, even if a little mischievous at times. She would miss them when the school year ended.

That evening, the Roberts took her to Clearmont to see a play. Emma rode back to Maryville on the bus, costing her forty cents. She spent the night with her mother for the first time since Christmas.

Emma shopped Saturday for summer clothes. She also visited the school administration office to obtain a list of schools with teaching vacancies. *I want to know my options before deciding whether or not to teach at Lone Valley another year.*

Later she rode the bus to her former high school stop, where Jacob picked her up in the wagon. She stayed all night at Jacob's house, joining Edith who had taken the bus down during the day.

Jacob took Emma back by wagon to the bus stop on Sunday morning. The mile and a half trip reminded Emma of all the cold, windy, rainy, muddy, snowy, sleety days she had walked the route to go to high school.

"My long walks seem worth the effort. I got to graduate from high school and now attend college. I just wish Dad could have been here to see me get my diploma," she remarked to Jacob.

She went alone to see *The Amazing Mrs. Holliday,* a comedy-drama movie starring Deanna Durbin, Edmond O'Brien, and Barry Fitzgerald. A young idealistic missionary smuggled a group of Chinese war orphans into America by posing as the wife of a wealthy commodore who went missing after his ship was sunk. Life got complicated after she placed the children in the commodore's family mansion, and then she fell in love with the commodore's grandson. Emma loved the music and plot twists as a great afternoon's distraction.

Peter's next letter arrived postmarked New Brunswick, New Jersey. His assignment would be overseas, but he could not say where for security reasons. The B-17 bomber group was leaving for true war action somewhere in Europe.

On April 28, Emma said aloud to herself, "It's been one year since Peter came home on furlough from Ft. Leavenworth. Now he's been back and forth across the country and is heading who knows where! Oh, why did this stupid war ever start?"

School lasted only a half day on April 30. Her one eighth-grade student had afternoon finals. Emma was proud of the girl who was to graduate.

That evening, Emma went with Owen, Melinda, and two friends to a square dance at the Maryville Armory. They danced until their feet ached, but the feeling of being alive and young and carefree was worth it. They finally took Emma to Edith's house, where she spent the night alone since Edith had stayed at Jacob's. Emma luxuriated in sleeping until nine Saturday morning, May 1.

Owen, Melinda, three friends, and Emma attended the midnight show *Star Spangled Rhythm*. Paramount Pictures made the all-star cast musical as a morale booster with songs by Harold Arlen and Johnny Mercer. "I hope Peter gets a chance to see the show, to know people at home are backing the troops' efforts," Emma remarked.

The school year was winding down. Emma's pupils practiced their upcoming spring program, with Mike absent with measles. One mother brought wieners, chips, and plates for the Tuesday afternoon school picnic in the Roberts' pasture. All had a wonderful time playing games, cooking food, eating, and talking about what they would do on summer vacation.

Emma looked on with pride and sadness. "I still don't know if I'll be back to teach them in the fall. I just feel like I can get more money at another school. I know money isn't why I teach, but it does help pay for college," she said to Ruth.

On Wednesday, Emma gave the fourth quarter tests, and the students practiced their spring program. Only a few school days remained.

Emma and her friends, the Smiths, went to Pickering to see the eighth-grade graduation exercises. Emma's student received her diplomas, with her proud parents watching. She had now had three students graduate in her two years of teaching.

Afterward, the rain pummeled down so hard Emma and the Smiths decided not to try driving home. "No way we're gonna make it home tonight. I'll pull into the Bishops' place up ahead and see if they'll put us up."

Ann and Paul were happy to keep the group safe. Such sleepovers were common when the weather turned roads into quagmires in northwestern Missouri. The war was killing enough people without their friends having car wrecks trying to drive in lousy visibility or on icy roads.

Rising early, Emma and the Smiths got to their house. Emma walked on to the Roberts' to change clothes before walking to school. Three students were absent the first half of the day but arrived for the afternoon. The class presented their original program, "The America Drill," late in the afternoon to seventeen parents and siblings. The parents brought potluck dishes, so everyone stayed for dinner.

May 7 was the last full day of school, and the students helped pack the schoolroom. Emma gave out the final grades before saying goodbye.

Emma cleaned the schoolhouse and packed away books and supplies for use in the fall. Slowly, she surveyed the room to memorize all its features. She had just completed her second full year of teaching, even without a teaching certificate since she did not have her college degree. Her pride in her teaching abilities had grown, proven by her students' grades and eagerness to learn. They had been through hard lessons, fun at recess and on field trips, various illnesses, critters around the school, and all kinds of weather. As she packed her personal items and books, Emma took a long last look at one more chapter of her life closing. *My world keeps shifting, whether I am ready for it to or not.*

The sprinkles ceased by the time Emma walked the three quarters of a mile back home. There she finished packing her clothing and toiletries. Melinda had promised to pick her up around seven Saturday morning and take her to Edith's to unload.

That evening, the Roberts presented Emma with a sugar and creamer set, Fiestaware salt and pepper shakers, a tea towel, and a nice card. Everyone wiped misty eyes at the thought of Emma's leaving, for the three of them had grown very close over the last two school years. If Tom had not risked his life to save Emma in that blizzard, she knew she would not be alive. And Emma had saved the Roberts' house from burning down by putting out the chimney fire. Those events and a million kindnesses meant the world to Emma. She had truly enjoyed a second home while boarding with them.

"I'm so sorry to be leaving, even for the summer," she said as she hugged Ruth and Tom. "I just can't make up my mind if I'm teaching here next fall."

"Well, as soon as you know," sniffed Ruth, dabbing her eyes with her hankie, "you just let us know. Your room'll be waiting. We'll see you in town often as we can."

On Saturday morning, Emma had Melinda drive her to the Watsons' house to leave her official school papers and the schoolhouse keys. The Watsons also pressed her to come back in the fall.

Emma left her few possessions with Edith, who was thrilled to have her back for the summer. Edith took one suitcase and rode with Emma and Melinda to the farmstead for the weekend.

For Mother's Day, all five adult children wished their mom well. Edith received a pin, picture, three cards, a dishpan, eggs, sausage, and cream. "Thank all of you for my gifts," she exclaimed. "You've become such wonderful grownups. Your dad and me had our doubts when you were little and ornery!" Even missing her husband every day, Edith knew she was loved.

Emma marked the day also as the one-year anniversary since Peter had entered Army basic training. She wished he were present to enjoy Mother's Day with her. With dreams of the children they would have, she wondered what her own future Mother's Days might be like. Many of her friends already had a child or two, leading fulfilled lives as wives and mothers. *When will my chance come?* she kept wondering.

Chapter 30

On Monday, May 10, 1943, Emma finally underwent a tonsillectomy at the Maryville hospital. Her throat had bothered her for months, and Dr. Jackson insisted her tonsils be removed.

Melinda took Emma to the hospital at nine in the morning. Dr. Jackson put her under at nine thirty, and she awakened about noon. Emma looked around, then quickly closed her eyes and slept until three. Mike and Kate visited late in the afternoon, and Melinda and Edith brought Emma ice cream for supper. Edith mailed the letter that Emma wrote to Peter telling him about the operation and that she would be fine. Emma knew the local grapevine would spread the news to the Paxtons and other friends, who might write Peter and worry him needlessly.

Dr. Jackson assessed Emma's throat Tuesday morning. "You can go home, young lady, but you're gonna feel real weak and need to rest for several days." Then he discharged her.

Bob and Linda, Jacob and Helen, plus others stopped by Wednesday. Even Mr. Gray from the Independence School District came by to see if he could persuade Emma to teach in one of their schools for fall. Emma used her throat to talk too much, making it hurt by evening.

On May 13, the radio announced great news. The Allies had finally forced the Germans to surrender in Tunisia and exit Libya. Nearly 240,000 Axis prisoners had been captured. The Allies now controlled Africa and could launch attacks into southern Europe. Finally, the Allies had won a major victory in the North African Campaign.

On Friday, Mr. Blake arrived to offer Emma the teaching position at Singery School. They would pay $90 per month, minus board. Emma seriously considered the offer.

Emma continued to recover through Saturday. She wrote letters to Peter, received well-wishers, and had a follow-up doctor's appointment. Emma paid $25.00 toward her medical bills.

Teachers never had health insurance in Emma's area. Roosevelt had decided not to include a large-scale health insurance program as part of the new 1935 Social Security program. When fringe benefits like health insurance were declared not to be considered wages that the government restricted during World War II, many employers offered such benefits to attract and keep workers. Small school districts could not compete. Emma knew she would have to pay her own medical bills over time as she could afford to do so.

On Sunday, Bob and Linda brought dinner. Afterward, Emma felt well enough to see the matinee of *Random Harvest.* Ronald Colman starred as a shell-shocked, amnesiac World War I soldier. Greer Garson portrayed his love interest.

How many young men will receive head wounds or other injuries from which they may never recover? She sent up a silent prayer for Peter's safety, as well as for all military personnel. She knew her prayer could not be answered for everyone, but she felt better for having tried to push the universe to protect those who served.

Emma's Great-aunt Nancy died on Monday at age eighty-seven. Edith mourned one of her favorite aunts in another life and death cycle on the home front. People were born; people died. But they were supposed to die of old age, at home, near relatives, and not in some distant place overseas in a war. *That is not a natural death. That is not how someone's life should end,* thought Emma.

By Tuesday evening, May 18, Mr. Kiser and Mike Trotter dropped by the house. They presented Emma with an offer of $105 per month to start teaching at Harmon School for the 1943–1944 school year.

Emma, shocked at the increasing salaries she was being offered, happily accepted the position. "How wonderful!" she exclaimed.

"You'll be able to board with me and Kate," replied Mike. "Our house is a short walk across the road to the east of the school. The school board still wants you to pay board, but you'll be with family."

"And I can spoil Tommy in the process," she said. She shook hands on the deal, grinning at her good fortune.

The next day, Edith and Emma walked wet streets to the train station heading to Bolckow. Edith, Grandma Bailey, and Emma got a ride to see Edith's brother Michael and his wife Janice where they would stay until after the funeral. Emma offset their sad feelings by buying some ice cream and sodas for everyone. Great-aunt Nancy's funeral on Wednesday received a sunny day. Losing one of the senior generation was always emotionally difficult since that source of wisdom and family history was gone forever. So few of the eldest relatives were left to enjoy.

Catching a ride with a relative to Midway, Emma then took the bus to Maryville. She telephoned Mae that evening. "My college registration is next week, and I want to keep earning money, if I can, while I attend summer classes. The money really goes fast after I pay for tuition, books, and other class expenses."

"Lordy, don't it go out the window as fast as we earn it," replied Mae. "I just get my paycheck from the restaurant and, zoom, it's gone again. My sisters and brothers are always needing somethin' for school and growin' fast as weeds. I can't make clothes fast enough for 'em before they've outgrown 'em."

Saturday arrived warm and mostly sunny. Emma washed clothes, ironed, washed five windows, and hung up the summer screens on Edith's house. That afternoon, she had fun shopping uptown.

"I'm going to do it. I need to update my wardrobe for summer activities. And I saw a navy-blue dress for $4.95 and a suit for $8.95 on sale. I'll just tighten up on other expenses so I can enjoy these new duds," she told Melinda on the phone.

On May 25, Emma walked to the college to receive her sixty-hour certificate to continue teaching. She filled out paperwork, paid her tuition, and turned in everything they required. Her excitement at going back to school made her feel younger, like one of her students.

Grandma Bailey came for a visit, so Emma went home to meet er. Together they walked uptown, where Emma registered for thirty pounds of canning sugar with her ration coupons. She also bought a white blouse, navy-blue slacks, hose, anklets, and nail polish. While frugal with her funds, Emma had decided to spend a little more on a summer wardrobe for college. *After all, I'm getting a big pay raise come fall,* she happily reminded herself.

The best part of the day was getting a V-mail letter from Peter. He had arrived in England but could not say where due to security concerns. He was safe and settling in for the duration of the war, or until his unit got transferred somewhere else.

Emma joined her classmates at eight thirty, May 26, for the first summer assembly. Afterward, she met briefly with her instructors to get book lists and course details. At four, she attended a practice teachers' meeting, for part of her coursework was to teach art and some reading to students at Horace

Mann Elementary School. She and her friend Debbie studied at the library that evening, beginning the summer's reading requirements. Before heading home, they enjoyed an ice cream cone and watched people dancing to radio music.

On her second day, Emma observed second grade students at work. She heard an abbreviated version of *War and Peace* by Tolstoy at four. Again, her evening was spent studying until eleven.

Melinda arrived to take Edith and Grandma Bailey home to her house for the evening. Emma had the freedom of the house to herself. *It's a rare thing for me to have a house to myself. How quiet it is! Now I can really get some work done!*

Friday morning, May 28, Edith arrived back in Maryville for her birthday. Emma gave her a $5.00 check, payable on October 5 when she would have her first fall paycheck, and a card. Grandma Bailey gave Edith a pair of hose.

Emma got a permanent at Powers Beauty Salon to curl her naturally very straight hair. "I know curls are the rage of the hair style world," Emma moaned to the stylist, "but my hair refuses to curl one twist without a permanent!" She loved the way the curls bounced against the sides and back of her head as she walked.

She celebrated with a matinee. *A Yank in the R.A.F.* showed an American pilot who joined the Royal Air Force (R.A.F.) while the United States was still neutral. Tyrone Power and Betty Grable starred. Emma had read how some American men had gone to Canada or England as early as 1939 to join the fight against Hitler.

On Sunday, she and her friend Debbie attended another matinee, *Reveille with Beverly.* Ann Mill and Franklin Pangborn starred in the movie based on the radio show "Reveille with Beverly." The movie featured many notable cameo appearances, such as Duke Ellington, Count Basie, Frank Sinatra, The Mills Brothers, and Bob Crosby. Emma loved the music and lyrics, feeling her patriotism rise, as the film producers intended. Many studios focused on semi-propaganda or increasing patriotism in their audiences during the war.

Emma taught her first art class on Tuesday, June 1. The class went well, for Emma loved artworks by famous painters and kept cutouts from magazines of important paintings and sculptures. She sold her enthusiasm to the second graders, again teaching art the next day and working on a poster. Late afternoon meant another teachers' meeting for further training.

Superintendent Dale of St. Jo spoke at assembly on Thursday. Later, after classes, Emma attended a book review led by Miss Bowman. *Beneath Another Sun,* a story about the despotic cruelty of the Nazis, showed the iron will of people who wanted to be free. People forcibly moved from their native countries to work for the Nazi war machine became a part of the European underground resistance. *I can't imagine having such terrible things happen in America. How did this madness ever get started, let alone expand so far?* she wondered.

Thunder and lightning with heavy rain began at four Friday morning. Emma studied then bought a brown suit at J. C. Penney for $2.98. In late afternoon, Emma boarded the bus to the Barnard Junction, where her friend Pearl met her. They danced to a country band for two hours in Barnard. Deciding to be wild and free, they headed for Del Rio, Missouri, to another dance.

"I don't believe this!" exclaimed Pearl. "We've just had the second flat tire since we left Barnard! Maybe somebody is trying to persuade us to forget this evening's fun."

"Let's see if the next car coming by will give us a lift," reasoned Emma. "We can get this flat off, take it to Midway, then try to get someone to bring us back to the car. We changed the first flat and put on the only spare. We certainly can't drive clear to the station on three round and one flat tire."

Since rubber rationing began, people had patched tire inner tubes until they were more patches than original rubber. Everyone who owned a car understood the frustration of a flat, which always occurred at the worst possible time. So it was easy for two young women to get a nice young man to drive them and the second flat to Midway. The mechanic knew Emma's and Pearl's families and was happy later to take them back to the car.

Emma caught the last bus to Maryville, arrived home at four thirty in the morning, and ran through pouring rain from the station. By the time she got home, she was drenched, exhausted, and laughing at the absurdity of the night's adventures.

She continued to write Peter nearly every day. The sporadic mail delivery meant she never knew when his letters would reach her, or her letters reach him. On June 7, Emma received seven letters at once. Sometimes they would arrive out of order, according to the dates they were written, but she cherished each one.

On June 10, Emma and Debbie went to *The Pride of the Yankees.* Gary Cooper portrayed Lou Gehrig in the tribute to the legendary New York Yankees' first baseman. At age thirty-seven, one year before the movie's release,

Gehrig had died from amyotrophic lateral sclerosis, which became known as "Lou Gehrig's disease." His death touched the entire nation, both for his baseball skills and for the courage with which he handled his disease. Emma, impressed by Cooper's great acting, could feel his pain and loss.

Emma used seventeen war shoe ration stamps to buy brown oxfords on June 14. It was her second pair of shoes for the year, so she could only buy one more pair in 1943.

Janie Paxton called June 15 to invite Emma to attend the Workman Chapel homecoming. Built in 1901, the one-room chapel sat off a gravel road near Burlington Junction, surrounded by cornfields and shadowed by large trees. Many area farm families had worshiped and married in the church and been buried by the small white building. The reunion provided a good excuse to enjoy home-cooked food, visit with people she hadn't seen for a long time, and spend a day outside in the fresh air.

Their friend Mike Noland was home on a week's furlough. Emma's friend Gladys and her parents drove to Kansas City to meet him. *I'm truly happy for Gladys, but I'm a little envious and miss Peter even more.*

People in Barnard declared a dance in Noland's honor on Thursday evening. Edith, Mae, and Emma joined Emma's brothers and their wives. They arrived back in Maryville in the early morning hours, happy but knowing Emma would get little sleep before Friday's classes.

Emma had to work four hours at Horace Mann Elementary School, plus take a Physical Science test that day. Sleepy though she was, Emma tried her best.

As the summer heat rose, Emma worked on her English lessons, taught reading, and gave a speech. She had to solve her own homework assignments, since no relative had ever completed high school, let alone gone to college. Occasionally, Emma asked advice from her city friends; some were happy to help, while others treated her like a country hick. *I don't care!* she told herself. *I'm going to get my degree.*

Emma knew how smart her brothers were and felt sorry their father had not allowed them to receive more schooling for they would have done well. As it was, they read modern farming magazines and attended local programs on the latest techniques. They certainly contributed to the war efforts through their long farming hours to increase production.

After taking a two-hour test in English, Emma talked Edith into going to a double feature on Friday, June 25. Emma again watched *They Died with Their*

Boots On, which Edith had not seen. Next came *Henry Aldrich Gets Glamour,* whereby Henry became the most sought-after man in town when he won a date with a movie star. The seriousness of the first movie got released in the laughter of the second. Both helped Emma relax after a long week of teaching and tests.

By July 3, Emma had painted three screen doors and the porch roof at Edith's house. She also cleaned the roof and gutters. Emma felt the main responsibility to maintain her mother's house, since her brothers had their farms and families to support. *If I do chores around the house, it's a way to pay back Mom for my board during summer school.*

After church on July 4, Bob and Linda visited. Everyone enjoyed buying ice cream to eat at Edith's house and going to *The Human Comedy* by William Saroyan. Mickey Rooney played Homer Macauley, a high school student working part-time as a wartime telegram delivery boy in California. Sentimental scenarios depicted the effects on the home front.

Emma could relate to the changes the war had brought to her life and the lives of people in and around the small town of Maryville, Missouri. No American city escaped the war's alterations. *I was with Peter one year ago on July fourth.* Emma felt sad at the uncontrollable changes in her world.

The number of men enlisting or being drafted had had serious repercussions for Northwest Missouri State Teachers College. Enrollment had dropped drastically, and the college faced extreme financial difficulties. From 712 students in 1940, the college had only 375 in 1943. Talk abounded the college might be forced to close, so administrators eagerly sought a solution.

The answer came through the Navy V-5 and V-12 programs. The V-5 program led young men to a commission in the Navy aviation branch. The V-12 program meant a commission as a regular line officer. The college worked out an agreement with the Navy to enroll 400 sailors. During World War II, Northwest Missouri State Teachers College became one of 131 colleges and universities nationally taking part in the V-12 Navy College Training Program.

Emma and her friends quickly became aware of another side effect of the Navy program. Many young, attractive, eligible young men now populated the campus. The ratio of men to women was now two to one. In short, unless women wanted to be alone, they were never without a date for dinner or a dance. College life for the women on campus had taken a turn for the more romantic aspects of life.

While Emma had little time for socializing, she did attend college dances when she felt caught up on her studies. While Barnard and smaller town dances usually had country bands, the college dances featured the music of popular swing bands. Tunes by Glenn Miller, Tommy Dorsey, Harry James, and other big band leaders blared out open windows on hot summer nights. Emma loved to dance and always could find a girlfriend to go with her.

Emma's friend Gladys accepted a teaching job at Lone Elm school for $95 per month. Emma helped Gladys see what needed to be done for cleaning and the seating layout.

Glady gushed with excitement. "Now we've both got guaranteed work this fall. While Mike's away some place I can't even find out about, I'll keep busy, at least during the day. Nights are still the hardest. I miss him so much!"

"I know what you mean," consoled Emma. "I love teaching my kids, but I want to marry Peter. I want to teach and have a home of my own. At least for a while, I want to do both."

Chapter 31

The radio crackled with good news. The invasion of Sicily began on July 9, 1943. Allies forces launched the attack from Tunisia, the closest land to Sicily. German ship passage to Egypt or the Balkans now became much more hazardous by passing through heavily reinforced Allied positions on Tunisia and Sicily. Controlling Sicily would allow expansion up the Italian peninsula into Europe. At last, the Allies had gained serious ground.

On July 21, Emma's brother Bob turned thirty-nine years old. He had been born in Oklahoma during the six years her parents farmed there. Now he had a farm and a wife and son. As the elder male in the family, he, too, felt responsible for Edith's and Emma's well-being. His advice provided good information when the two women needed it. Sometimes, though, he acted more like Emma's father, wanting to issue directives rather than advice.

More radio news broke on July 25. Mussolini had been overthrown and imprisoned. The Fascist Grand Council had taken over. Italy was still an Axis ally, but the hated Mussolini was gone from power.

All summer, Emma studied hard, typed papers, helped with housework, visited with friends, and set friends' hair. Letters to and from Peter kept the mailman busy. Emma attended and sometimes gave reports at teachers' meetings. She broke up the busy routine with movie escapes, including *What's Buzzin', Cousin?* The musical comedy starred Ann Miller and Eddie "Rochester" Anderson (who played Rochester on the Jack Benny radio show) as a chorus girl and a band leader who tried to fix up an inherited hotel and convert it into a vacation hotel with a nightclub.

On Tuesday, July 27, the sultry day drove Emma to study in the city park. Later she bought a reversible raincoat for $10.95 and picked up groceries on her way home.

President Roosevelt spoke that evening and announced coffee had been dropped from the ration list. Emma could practically hear the cheers up and down the street. She giggled and said to Edith, "Owen will be thrilled he can have his morning coffee without having to ration his cup size. He'll probably buy the biggest cup he can find, fill it to the brim, and have a second cup each day for a month!"

Finally, on July 30, Emma moved her possessions out of her college locker. She took three exams that day to finish her summer course work and bought a Webster Collegiate Dictionary for $3.50. She and her college friend Gracie had a final dinner together at the bookstore before Gracie moved away. Emma would sincerely miss her friend, who had received an offer to teach in Kansas City for more money.

Also late July 1943, Mike looked up in surprise to see little Tommy racing across the field as fast as his chubby legs would carry him. "We got lights! We got lights!" he yelled as he ran. Mike swung him up, hopped on his tractor, and drove back to his house. Yes, the electric company had finally installed electricity in their area. They had dug post holes, inserted tall poles, and strung wires all the way from Midway to his farmhouse. At last, they had one bare lightbulb hanging in the middle of each room and one electric outlet to plug in appliances.

"Now maybe we can get an electric icebox," said Kate, looking hopeful.

Mike could see one more bill arriving each month for electricity, plus a radio, more than one fan for summer heat, and other gadgets. "I'm not sure electricity is such a good thing," he joked.

Emma had received fifty overseas letters from Peter. She had written him at least as many. Missing her deeply, he would reread her letters many times. Then, because everything had to be packed into one duffle bag, he would tear up the letters or throw them into the stove to keep others from reading them.

Janie Paxton broke her wrist on August 1. Dr. Jackson had applied a cast.

"Oh, dear," moaned Janie.

"Are you hurting?" worried Emma.

"No, darlin'. It's just I can't write to Peter for a while," she sighed. "I try and write him ne'r ever' day, and now I can't! And Gene's no good a hand at writin' letters."

Emma thought a moment. "I write Peter nearly every day. Why don't we talk on the phone every day or so, and I'll add what you want him to know in my letters. That way he'll keep up with your news while your hand heals."

"Would you?" Janie gushed. "That would be wonderful. Can you write him tonight and tell him not to worry, that I'll be okay in a few weeks? And tell him it don' hurt too much, and I love him, and I want him home soon."

As the summer dragged on, friends married, had babies, or died. Emma thought about the usual order of life with parents seeing their children grow to adulthood, marry, start families, and continue their lives for many years to come.

It didn't seem natural for parents to bury their children, but the war had changed that dynamic. Too many parents had already lost their young men, buried overseas in locations the parents had never heard of and where they would never get to see their children's graves. They had to grieve without a chance to see their children's coffins lowered into the ground, to place flowers on their gravesites, or to visit on their children's birthdays. They had lost their children without one last look at their faces, to hold their hands and tell them they loved them. Many parents knew their children had no graves, for they had seen enough newsreels to know bodies blown apart by land mines and artillery shells did not have enough pieces left to identify, let alone bury, as a whole person. That was the worst loss of all, to know no grave comforted their loved ones.

While Emma envied her female friends who had gotten married and maybe had a child by now, she knew their stress grew each day the war extended. Even if their husbands had been exempted as farmers, who knew if the government might rescind those exemptions and draft their men? Also, some who had received exemptions, like Peter, felt obligated to join the military to do their part to win the war. Other women, as Emma had done, pleaded with their loved ones to stay home, but the urge to serve was too great. At those times, women could not understand male pride when it meant they would leave their wives and young children home alone. If the men gave their lives for their country, how would their families survive without their support?

The war had changed many facts of life. Sometimes Emma believed only chaos reigned now, with no structure to the future and no way to plan one's life and expect most of those plans would come true.

Emma viewed her daily life of school, home, and community as almost artificial. She felt safe and knew what she had planned for the fall. Yet thousands overseas and at home had no idea where they would be in a week, let alone a month, or even if they would be alive. The newspapers and radio reports daily blared the number of dead and wounded, as well as could be counted. How could they possibly know how many civilians had been killed, with so many people displaced from their homes? The military dead and wounded were easier to count, since the men in each unit could relay to headquarters the names of those who had been lost each day or week. Civilians had no one to account for their lives, for relatives were scattered across the countryside and national borders. Many hometowns had been bombed into rubble piles, with no houses to find if the war ever ended.

Emma carried on as best as she could. She spent weekends with the Paxtons to churn butter and comb Mrs. Paxton's hair during the weeks Janie wore her cast. Emma cooked and washed dishes, leaving enough food prepared for several days. Neighbors also visited to bring food and help with laundry and housekeeping. Such was expected of small-town friends and neighbors, for everyone knew sooner or later they, too, would need help.

Monday morning, August 9, produced a rain shower. Emma bought pajama material and got Peter a tie clip, cigarettes, and a birthday card. She still had to mail special occasion presents early, since she never knew how quickly the military mail service would get her packages to Peter.

Emma picked up the Harmon schoolhouse key on Thursday. Tommy tagged along. He wanted to be old enough to go to school with his favorite aunt as his teacher, but he had a few years to wait yet. While Emma would miss teaching at Lone Valley and staying with the Roberts, she loved the idea of making $35 more a month.

More radio news broke on August 17, 1943. The Battle of Sicily had ended as American troops entered Messina. Sicily was controlled by the Allies, who could now invade the Italian peninsula.

Let the war end by Christmas and Peter can come home! prayed Emma.

Chapter 32

Emma's sister-in-law Linda had not felt well for several months. Local doctors were stymied and recommended Linda go to the Mayo Clinic in Rochester, Minnesota. The news nearly devastated Bob and Linda, for everyone knew only the most serious illnesses were referred to the Mayo Clinic.

Bob worried, "I've got to stay on the farm because crops are ready to harvest and livestock gotta be fed. Can you go with Linda?" Emma agreed to go but had to borrow $50 from Edith to pay for the trip, with Bob adding $5 more.

Linda and Emma rode the bus all night, arriving in Rochester at eight fifteen Wednesday morning, August 18. Going straight to the Mayo Clinic, they registered before getting a late breakfast. Then they found for an apartment at 120 5th Street Southwest. Emma walked to a nearby post office for postcards and sent notes to relatives. Picking up supper, Linda and Emma ate at the apartment, later walking uptown to buy a few groceries.

The next day, they arrived early at the clinic, but the first assessment appointment was Monday morning at seven thirty. Disappointed, they treated themselves to a movie, *The Navy Comes Through,* starring Pat O'Brien, George Murphy, and Jane Wyatt. Based on a short story, it was the first movie where RKO Pictures used its new radio signal trademark spelling out "victory" in Morse code.

They tried to keep busy each day to distract themselves from a potential surgery. Linda wasn't in a party mood for her birthday on Friday, but they did call friends in Guilford to cheer her up. They walked to Soldiers Field Park two blocks south of their apartment and attended an old-time Saturday dance at the Armory. Sunday was spent in church, praying for good medical results, and walking eight blocks northeast to Mayo Park for a band concert and sermon.

Emma did what she could to raise Linda's spirits. The longer it took to get the testing done and analyzed, the more the strain affected them both.

By Monday, Linda was sick to her stomach, arriving at the clinic without breakfast. Doctors began to assess her health issue. Later, Linda and Emma bought some small souvenirs and ate at the Vague Sweet shop. The next day, Linda had more early clinic tests.

On Tuesday, Emma accidentally locked herself out of the apartment. She finally found a painter in the building who unlocked the door. "I feel so foolish," she admitted, "but my mind has been on so many other problems!" She relaxed by going to Silver Lake and an evening concert at Mayo Park before Rochester had a practice blackout that night.

The medical opinion was Linda's gall bladder was causing her severe symptoms and had to come out. Linda then registered and filled out paperwork at St. Mary's Hospital in the Mayo complex. The women had already been in Rochester a week and now faced more time for the surgery and recovery. Putting her teaching duties on hold to care for her sister-in-law's needs, Emma thought, *I feel guilty for not being with my pupils in my new school.*

Arriving at the clinic at four Friday afternoon, Linda checked into her room at Kahler Hospital, also part of the Mayo complex. The surgery would be the next day. Emma walked home alone. *But I know Linda feels even more isolated without Bob for moral support.*

Emma walked to the hospital at eight Saturday morning. Linda was already on the eleventh floor for her operation and two-hour recovery period. Emma, overcome with emotion, nearly fainted in Linda's room. She managed to eat breakfast at Ted's Store during the operation. She realized she had missed her teachers' meeting in Maryville. I wish I could go home to my school and that Linda had never been ill in the first place.

By Sunday, Linda became terribly sick. Emma sent a telegram to Bob to come to Rochester quickly. The hospital staff placed Linda in an oxygen tent at seven that night with special nurses to cover her care. Emma stayed by Linda's side.

Emma met the train at seven fifteen Monday morning, thinking Bob might be on it, but he finally arrived about eight. At the hospital, they both stayed until nine thirty at night. Bob paid the two nurses $11 and $6 for the special care Linda required. Finally, Emma was able to send a telegram to her mother explaining Linda had begun to recover. By the next day, "My hand's cramping from all the postcards I've written to friends and relatives about Linda's situation," she admitted to Bob.

Bob slept all morning at the apartment. On Wednesday, September 1, Emma cleaned up the room and packed her suitcase. She made breakfast for Bob, then he took her to the train depot. Bob had decided to stay in Rochester, so Emma was free to return to Barnard and begin her school year. Her afternoon train left at five thirty, with her relieved to be heading south.

Eating a dinner and reading a newspaper she bought before boarding, she enjoyed talking with a WAAC who rode the train from Des Moines, Iowa, to Conception Junction, Missouri. There, Emma caught the late Wabash train to Maryville.

Reaching Edith's house at five thirty in the morning, Emma thrilled to find six letters from Peter. She read them all before going to bed, even though her tired body just wanted sleep. Peter had sent her a lovely bracelet, which she wore to bed. She managed to doze until eleven.

Emma finally made it to school on Friday, September 3. The hot sun lessened when sliding behind clouds, then peaked out again to brighten her day. Emma had nine students from four families at Harmon District 176 school. She realized she had started her own elementary school career fifteen years ago that day. Her students included Mae's brother Gary and sister Lucy Beckett; Debbie, Earl, and Ben Morton; Tyler and Doyle Falcon; and Mary and Linda Cooper. Such a large class would keep Emma busy, so she was pleased she had only a short walk. *I'll be on my feet a lot more this year. That many kids will have lots of questions, so I'll be walking back and forth to their desks more often.*

To make up some days Emma had missed, school was held on Saturday. Emma began to learn her students' moods and attitudes, giving them homework to make up for lost time.

That evening, Mae, Emma, and four friends went to Savannah to see *My Heart Belongs to Daddy,* a comedy film about a man who was found murdered. Witnesses were convinced about the woman they saw leaving his apartment, but later the script revealed the woman had a twin. Emma needed the funny relief after the strain of nearly two weeks in Rochester.

Putting chains on his car, Mike drove to Maryville to pick up Emma on Sunday. The wind and rainstorm around six in the evening left the roads to Mike's house a muddy mess, but he got Emma home so she could teach the next day.

By Tuesday evening, she took a break to attend a Barnard dance. "Oh, I shouldn't have stayed so late, but I was having so much fun," moaned Emma as she glanced at her clock and crawled into bed. "It can't be two in the morning! How am I ever going to make it through the day?" When her alarm sounded, however, she pried open her eyes and headed out the door.

Her new students worked hard. Six of the nine had perfect spelling scores on the next test. Emma worked late that afternoon, and Mae appeared to help her sweep the dried mud out of the building.

"If I'm not killing flies in the classroom, I'm sweeping out mud every time it rains. The kids try, but don't use the boot scraper very well," Emma complained.

"Yep, the young'uns never seem to remember," laughed Mae, who always seemed in a good mood. "At home, I'm always a gittin' after 'em to wipe their muddy boots."

Together, they drove to Savannah to see *Hello, Frisco, Hello,* a musical film starring Alice Faye and John Payne. Made in a new process called Technicolor, the movie was one of Faye's last musicals at 20th Century-Fox and became one of Faye's highest-grossing pictures for Fox. The script covered the life of vaudeville performers in San Francisco during the 1915 Panama Pacific Exposition when Alexander Graham Bell made the first transcontinental phone call from New York City to San Francisco. Emma marveled at the color quality, wishing someday she could see San Francisco, the city by the bay.

Also September 8, 1943, the Italian Badoglio government gave up unconditionally to the Allies. Although Germany and Italy had been allies, Italy switched sides after it surrendered. Immediately, the Germans seized control of Rome and northern Italy. They established a puppet Fascist regime under Mussolini, who was freed from imprisonment by German commandos on September 12.

On September 9, Allied troops landed on the beaches of Salerno near Naples. The drive up the Italian boot could begin in earnest to rout the remaining German troops. Hard fighting would be required to take southern Italy, but the Allies were advancing again.

Emma's days blended together. Some went smoothly, and some made her wonder why she had chosen teaching as a profession. She made arithmetic charts and geography tests, washed shelves, brought in coal and corn cobs for the stove, graded papers, and finished other school responsibilities. Anything to keep her mind off missing Peter, at least for a few hours a day.

September 15 was Peter's birthday. She had sent a package two weeks earlier to ensure a timely arrival. In her daily messages, she described her life, her students and their antics, and how much she missed him. He had been overseas five months. When would the war end?

Linda finally returned home the next day. She looked better than when

Emma had last seen her, but she still needed recuperation time. Emma spent Friday night at Bob's house to help Linda with the cooking, dishes, and washing. She even cleaned the house despite having a sore throat. On Sunday evening, Bob brought her back to Mike's so she could teach the next day.

The following Saturday, she got a ride to Maryville for photos of herself at Carpenter's studio to send a new picture to Peter. She also bought six packages of paper towels for her school from her supplies allotment.

After she built the first stove fire on Monday, the heat felt good on her sore throat. Doyle got sick at school, and Emma thought he had fainted at one point. She made a pallet of blankets for him to rest upon until school ended.

Mike's handyman Dale had decided to join the Army Air Corps. Emma and Dale had helped Mike do chores over the years, and she would miss his friendship. Mike faced the task of finding a new farm hand, made difficult due to so many young men enlisting.

The fall weather continued to vary between nice and rainy. The next day was damp and chilly, so the stove burned all day. That evening, Mike took his family and Emma to visit friends and practice songs for the fall program. The rain poured so heavily that Mike had to chain up the tires to make it home over the soggy roads.

On Thursday evening, the local community gathered for the fall program. Nearly forty people attended, a much larger crowd than Emma had ever had at Lone Valley. Doyle's mother played the piano for "Dancing in the Sunbeams." Mike, Kate, and two friends sang "San Antonio Rose" and "Why Don't You Fall in Love with Me?" Everyone enjoyed coffee, cookies, and sandwiches. Program evenings gave Emma a chance to meet parents and answer questions about their children's schooling.

The students enjoyed a break from the daily routine the next day. They helped Emma clean the dirty dishes and muddy floors before working diligently on their regular studies. Emma's cold was finally getting better, just in time to enjoy her first pay warrant.

Mike drove Emma to Midway early Saturday morning, where she caught the four-twenty bus to Maryville to attend the monthly teachers' meeting. She and Gladys ate uptown and shopped all afternoon.

Emma was thrilled to sleep in Sunday morning at Gladys' house, then rode horses with her and her family. She felt tired but re-energized from having a lovely weekend with friends.

The next Saturday arrived chilly. Mike took Tommy and Emma to Midway by wagon. There Bob picked them up in his car for a ride to Maryville. Emma picked up her photos and new arithmetic books. She found a letter from Peter waiting for her at Edith's.

Bob took Emma home to help with housework Sunday morning, then Emma and Doug rode to the river on horseback. They all went to Bethany on Sunday evening for a revival meeting. Emma wished for the war to end to create a married life with Peter, and the constant uncertainty of when he would return taxed her mood.

Mike drove Emma to Maryville on Thursday afternoon to a special district teachers' meeting. Then she and Gladys went to see *Seven Days' Leave*. Victor Mature starred in the musical comedy about a soldier who had seven days to marry an heiress, played by Lucille Ball, in order to inherit $100,000. Emma laughed and said, "What would so much money even look like? If I had that much, I'd have my own car, only live on gravel or paved roads, and never walk in mud again!"

Emma enjoyed spending Friday night and Saturday with Peter's parents. She helped milk and had fun visiting. They, too, were desperately missing their oldest child, and their time with Emma gave them some comfort.

Emma and Edith enjoyed *Wintertime*. The Sonja Henie and Cesar Romero film featured Woody Herman and his orchestra. Sonja had won more Olympic and world ice skating titles than any other figure skater. As an actress, she became one of the highest paid Hollywood stars at her career peak. In the movie, Sonja schemed to get her Norwegian millionaire uncle to invest in hotel improvements. Emma admitted she could barely ice skate, so she appreciated Sonja's talents.

On October 19, 1942, the War Production Board ordered mandatory collection of discarded tin cans in any city with a population of 25,000 or more. Maryville's population in 1940 was 5,700, but its citizens eagerly joined the tin scrap drive. The scrap drives made even children feel part of the war effort on the home front.

Emma's students dragged tin cans to school in burlap sacks or baskets, dumping them in a pile outside the schoolhouse. Someone with a truck would come by and collect the cans to be recycled. Emma's pride in her students' efforts showed as she watched them lug their containers to school.

On Monday, October 11, Emma had mailed Peter's Christmas package. The military had announced all holiday packages needed to be mailed very early to ensure delivery by Christmas. Such gifts from home were essential to troop morale, especially during the holidays. Emma sent him her photograph, shaving soap, hand cream, candy, razor blades, talc powder, and caramels. The postage to England cost thirty-one cents. *I wish I could be with Peter when he opens the box. I've never spent one Christmas with him since he enlisted. He left for the Army before our first holiday together.*

By mid-month, Emma was writing parts for the Halloween program. She and her students made room decorations and rehearsed play roles. Mr. Keyton brought two sacks of corn cobs for the stove. Each day seemed slightly chillier, so the stove glowed most days. That meant more ashes for Emma to clean out before restocking the stove for the next day.

Emma managed to make it through her Saturday dental appointment for fillings in two teeth, and she hated going to the dentist. "To reward myself, I bought a pink sweater, red blouse, blue purse, Halloween decorations, and some Christmas gifts," she told Edith at lunch at Kresge's department store.

Bob had been in Maryville shopping and took Emma home for the night. Bob, Linda, and Emma had fun at a Barnard dance, where Emma enjoyed ice cream and the unique flavor of her first Cleo Cola. In 1935, the Whistle Cola company introduced Cleo Cola, named after the owner's favorite cigar and used Cleopatra as a trademark.

Emma, Mike, and Kate went to Savannah on Tuesday evening. *Stage Door Canteen* had musical numbers interspersed with more serious scenes. Produced as an American propaganda film, the scene was a famed New York City restaurant and nightclub for American and Allied servicemen. Emma imagined Peter enjoying USO shows in England, wanting to dance with him.

Three people arrived at the schoolhouse Friday afternoon to help Emma register seventy-six local adults for Ration Book 4. Printed in red, blue, and green, each stamp illustrated a military symbol such as a naval ship, airplane, tank, gun, horn of plenty, or torch of liberty. The book contained red and blue cardboard tokens, each valued at one point to be used as change for ration coupon purchases. Before Ration Book 4, people had to use precisely the right number of ration points, or they lost the difference. The new tokens never expired and had spare stamps to be used occasionally to buy five extra pounds of pork. People were accustomed to getting new ration books periodically but still found it frustrating to learn a new system with each edition.

As Halloween neared, Emma and her students made a fence leading to the schoolhouse using jack-o'-lanterns, bats, witches, and black cats. In the evening, Emma and Mike cut fodder to decorate inside the schoolhouse. They added ribbons and some borrowed lights, creating a visually fun place.

On Thursday evening, October 28, 1943, those attending showed their appreciation of the children's efforts by hearty applause. Afterward, they enjoyed treats and a chance to talk with neighbors.

The children helped Emma clean the schoolhouse twice the next day. Students were willing to help because it got them out of regular lessons. They didn't realize Emma would just send the work home with them later.

Emma packed a suitcase, got Mike to drive her to Midway, and intended to catch a bus to Maryville. She wanted to spend Friday night and the weekend with Edith. Before the bus arrived, the Red Ball truck pulled into the station. American Red Ball, an essential war moving business, had to report the number of miles for each trip and was then issued enough stamps, at five gallons of gas per stamp, to complete the run. A certain number of reported miles were required before new tires could be issued to the moving company. Emma knew the driver, who happily accepted her company. He drove so many miles alone each week he enjoyed talking with someone.

Melinda's father died that week. Edith's family ordered a wreath for his funeral at Workman Chapel. Mike and Bob attended, with Owen helping Melinda deal with her loss. Emma thought, *One person's death means so much to a family, yet thousands are dying each day overseas, too many to comprehend. Why aren't people crying constantly over so many losses? Maybe each loss at home and the tears involved can stand as a symbol for the many deaths in distant places.*

On November 6, 1943, Soviet troops liberated Kiev from Nazi control. The radio announcer was thrilled the Soviets were pushing back the Nazis. German supply lines were constantly attacked, resulting in increasingly high death tolls due to illness and lack of military arsenal refits. The Germans faced defeats on their Eastern and Southern fronts. Only their Western front seemed secure.

Dale had not yet left for the Army Air Corps. He and Mike were busy shucking corn by hand. One evening, he warmed up too close to the stove.

"Owww!" Dale yelled, "My overalls are on fire!" Quickly he and Mike began to beat out the flames. Dale wasn't seriously injured because his work boots protected his legs, but Mike's house filled with smoke. They opened all the windows and doors to allow the cold fresh air to overcome the smell. Everyone stayed up past their usual bedtimes until the odor dissipated somewhat.

By Friday, Emma managed to get one dress nearly odor free. Another friend had been home on leave, which gave everyone an excuse for a Barnard dance. Emma rode home with Jacob and Helen at two in the morning.

The rain overnight had turned the roads muddy again, with a cold morning turning even colder as the day progressed. Emma's head cold stayed the same, but she enjoyed popped corn and listening to the radio.

Sunday brought snow and colder temperatures. The roads had not frozen, so the mud lay too thick even for cars with chains on them. Jacob and Emma rode to Highway 71 on horses. There Mike met them with his horses, so Emma rode all the way home in frigid air, which did not improve her cold.

The school day started with strong northwest winds and a three-inch snow. The two Cooper girls were absent. Everyone studied hard, listening to the wind howl around the thin schoolhouse walls and watching the snow pile into drifts outside. The children made fast dashes to the outhouse when necessary, but Emma didn't have to worry about them lingering there. The cold wind whistling up their backsides would urge them into the relative warmth of the schoolhouse.

"Have you heard? The Globe Theatre in Savannah burned down." Word traveled along telephone party lines more quickly than a radio broadcast. Emma thought of all the movies she and her friends had seen there. Although built for silent movies, it was converted to sound in 1928. Now war shortages of materials did not allow for a new building to replace it, but Savannah still had another theater standing.

While people struggled with ration books and rationed goods, they relied on movie theaters. Movies provided a mental break from the war's constant worrisome news, a shelter of fantasy for two hours. The comedies and musicals kept up home front morale, while the war films demonstrated, even by Hollywood standards, some of what their relatives were enduring overseas. To lose a movie house meant a psychological loss for the entire community.

People celebrated Thursday, November 11, 1943, as Armistice Day for World War I. Emma and the family listened to radio programs. *Why can't tonight be Armistice Day for World War II and bring Peter safely home?*

Chapter 33

Emma packed after the school week, and Mike drove her to Midway at nine in the morning. At twelve twenty, the bus finally arrived, so Emma was able to enjoy a late lunch with Edith in Maryville. They talked about how November 12 would have been Rose's birthday. "I wish I had had an older sister, someone to give me life advice. My sisters-in-law are understanding and helpful but not the same as having a sister."

After Emma scrubbed Edith's basement and stairway, she set her mother's hair and went uptown twice for things Edith needed. While there, she registered her school for sugar rations. Later, Emma joined Jacob and Helen at the midnight show, Northern Pursuit. Errol Flynn, as a member of the Royal Canadian Mounted Police, tried to uncover a Nazi plot against the Allied effort in the early war years. *I wonder how many real spy plots have been or are being tried around the country,* thought Emma.

All of Emma's brothers and their families arrived at Jacob's house on Sunday. Helen had won a goose at bingo, which they shared as their Thanksgiving family dinner. As three brothers drove off, all of their cars got stuck in the mud at the corner a half mile north of the house. Jacob brought his horses and chains to pull out the cars and get them on the muddy one-mile road east to Highway 71. Rural Missouri roads were always unpredictable and frustrating.

After school Monday, Kate and Edith began shucking by hand corn that Mike had twisted off the stalks. Emma worked on making a magazine rack and a shelf for Christmas at school. She got a ride into Barnard and brought back some ice cream she mixed into malts for the hard-working women. Their arms and hands might be sore from twisting the rough, dried husks off the corn ears, but the thought of ice cream waiting made the chore go faster.

In town, Emma learned two local young men were home. One had a regular furlough, and the other, a distant cousin of Emma's, had a medical discharge. Though he had survived, his medical condition had been serious enough he would not be rejoining his Army unit. *Will Peter come home whole and able to work his family's farm again?*

Dale left for training at Fort Leavenworth on Tuesday, November 16. That meant Mike had to shuck corn almost constantly since he had lost his hired hand. He had tried to find a replacement, but so far, all extra men around Barnard were already working for other farmers. The war farm labor shortage became increasingly serious, with more farmers losing hired hands the longer the war lasted. Farmers were expected to produce bumper crops, but how could they if they couldn't find enough help to harvest the extra acreages?

Emma and Gladys attended the Saturday teachers' meeting, then enjoyed lunch together, chatting with several friends. Next they splurged on a movie. *The Devil with Hitler* was a short, black and white comedy propaganda film. The board of directors of Hell wanted Adolf Hitler to take charge, but the devil tried to keep his job by making Hitler perform a good deed.

"I may enjoy the movie, but I'll never believe for one second that Hitler could ever do a good deed," Emma told Gladys.

That day, November 20, was Emma's birthday. After the movie, Emma rode with Owen and Melinda to Edith's and shared an entire quart of ice cream with Owen. Emma received several presents: two cards, a baking dish set, and one pound of candy. She added the dish set to her hope chest and happily described her fun day in a letter to Peter.

Mike finally hired a fifteen-year-old boy named Norman as a corn shucker. When they finished a large load, they filled gunny sacks with cobs. They delivered the cobs to Emma's school, along with the Tuesday coal delivery. The weather was constantly cold in late November, so the stove fire burned all day.

Emma received a card and three linen handkerchiefs made in Ireland from Peter. She was truly touched by his gifts, a rarity in rural Missouri. *I'll keep one handkerchief new to use when Peter comes home and takes me to our first dance.*

As a treat, Emma slept in Thanksgiving morning until nine. She cleaned her room, then washed and ironed her clothes. Later, she and Mike shucked nearly forty bushels of corn before a neighbor arrived and helped them finish.

On Friday, Emma got a ride to Barnard, where she bought thirteen pounds of sugar for her school using some of her school's precious ration cards. She, her family, and some friends drew names to exchange Christmas gifts.

On Saturday, Emma cleaned up and joined Mae after lunch, getting a ride to Midway to catch the bus to St. Jo. The bus arrived over two and a half hours late, completely loaded. Disappointed, the two women gave up their plans for a special evening in St. Jo, finally getting a ride to Maryville. "If I had a car," remarked Emma, "we wouldn't have to wait on a darn old bus to have fun!"

Radio news described the Cairo Conference being held from November 22 through November 26, 1943. President Roosevelt, Prime Minister Churchill, and Chiang Kai-shek agreed to defeat Japan and free Korea. Now the Allies had China working to bring victory in the Far East.

While Emma tried to stay informed about war news in the Pacific Theater, she paid more attention to the European fronts. *Defeating Germany means Peter can come home.*

Emma wrote a Christmas program and worked on her presents. Her students became excited to learn their new parts, plus the play practice gave them a break from the usual routine. They still studied hard, for Emma always pushed them to excel, but any schedule alteration brought enthusiasm.

December 1, 1943, arrived mild and clear. The year was nearing a close, but the war continued. Emma wondered when, and if, the fighting would ever stop.

Two days later, Emma received her Christmas card from Peter. After school each day, she hurried home to see if any letters had come from England. Sometimes she got one, or none, but on the best days, she might get five. Carefully, she reread each one, then stored them in bundles tied with string.

Emma shopped for and wrapped Christmas presents as she had time. While loving the holiday season, her mood remained unenthusiastic. The war news dragged on, making the holiday separation much worse. Often, she felt her nerves would snap from the tension. Each morning, she hoped Peter would be safe that day. Each night, Emma penned a letter, trying to keep her news light and funny, but not sure she succeeded.

She wrote a number in pencil on each envelope she received from Peter. By the time his letter postmarked Tuesday, December 7, 1943, arrived, Peter had written her 157 letters since he had gone to England in late April. *I know how lucky I am that Peter wasn't sent overseas sooner, as many local men were. But I feel the separation just as keenly, whether it's been a few months or years. Either way, I want Peter home so we can begin our married life.*

At school, Debbie Morton celebrated the second anniversary of the

Pearl Harbor attack by throwing up. Her brother Earl took her home at noon along muddy roads. Emma cleaned up the mess, hoping she and the other students didn't catch whatever sickness Debbie had. Ordinary life continued on the home front even if the war raged overseas.

Mike and Kate shopped in Maryville for Christmas gifts on Wednesday. Since the roads were muddy pits, they left their car and walked a mile from the gravel road to their house. They would retrieve the car whenever the roads froze. All over the countryside, people abandoned cars by roadsides when even chains couldn't get them home through the mud. As soon as the roads froze or dried out, people reclaimed their autos.

Snow began to fall the next day, and by Friday, Emma knew she had another cold. Still she walked to school with the snow over the tops of her overshoes. Her feet and legs were soaked by the time she got the schoolhouse fire roaring.

Mae picked up Emma in her buggy after school. They enjoyed supper at Mae's house, then Emma walked back to Mike's in the moonlight. Even the mailman couldn't come because of the muddy roads, so Emma's outgoing letters remained in the mailbox when she checked.

A cold south wind blew and there was no mail service Saturday. Emma slept late to doctor her cold but went to school at two thirty to work. She again walked to Mae's house, with both of them walking to Midway to catch the bus to Maryville. Emma needed new overshoes, since her old ones had too many holes in the soles.

Mike took Emma to visit Grandma Bailey in Bolckow on Sunday. On the way back, she took the train to Barnard, then walked to Mike's in the mud. She managed to cut her leg on a fence, making her feel more discouraged than her head cold did. By evening, Emma was sick to her stomach. *I know such things happen, but I wish Peter was here to take care of me.*

Monday was the coldest day so far. The temperature only rose one degree on the south side of buildings. Emma dragged herself to school, where she helped the girls sew their projects. Her stomach bothered her all day, so she ate little and felt very weak. She tried to sit as much as possible. The only good part of the day occurred when she found five letters from Peter waiting at home.

Wednesday morning showed thirteen degrees below zero on the thermometer, especially cold for mid-December. Emma got to school early to ensure the stove had a good fire before the students arrived. Emma couldn't blame the Coopers for keeping their children home in the bitterly cold weather, since they had the farthest to walk. Frostbite for small noses and fingers lurked in the frigid air.

Emma had to walk to the neighbors' farmhouse after school to pick up Tommy. Mike and Kate had gone to St. Jo, not expecting to get home until late. Tommy gushed "I got you all to myself" as they shared their supper.

Norman helped finish corn shucking by December 16. The war labor shortage for farm workers continued. Where farmers typically worked from sunup to sundown in pre-war years, now they struggled beyond sundown with whatever lights they could rig to gather crops.

On Friday, December 17, Emma finished the week, and Mike and his family drove her to Barnard to pick up her fourth warrant. She caught the train to Maryville, then carried two suitcases from the depot to Edith's house. The temperature still hovered around zero, but she didn't feel the cold as much as when the bitter chills had first arrived a few days ago.

Emma washed clothes, ironed, washed dishes, cleaned the house, took a bath, and set a neighbor lady's hair on Saturday. By afternoon, Emma celebrated by shopping and bought herself a new hat for $2.50 and a dress for $7.90. Also, she turned in $3.03 of Christmas Seals money.

Owen and Melinda arrived for supper with Melinda's mother, then everyone saw *Corvette K-225*. Randolph Scott played a Navy lieutenant commander who lost his ship and most of his crew to a German attack. Robert Mitchum had a minor supporting role, one of twenty films he made in 1943. Emma was so glad Peter stayed on land to maintain B-17 bombers. *I can't imagine a more horrible way to die than abandoning a sinking ship, only to be machine gunned by Nazi submariners.*

The next day, she went to the movie *This Is the Army*. The musical comedy was designed to boost U.S. morale with music by Irving Berlin. The large ensemble cast included George Murphy; Ronald Reagan; Alan Hale, Sr.; and Rosemary DeCamp. Also many U.S. Army soldiers who were actors and performers in civilian life had parts. Emma appreciated the lighter comedy after the dramatic Saturday movie, so Hollywood's attempt to lift her morale worked well.

The last week before Christmas break continued cold with a sharp north wind. The students practiced their roles, and the music teacher led them in holiday songs. They also decorated the tree Mike brought, with Tommy visiting all afternoon.

Local folks packed the schoolroom for the evening program, making space for Santa Claus when he arrived. Her students gave Emma a set of glasses, a dish, a salt and pepper set, three makeup kits, and a perfumed lamp. Emma had bought pocketknives for the boys, makeup and brush sets for the older girls, paints and book sets for the younger children, plus candy and oranges for all pupils. Everyone laughed and shouted "Merry Christmas" as they left the schoolyard. At least the roads were frozen, so everyone easily got home.

The next day, Emma still had a bad cold and felt rocky but rode to Maryville to spend the holiday with Edith. Some friends had sent Emma a box with four cereal bowls, a box of chocolates, and a white collar to wear on a plain dress or blouse. Emma carefully added the cereal bowls and her school gifts to her hope chest. She wanted to have a good supply of housewares to furnish her home with Peter.

On Christmas Eve, Edith and Emma decorated the tree Jacob had brought. Emma rode with Jacob's family to Grandma Bailey's in Bolckow, while Edith went home with Owen. Mike's family had illnesses, so they couldn't go to Bolckow to celebrate with the remaining family. Emma received plates, a meat platter, two stationery sets, a dresser set from Peter, a pin, a bath cloth, a teapot with a sugar and creamer set, a nightgown, towel set, deodorant, and toilet water. How different those gifts were from the one or two gifts she had been lucky to receive during the Depression. With the higher war prices for crops, her brothers' income had risen.

Emma stood on the capacity-crowded bus from Maryville to Midway on Sunday, December 26. She had left her presents carefully packed at Edith's house, but still brought two suitcases. Mike picked her up, but Kate and Tommy were in bed with the flu and croup. Winter illnesses never took a holiday.

Edith helped Kate by washing dishes and popping corn, and she wrote Peter and washed her hair. She even cooked breakfast before Mike took her to school at a quarter of nine. By evening, Emma had washed the noon and evening dishes, studied the next day's lessons, and written Peter. She received four letters that day.

The month closed beautifully. December 29 had heavy frost glazing the land with white froth. The glorious landscape took everyone's mind off doing outside chores in the cold.

Friday, December 31, 1943, finished the quarter at school. The children were eager for New Year's Eve parties, if they were old enough to be allowed to stay up until midnight and listen to the radio. Most farm families never lasted that long, having been up early to do chores even in the winter. Emma celebrated with her students by making ice cream at school that afternoon.

At the stroke of midnight, Emma's thoughts turned to wish Peter a Happy New Year. *I'm lucky. At least I know he's somewhere in England. May the war end soon, my dear Peter, and you return to me before Easter.*

Chapter 34

Edith enjoyed Emma's company on New Year's Day 1944. They talked for hours while they took down the Christmas tree.

Owen and Melinda came to Maryville for church and ate dinner with Emma and Edith. Then everyone went to see *Crazy House*. The comedy starred Ole Olsen and Chic Johnson as Broadway stars returning to Universal Studios to make another movie. The film had an impressive cast of famous supporting comedians, and Emma and her family roared with laughter at their antics. Anything to extend the good Christmas mood awhile longer, before thoughts of the war again overtook their emotions.

Back in school on Monday, January 3, Emma wrote and gave tests. Her class averaged two of nine students absent due to illnesses each day the first week.

Bob and Linda took her to the Barnard dance on Friday evening. "I'm having a fantastic time! I want to forget all about sick kids, the war, and anything else negative," she told Linda. She even celebrated with a pineapple malt. She just wanted to dance and did until a quarter of four in the morning.

By early Saturday afternoon, Emma rode the bus to Maryville to have a late lunch with Edith. Emma shopped, returning some overshoes, and spent $4.03 on other items. Edith and Emma splurged on oyster soup for dinner.

Sunday was a typical day for Emma while at Edith's house. She attended Sunday School, helped cook three meals, scrubbed two rooms, and washed curtains. Edith kept house well, but she was getting older, now nearly sixty-two. Emma tried to do some of the harder cleaning whenever she was home.

Geography, agriculture, math, spelling, health, and writing tests were given throughout the school year. Emma had to compose most of them, hoping her pupils grasped the concepts. Luckily, parents were very supportive of schooling, so Emma had good backing when she sent homework. All her students had farm chores to do but were still expected to perform as well as they could at school.

On January 11, Emma passed out grade cards and sent a formal report to Mr. Burr. So far, the children were doing well. Also, everyone had been present for the first time in six school days.

Emma closed school at noon Wednesday. One student's father, Mr. Morton, had died. Emma and many residents attended the Barnard funeral and nearly froze at the gravesite. Emma always felt it was harder to say goodbye to a loved one during rainy or cold weather.

Afterward, she stopped in town to ask the sheriff about picking up any salvaged paper he might have. The war recycling efforts continued on all kinds of goods.

She barely got to Midway in time to catch the bus to Maryville on Friday evening. Temperatures had risen dramatically, almost feeling spring-like in mid-January, so she left without her overshoes or slacks. Tommy accompanied Emma to spend the weekend with his Grandma Edith.

After church that Sunday, Emma, Edith, and Tommy attended the matinee *A Lady Takes a Chance*. The romantic comedy starred Jean Arthur and John Wayne. A New York working girl traveled to the American West on a bus tour, falling in love with a handsome rodeo cowboy. "Can you believe a huge star like John Wayne was born in Winterset, Iowa, about three hours from our house in northwest Missouri?" asked Emma.

Emma and Tommy tried to take the late afternoon bus to Midway. The bus arrived completely jammed with passengers, so they spent Sunday night with Edith. To teach Monday morning, she and Tommy took an early taxi to the Maryville train depot. They managed to get on the train to Barnard, accompanied by Edith, who continued on to Bolckow to see her mother. Mike picked up Emma and Tommy at the depot, getting her to school by nine.

Two students beat her there. The schoolhouse stayed cold most of the morning because Emma hadn't arrived early to light the stove. She felt guilty, but there was nothing she could have done to get from Maryville to Barnard any sooner. *If only I had my own car! I wouldn't have to wait for rides or the bus or the train.*

All week, Emma had a headache and cold. No substitutes were available for one-room country schoolteachers. Unless they were seriously ill, they just managed to make it through the school day.

On January 22, 1944, the radio announced the momentous news that Allied troops had landed near Anzio, south of Rome. They held the beachhead and were unloading more men and supplies every hour. The invasion of the Italian peninsula had begun.

Also that day, Emma finally bought a car. The urge had been growing for months. On Thursday, she got a letter from Owen telling about a neighbor who had a car for sale. Owen picked her up Friday after school. Using money she borrowed from Edith, by midmorning Saturday, Emma owned a 1935 Ford Tudor sedan. Its blunt front end resembled like a flat nose with two headlight eyes midway down on the sides. The Flathead V8 engine looked powerful. Rounded bumpers covered four white-walled tires with spoke hubcaps. Two silver latches held the trunk lid shut, and two small taillights extended above the rear bumper. The car even had a radio.

Emma slid into the driver's seat, gently grasping the slender steering wheel. She put her right foot on the brake and her left foot on the clutch, then worked the gearshift to get accustomed to the feel with the engine off. Emma finally had the freedom of her own transportation.

She drove from Midway station to Maryville that afternoon to get her application receipt for her first driver's license. She and Owen ran into her other three brothers and two of their wives. Everyone kidded her about getting her own "wheels."

"Will you look at that," remarked Mike. "Our kid sister's got a car. Wonder if she can drive it. You know she has trouble steering a horse when she rides, so how can she handle a car going thirty-five miles an hour down a road?" he teased.

Jacob studied her and the car in mock seriousness. "I think she should've asked our opinions before she bought a piece of junk. It looks like it will barely get out of the driveway before it breaks down!"

Even Bob added his two bits. "She's just too young to have a car. She's only twenty-two. And why did the state ever allow women to get a driver's license anyway?"

"You just wait until you need my help getting someplace," Emma retorted. "Then you'll be glad I've got a car. Besides, now you won't have to drive me to Midway or Maryville."

In the evening, most of them went to see *The Heat's On* with Mae West, William Gaxton, and Victor Moore. A temperamental diva was reluctantly persuaded by a Broadway producer to star in his latest production. Emma could not imagine being as beautiful and self-assured as Mae West portrayed.

On Sunday, Emma drove her car to see Gene and Janie Paxton, who raved about it. Janie said, "I always was too scared to learn to drive. But you sure got the courage to do it."

255

"Wait until Peter sees me driving," Emma replied. "I hope he'll be proud of me for taking care of myself and getting around when I want to."

Late January brought mild temperatures but strong winds. Although frost had arrived, the roads still were deeply covered in mud.

At school, Emma played Andy Over with the students at recess. Half of her students stood on each side of the schoolhouse. One student would throw a ball over the roof, and if the other side caught it before it hit the ground, they yelled, "Andy Over." Then the catcher would run around the schoolhouse and tag someone on the other team, who then joined the catcher's team. The game continued until only one person remained on one side. Emma managed to catch the ball twice, a record for her.

Emma and Mike went to Savannah to the movie Dixie on Thursday evening. The American biographic film of songwriter Daniel Decatur Emmet starred Bing Crosby and Dorothy Lamour. The movie contained a song that would become one of Crosby's most popular, "Sunday, Monday, or Always." *I feel so dreamy whenever Bing sings.*

After school Friday, Emma drove to Bolckow and stopped at Criss' repair shop to rotate the tires. On Saturday in Maryville, Emma had the mechanic grease the car chassis and other parts. The tires were inspected officially and passed. Emma was beginning to understand car ownership and some of the costs involved. *It's a good thing I've been saving my money and got a raise. This car is going to eat into my bank account. But it's worth it!*

Emma couldn't get the car started on Sunday, January 30, 1944. It was out of gas. She walked uptown to the gas station, then lugged the gas can home to empty into the tank. She had to wait for gravity to work the gas through the lines before the engine would turn over.

Oh, I hope the gas station guy won't tell my brothers about running out of gas. I'll never hear the end of it if he does! But she knew they were friends, so she steeled herself for more ribbing from the four of them.

Wednesday was misty and foggy with a chilly wind. That evening, Emma and some friends went to Savannah to see *So Proudly We Hail!* Claudette Colbert, Paulette Goddard, and Veronica Lake served as military nurses sent to the Philippines during the early days of World War II. The movie was partly based on two books, one by a World War II nurse who served during the battle for Bataan and Corregidor called *Angels of Bataan,* and *I Served on Bataan.* The true horror of the Bataan Death March had just been announced by the government on January 27.

Emma drove to Grandma Bailey's house for a short visit that Friday. She almost made it back to Mike's, but the car engine died a quarter mile away. She walked to the house in the dark, and Mike pushed the car while she steered with the gear in neutral to get the automobile into the driveway. She knew she was in for some serious teasing about her aging car. *Between running out of gas and the engine dying, I'll have to go into hiding to escape their jokes!*

Emma, with Mike pushing, managed to get the V8 started by coasting it downhill the next day. She drove to Maryville to change the car license tags and washed the windows inside. She added the required car stickers, then enjoyed a malt to celebrate having her car officially registered in her name.

Mae asked Emma to supper on Monday. Her brother Dean had a furlough from the Army. They played pinochle and pitch until late, and Dean presented Emma with his photo. She knew she would treasure it due to their friendship, but also because one never knew if the photo would be the last one Dean might ever have taken. Life in the military was very tenuous those days.

Emma stayed home with Tommy while Mike and Kate attended a Barnard dance on Wednesday. Tommy accidentally threw a baseball in the house, breaking the east window. As fierce wind blew in, snow drifted onto the floor. Emma hammered a blanket over the opening until Mike returned to nail up a tarp and boards to keep out the snow. It ended a bad day, for Emma had broken her glasses in the morning and fought a cold all week.

Fierce wind continued the next morning. The snowplow didn't arrive until Friday morning when seven of nine pupils attended. Emma stayed after school, sweeping the mud clods and dust off the floor and washing the blackboard. Often the students enjoyed washing the blackboard, but the weather was too cold to allow anyone to stay late.

By Saturday morning, the thermometer dipped to nineteen below zero and snow continued. Mike finally cranked the V8 engine to life, and Emma packed her bag to drive to Edith's. In Maryville, she had the car's oil changed and added alcohol to the radiator to prevent freezing. She even bought a new battery at Montgomery Ward. She proudly drove Owen to his house, returning the favor after he had driven her so many times since she had begun teaching at Lone Valley.

After dinner on Monday, Emma returned to the schoolhouse. Four students had formed a quartet and needed to practice for the program Tuesday evening. The next morning, Emma paid one boy fifty cents to shovel the school driveway. Before the program, Emma had intended to drive to pick up Mae, but her car ran out of gas. She had to walk back to the schoolhouse. Mae got a ride with other friends but had a good laugh at Emma's expense. Emma again faced ribbing for a second empty gas tank.

Their day after Valentine's program was called "The Tea Party" with an all-boy five-student cast. Then everyone exchanged valentines.

On most evenings, Emma, Mike, and Kate listened to the radio. The war news sounded a bit more hopeful. The Allies continued to gain ground in Europe.

Mike and Kate celebrated their eighth wedding anniversary on Friday, February 18. They took Emma to see *Dancing Masters* in Savannah. Laurel and Hardy starred as two bumbling dance teachers who helped an awkward inventor sell his new invention and facilitated his wooing of a beautiful socialite. The film was perfectly hilarious, and Emma wished Peter could have shared it with her.

She cleaned her room at Mike's the next morning, then drove to Bob's house. Bob, Linda, and Emma drove to Maryville to shop and buy Edith some jars to use canning meat. By evening, they went to a Barnard dance, splurging on ice cream and Pepsi-Cola before they left town. Emma declared, "I'm celebrating! I officially got my driver's license."

Sunday's thaw didn't happen until Emma got to Sunday School at Salem. By the time she drove to visit Bob and Linda, he had to chain up Emma's car to get her up the sloping driveway. Later, Emma drove to Bolckow for dinner with Edith and Grandma Bailey. She waited for the roads to freeze to drive back to Mike's.

A strong wind blew the children to school on Tuesday. Emma and her students tried to make ice cream but couldn't get it hard. They didn't seem to mind, since it tasted great even if a little thin. Emma's sore throat continued all week, worsening into a cold.

Mae and Emma went to see *Thank Your Lucky Stars* on Thursday evening. The musical comedy was a Warner Brothers' World War II fundraiser. The film headliners donated their salaries to the Hollywood Canteen, which was founded by John Garfield and Bette Davis. Emma felt lucky to enjoy the movie and contribute to the war effort.

A Valentine's present arrived on Friday, February 25. Peter sent a silk scarf from London and a long letter. Emma was thrilled.

A cloudy sky and cold strong wind slammed Mae and Emma as they drove to Maryville for the weekend. The midnight musical *Higher and Higher* featured Michele Morgan, Jack Haley, and Frank Sinatra in his film debut. The household staff of a millionaire discovered they were not going to get their months-overdue backpay because their boss was bankrupt. The boss took his wife, plain-looking daughter, and attractive maid on a long trip abroad. He tried to pass off the maid as their socialite daughter to marry her to a rich man to get money for everyone. Emma could relate to being broke, since money had been extremely tight most of her life.

The next day, Mae and Emma saw the matinee *Lifeboat*. Alfred Hitchcock directed the survival drama movie based on a story by John Steinbeck. Tallulah Bankhead and William Bendix starred. The entire film took place on a lifeboat launched from a sinking passenger liner after a World War II German naval attack. Emma had never been on a large body of water and had no desire to try surviving in a lifeboat at sea. *I feel sorry for all of the sailors and marines who face similar situations after a sea battle.*

Emma worked through Wednesday, March 1, but felt very lonesome for some reason. She couldn't shake her miserable mood, although usually she could force such emotions away through work.

The next day, her mood had not improved. She gave spelling and arithmetic tests. The children worked on an Indian scene for a tabletop display. Janie Paxton called in the evening to say she had also received a scarf Peter had sent for Valentine's. Emma felt a little brighter, remembering how thoughtful Peter was and how fond of his parents.

But Friday afternoon, Emma dodged hail and hard rain as she made her way home over slippery muddy roads. She was soaked and cold by the time she got inside.

The cloudy skies and chilly wind served to keep Emma's mood down. She did clean the mud from her car mats and straightened her room. Tommy had been sick all the previous night and Saturday morning, so no one had gotten much sleep. Still, Emma packed her suitcase into the Ford's trunk, swerved along the muddy roads, and arrived in Bolckow to spend the night with her mother and grandmother.

The next day, Emma drove to Bob's. His hired hand put chains on her car, but the car lost a chain on the muddy road. Luckily, a neighbor came along and fastened it back on the tire. *I hate having to install chains on a muddy road, with mud all over the tire, the chain, and my hands and clothes before I can finish.*

Frustrated, Emma finally exploded to herself. *Here I am working on a college degree, teaching school, and dealing with muddy slime up to my knees way too often. And Peter's just got an eighth-grade education, but he's working on the most advanced bomber ever made and never has to walk through mud. It isn't fair!*

Tuesday, March 7, arrived at zero degrees. Mike had been sick during the night, so Emma fixed breakfast for him and Norman. Kate had stayed overnight with relatives. Mike said he would feel better by noon, so Emma went to school and left Tommy with him.

The weather moderated by Thursday. After school, Emma mopped and oiled the schoolhouse floor. Then she washed dishes after supper. Mike removed the car's chains, and Emma drove to Midway to shake off the dried mud.

Then Emma motored to the school board president's house so he could sign her seventh pay warrant. She paid Kate for three months' back board and for April. While Mike and Kate would expect any boarder to pay, they did not like to charge Emma for room and board since Emma worked so much around the house. Emma, however, insisted.

That afternoon, Emma drove to Jacob's house and picked up her niece Alice. Although she loved to roller skate, Alice needed a lot more practice to pass the novice stage.

Emma went to the afternoon matinees, *Silver Spurs* and *The Sea Hawk*. The first was a Western starring Roy Rogers and Trigger. Roy's boss inherited a huge ranch but the will denied him from selling it; however, the boss's widow could. John Carradine, the villain, tried to gain control of the ranch at any cost. Emma loved Westerns and Roy Rogers' singing. The second black and white film featured Errol Flynn as an English privateer who defended his nation's interests just before the Spanish Armada arrived. The swashbuckling adventure on the high seas was a great way to end a Saturday afternoon.

Emma lost track of how many letters she had written since Peter joined the Army. However many they were, they were too many. *I want you home and safe. A letter can't replace feeling your arms holding me tightly.*

Chapter 35

Wednesday, March 15, 1944, brought light snow, cloudy skies, and the first B-12 ration coupons.

Mike, Kate, and Emma drove to Savannah Thursday evening for *Let's Face It*. Cole Porter wrote the music and lyrics for the 1941 Broadway hit before the 1943 film was made. Three suspicious wives invited three Army draftees to a summer house in Southampton, Long Island, to make their husbands jealous. Of course, nothing illicit occurred, but the evening's entertainment was worth getting to bed late for Emma.

After a teachers' meeting on Saturday, Emma took a couple of friends on a long drive, enjoying the freedom of the countryside. Owen and Melinda arrived in the evening at Edith's, and everyone went to the midnight show *The Iron Major*. The movie was a biographical film about the famed college football coach and World War I hero, Frank Cavanaugh. Pat O'Brien headlined with Ruth Warrick and Robert Ryan. Although the father of seven children and a football coach, Cavanaugh enlisted in World War I. As a major, he saw heavy combat, becoming seriously wounded but recovering, thus earning his nickname. Emma wondered how many thousands of military men and women had faced similar wounds. *How can the country ever care for so many veterans when they all return home?*

After sleeping late Sunday morning, Emma drove to the Paxtons to spend the afternoon and to eat dinner. They even made ice cream, stuffing themselves until Emma left for the late show, The *Miracle of Morgan's Creek*. The screwball comedy starred Eddie Bracken and Betty Hutton. A small-town girl had a soft heart for soldiers. After a wild, drunken farewell party for a group of them, she awoke to find she had married a soldier but can't remember his name or what he looked like. She later found herself pregnant, giving birth to sextuplet sons. Finally, a local 4-F boy who had loved Trudy for years stepped in for a happy ending. *I want children by Peter, but I never want more than one baby at a time!*

One girl was absent with chickenpox on March 22. The winter round of illnesses had mostly ended, but the spring health surprises had begun.

Mike posted the school board elections notice on the door. Everyone in the local district for Maple Grove and Harmon could vote on April 4. Since there were usually few candidates, the voting process often went quickly.

On Friday, the roads were rutted but dry. By Saturday, six inches of snow had melted during the night. Emma's car overcame nearly being buried in mud when she went after Mae. They drove on to Savannah and took the bus to St. Jo. Emma had to see a dentist but found he couldn't fill her teeth that day.

After spending the night at her grandmother's, Emma drove to Mike's Sunday morning. Mike had had a farming accident, getting a piece of steel stabbed into his leg. He would be alright but would be sore for several days. Mike could barely limp around the house, so Emma helped Norman do chores.

She tried to drive to Barnard, but the car got stuck at the river bridge. She had to get out, wade into the mud, and chain up the tires. Afterward, her hands and boots were covered with mud, most of which she managed to scrap off by rubbing her hands and feet among dried grasses. Overall, Sunday had not been a delightful day.

Tuesday, March 28, held a strong, cold, north wind, with temperatures dropping all day until snow fell. Only four students attended school the next day. More absences from illnesses continued until Friday when everyone finally appeared. Emma had to write homework assignments for lessons they had missed.

Emma paid $4.00 for a permanent on Saturday, envying women with naturally curly hair. Her car repairs cost her another $6.35. Later she cleaned the car inside and out, even scrubbing the mud off the wheels. She knew it was a useless effort. *Even for a few hours, I want a clean car! These country roads always make my car look like a hog wallowing in mud!*

Emma joined Bob's family for Sunday School at Salem Church. They stayed for a duck dinner, and later she helped Bob with his chores. When she got ready to leave, a gear came off the car, but Bob managed to fix it. All she could do was put up with her brothers' teasing, since she loved having a car and the freedom to go whenever she wanted. That is, if the car cooperated and decided to work that day!

Emma held her classes in the school basement for a few hours, so elections could be held upstairs on April 4. Finally, the current board closed the elections, since only four people voted.

Thursday found Emma and her students painting real Easter eggs. They had boiled farm eggs in the morning, letting them cool over the lunch hour. By afternoon, the eggs had received their festive colorings.

Later, Emma spilled almost a gallon of gas inside her car. When she picked up Mae and her sister, they had to drive to Savannah with the windows rolled down. They wanted to see *Thousands Cheer* and didn't want gasoline fumes deterring them. The musical comedy was a morale booster for American troops and their families. Gene Kelly played an aerialist who became an Army draftee and fell in love with his commanding officer's daughter (Kathryn Grayson). The second half was a variety showcase for soldiers featuring Metro-Goldwyn-Mayer musical and comedy actors, which Mickey Rooney hosted. Emma knew Peter got to see some USO shows at his English base, but usually he wrote they were not good for performers or production quality. *I wish he could see a wonderful show like the movie portrayed.*

The children's illnesses finally conquered Emma's efforts to resist. By Friday, April 7, Emma was showing signs of chickenpox. Feeling terrible, she managed to host the school's Easter party. She picked up her eighth pay warrant, drove to Bolckow to get Edith and to Maryville, then fell into bed to stay. Edith had had chickenpox years ago, so she cared for Emma.

By Saturday evening, Emma's body was covered with pox marks and high fever kept her down. On Sunday, Owen and Melinda came to see Edith but stayed outside since Owen had never had chickenpox. Emma had no energy, a fever, and felt and looked terrible. Since she couldn't work because her mind wouldn't focus, she laid around doing nothing.

Edith said, "Just what your body needs! Quit worrying about not bein' able to teach school. The kids will enjoy a few days off."

Emma felt much better by Tuesday, reading a little and resting. The next day, she managed to wash her clothes and take a bath. She even drove Edith uptown, where they visited with Jacob and Helen. Emma ate a hamburger, which tasted delicious after only eating light food for four days. Emma, however, decided not to teach that week and called Mike to post a sign on the schoolhouse and to call the families who had telephones.

Emma realized she had overdone her activities uptown and felt poorly on Thursday. Mike and Owen visited, bringing six letters from Peter, before heading home to farm tasks. Emma began easing into activities by ironing and mending clothes, reading, and assembling a jigsaw puzzle.

On Sunday, April 16, Emma packed her bags. At Midway, a friend helped her chain up the tires for the muddy drive to Mike's. Emma saw Dr. Humbred in Barnard that afternoon, and he told her she was not yet over the chickenpox.

Still, Emma went to school on Monday in the snow, wind, and rain. Mike wouldn't let her walk home, so he picked her up. Emma happily rested in bed as soon as they arrived home, even eating supper there. The last chickenpox scale fell off Emma's face on Wednesday, April 19. *I want to scream for happiness because that itching has finally stopped!*

Spring weather continued rainy off and on all week. The roads formed deep muddy tracks and were so bad the mail carrier couldn't come on Tuesday.

By Saturday, April 22, 1944, Mike, Kate, and Tommy all had chickenpox. Feeling guilty for exposing them, Emma cooked meals, washed dishes, and did chores. Mike managed to work some the next day, but Norman did most of the jobs.

Emma drove to school on Monday. The chilly wind had dried a deep road track. Also, the building had water in the basement from the recent rains. Emma and her students swept and toted buckets of water out of the basement twice that day.

Her car made it to school, then decided to have a flat tire during the day. When Emma wanted to leave, she discovered the problem and managed to jack up the car. Luckily, one set of parents came by, removed the chains, and helped Emma pump up the tires. Then she drove to Barnard to get the tire fixed. *Between chains, repairs, flat tires, licenses, and more, I can't decide if buying a car was a wise decision.*

By Monday evening after the car fiasco, Emma found Mike feeling better. Kate still had no energy. Tommy had never felt badly from the chickenpox, just being a little grumpier than usual.

April 17 marked eight years since their father had died. April 24, 1944, marked two years since Peter had gone into the Army. Emma missed him so much, but she wouldn't let her emotions get her down. Spring was here, the end of school neared, and the war couldn't last forever, could it?

On the last Saturday in April, Emma shopped for new slippers and watched some schoolgirls roller skate at the pavilion. Later she wrote parts for the final school play. On Sunday, she began packing her belongings at Mike's house to return to Maryville. She stopped by Bob's for a visit, where her car got stuck in the driveway. Bob used his tractor to free it, but she suffered more joking about her ability to handle a powerful V8 in the mud.

May 1 and 2 brought heavy rain. The 102 River overflowed its banks in several towns. Over an inch of water again filled the schoolhouse basement. Emma moved all the school's belongings upstairs to keep them dry and prevent molding. Mike and Norman rode to Barnard on horseback for supplies. By Wednesday night, the river crested, slowly withdrawing into its normal banks.

The final school play actually had two productions. Some local folks had parts and came to school for Thursday's practice. By Friday, the students finished up lessons and practiced their play parts, and Mary Cooper fainted that morning.

Emma decided to rent a house across the road from Harmon school for her and Edith. Edith still owned her house in Maryville, which she could rent out. On Friday, May 5, Emma drove to Barnard to pick up groceries to feed the people who would help them move on Saturday. Some helpers had brought part of Edith's furniture from Maryville by evening, along with coal for the stove.

Saturday was sunny all day, but still chilly. Mike drove Tommy to Jacob's house to stay during the move, but Tommy protested, "I can help a lot if I stay with Aunt Emma!" Owen, Mike, and Jacob, plus some neighbors, helped Edith move her things from Maryville and Emma's things from Mike's. Kate, Edith, and Emma put up beds and cleaned the living room. The cooking and heating stoves had been installed by day's end. By dark, a very tired crew of people finished getting everything into the house.

Emma began the last week of school on Monday. Students practiced the closing play and took four tests, with everyone anxious to get out for the summer. After school, Emma only had to walk across the road to her newly rented home.

She decided to drive over to the Cooper's after some setting eggs so she could raise her own chickens. Sunday's rain had made a mess of the roads and her car got stuck at the corner, with Mr. Cooper and Mike pulling it out with a tractor. *I may have to endure more ribbing about being a poor mud driver. But I can remind the three of them they all got stuck last November!*

On May 9, Emma surprised her class. While they practiced their program songs with Mrs. Harwood in the morning, Emma cleaned the mud from the car wheels. She drove all her students and Mae to the city Roadside Park for lunch and to a free show, *Ali Baba and the Forty Thieves,* which the students loved. Some pupils had never been to a movie, so they were awed by the production.

They had their last program rehearsal Friday. Even Tommy was in the play for a song and a little drill routine. Everyone helped put away books and clean the schoolhouse.

That evening, Harmon school produced its last two programs of the year. Kate and her cousin Flynn sang, others performed piano solos, and everyone had a great time. They also ate all ten gallons of ice cream. Everyone finished and got home before it rained again.

Emma drove to Owen's house to celebrate Mother's Day with the family. When Emma headed back to Maryville, her car died. Luckily, a man came by and fixed it on the spot, since only a wire had come loose. She managed to get back to her house. She took the car in Monday for repairs but found the mechanic gone. *I'm getting frustrated at keeping this car working!*

Later at home, a neighbor brought her a lovely bouquet of purple lilacs, and their wonderful aroma lifted her spirits. On Thursday, Bob brought some irises that Linda loved to cultivate so Emma could plant them at her new home.

All week, Emma painted Mike's brooder house and ironed clothes. Her house was so close to Mike's she still felt she lived there sometimes and enjoyed helping out. Mike planted corn with his tractor, and Emma hauled seed corn and water to him as needed.

Emma, Linda, and Edith celebrated the week's hard work by going to a Barnard dance on Saturday. As they laughed and danced, a terrible rainstorm blew into town, hammering the old building and pounding the roof in waves. After the dance, the rain deluge continued. As Emma ran to get the car and bring it up for the two women, she slipped on the wet ground, falling hard. She struck her head on a thick clump of rain-soaked weeds, resulting in a serious headache. She managed to drive them back to Bob's house, then fell into bed exhausted.

On Monday, Edith and three sisters-in-law helped Emma hang wallpaper. By late afternoon, they had finished the west bedroom and seven strips in the living room. They enjoyed supper at Bob's, and he gave Edith twenty-five chickens and Emma one chicken to have for egg laying. Emma borrowed a chicken coop for her little hen.

Emma felt like celebrating on the next day. She made her last payment on her car to Edith, officially owning it free and clear. Her hard work teaching had brought one of her dreams, to have her own wheels so she didn't have to depend on others.

Edith helped Emma work on her house. They finished papering the living room, then installed bedroom and living room shades. Edith even made new bedroom drapes. Emma cleaned the dirty attic and burned junk items out back on the trash pile. She also mopped her bedroom and all woodwork and finally unpacked bedroom items.

On Saturday, Emma and Mike filled out end-of-year school reports for the local school board records. After Emma drove Mike to Maryville, Owen helped them tear down the old coal shed on Edith's property. On the way home, Emma had to stop and chain up the car's tires to reach her house. Just as she was driving between her garage doors, the car died—again. Feeling tired, frustrated, and single without a man around, Emma slammed the palm of her hand hard against the steering wheel.

Sunday, May 28, 1944, was Edith's sixty-second birthday. Owen and Melinda came for lunch and brought ice cream. Mike and Kate later brought Tommy to visit. Then Jacob, Helen, and Alice came before supper. Everyone brought Edith a present. She was delighted to see three of her four "boys" and their families, for she would always call them her boys, no matter how old they were.

The next day, Emma's little chickens hatched. She thrilled to watch them struggle out of their shells. Although she had seen chicks hatch since she was little, she was always fascinated at their arrival in the world. They were so small, soft yellow, and warm, just wanting to say "cheep" and find something to eat. Soon they would be running all over her small brood house and climbing on everything their tiny wings could help them reach.

Mike and Tommy drove their pickup over to Emma's house. They hooked up a chain and dragged the V8 to Barnard so the mechanic could figure out why it died. He concluded the 1935 fuel pump had failed, and by Wednesday, managed to find one for that model. Emma was happy to have her wheels back and actually running well.

Emma had decided not to attend college that summer. She wanted to settle into her own home, help her brothers and Edith, and just spend family time. Working nine months each year, then going to summer school for several years, had mentally drained her.

Emma helped Jacob shell some of last year's corn on Tuesday. They had intended to visit local cemeteries in Barnard and Bolckow for Memorial

Day, but an afternoon shower delayed their trip until evening. They took water buckets to keep the irises, roses, and peonies fresh to lay on relatives' gravesites. At Daniel Trotter's burial plot, they placed a wreath with "Father" in big letters. Emma deeply missed her father.

A neighbor had two extra chicken coops, so Mike drove his pickup to pick up one for Emma's chickens. They were growing fast and needed more room than the small brooder provided.

Edith also wanted to wallpaper her house in Maryville. Emma helped patch the plastering and hung two strips in the living room. Later they finished the ceiling, and the north and east walls. As Emma drove back to her house, her car began acting up again! This time, she figured it was the carburetor, but managed to nudge it home.

On Friday, Emma walked a mile and a half to Mike's corn field. She helped him drill about twenty miles of corn rows that day. Their reward was homemade strawberry shortcake Kate had made for lunch and supper both. Emma got to bring some strawberries home.

Emma left early Saturday morning to drive her ailing car to Bolckow for a mechanic to fix. Then Emma again rode the planter behind Mike's tractor all afternoon. Mike paid her $10 for her help and drove her back to Bolckow to retrieve her car.

Excited radio announcements came on Sunday, June 4, 1944. Allied troops had just liberated Rome. Southern Italy was now in Allied hands. For the first time, masses of Anglo-American planes would be heavily bombing eastern Germany. The Allies were gaining true headway toward defeating the Nazis.

More chores captured her attention the next week. Emma painted Mike's outhouse and mailbox. She got dinner for Kate and used any excuse to avoid remembering she had not received any mail from Peter for over a week. She would soon discover why.

Chapter 36

The radio reporter announced that D-Day, the invasion of Europe through Normandy near Le Havre, France, had begun on June 6, 1944. U.S. citizens listened to radios whenever they could. The Allies fooled the Germans into believing the invasion would come through Calais, the closest land point to England. The "Second Front" had been opened on the Atlantic side. Finally, the Allies were grabbing a toehold on western European soil, but everyone feared the cost in young men's lives would be extremely high.

Many local men served scattered all over the world, but families rarely knew exactly where their relatives were stationed. Even Peter's letters to Emma always bore the heading "Somewhere in England." None of the military men could tell their parents where they were stationed beyond something vague like "Europe" or the "Pacific." While mail deliveries had slightly improved, it still could be days or a week before any mail arrived. Each letter was treasured because it meant a father, brother, son, cousin, or friend had been alive on the day the letter had been written.

On Friday, June 9, Emma received her first letter from Peter in over two weeks. The envelope was dated May 23, but Emma didn't care. She slit open one end as she always did and read and reread the letter with delight. Peter was okay. Things were normal there, or at least they seemed to be. Surely, his base must have been in an uproar with the invasion nearing, but he couldn't write anything about their activities because the censors would never have cleared the content. At least she knew Peter was alive on May 23.

Ordinary daily life continued, while war news blasted from the radio each evening about the European invasion's progress. Emma helped Bob hay, Mike drill corn rows, and Kate pick strawberries. She cleaned her fishbowl at home, washed and ironed her clothes, cleaned her house, and built her own stove fires when needed on chilly evenings. Emma sewed a plaid skirt, even making the buttonholes herself. Mike repaired her ironing board and put up a shelf for her knickknacks. Kate gave her quarts of milk, since they always had extra. Emma helped can strawberries and pick vegetables as they ripened.

Mrs. Benton gave Emma a spare rug. Emma washed it with soap, used a scrub brush to dig deeply into the pile, and dried it in the sun. Now she had a bedroom rug so her toes would be warm each time she got out of bed. The bare linoleum floors were cool, even in summer.

By Saturday, Emma picked strawberries and helped Bob hay, then went to Maryville to see *Up in Arms*. Danny Kaye operated an elevator in a New York medical building, where he got free advice from doctors who thought he was a hypochondriac. After he received his draft notice, he was devastated, with hilarious results. Emma needed the laughter release after the tensions of the past weeks from the war and waiting for a letter from Peter.

On Sunday, June 11, church attendance rose higher than normal, since everyone prayed the war's end was near. While realizing an advance from the Atlantic coast to Berlin would not happen overnight, they still felt elated the Allies now owned ground in Europe, instead of having to fly over it from England and elsewhere. Hope had returned, even just a little, that their loved ones might be home by Christmas 1944. Please. "Just at least get my boy/father/brother/cousin home! I know it's selfish, but he's such a special person and we need him here." So many sentiments. So many worried hearts.

The car lights became the next repairs. Emma had them fixed while she shopped for feed and groceries in Bolckow. The next day, Emma helped mow, bunch, and pitch hay to Mike in the wagon. By dark, she couldn't move her aching arms.

On Thursday, Emma helped Mike plan the garden and start planting potatoes. She also rode the go-devil cultivator, loosening corn row soil in the area northwest of the river. Later she drove their Chevrolet to Barnard so Kate could get some ice cream to celebrate the day's hard work.

Emma arrived at her house to find the lights were out, which happened fairly frequently. *Oh, well, that's why I keep candles and kerosene lamps.*

For two more days, Emma rode the planter or go-devil. In one morning, they managed to plant twelve acres north of the barn. The good farming weather continued, so they kept working even when bone tired. Who knew when the weather would turn against them, making planting difficult or delayed?

By Saturday evening, Owen, Melinda, and Emma watched *Rationing,* a comedy featuring Wallace Beery and Marjorie Main. Wallace, a grocer, tried to get gas coupons from the female director of the local rationing board. Instead, she, who had been his enemy for twenty years, lectured him on thrift.

Also, he learned his adopted son had joined the Army and was marrying his high school sweetheart, who was the woman's daughter. Emma loved Peter's mother and father and knew her mother loved Peter. She felt they would never have the comedic interfamily issues Wallace and Marjorie faced in the movie.

Emma enjoyed Sunday dinner with the Paxtons. They talked and laughed and decided plans they wanted to do as soon as Peter got home. Even though they didn't know when that might be, they still had fun thinking about the good times to come.

Owen, Melinda, and Emma drove to Hopkins to see *None Shall Escape* on Sunday evening. The setting was a war crimes trial of a Nazi officer. Several witnesses, including a Catholic priest, the officer's brother, and his former fiancé, provided the unfolding story. Emma had read newspaper accounts of war atrocities but hoped at least half of them were untrue. How could people possibly be so cruel to others?

Kate's grandmother died June 17, with the funeral on Monday, June 19. Starting at daylight on Monday, Emma painted a shed and hoed potatoes. Then they all cleaned up for the afternoon funeral. Even with a family funeral looming, farm work had to be done. Young Doug turned twelve years old the same day, growing tall like his father Bob.

By evening, Emma drove home exhausted. Besides the physical work, the emotional reactions to the funeral had drained her. She understood Kate's grandmother had been quite elderly. She couldn't bear the thought of having to go to a funeral for someone close to her again. Losing her father had been a real trauma, so Emma understood, but disliked, the parting funeral rites when people died.

Her reward for her fortitude came when she arrived home to find four little banties had hatched. Her chicken family had increased. Life replaced death once again. She had something of her own to nurture and grow. "Of course, Peter," she said aloud to the empty living room, "I would rather have one of your children to be raising. But chickens will have to do until you get back and marry me!"

The radio announcer brought more good news on Thursday, June 22, 1944. The Soviets had launched a massive offensive in eastern Belarus, destroying the German Army Group Center. By August 1, they expected to be driving westward and nearing Warsaw, Poland. Germany was being squeezed from the east by the Soviets, south and west by the Allies. Surely the final defeat of the Nazis would be inevitable.

June brought more field work for Emma. She rode the planter and go-devil; mowed, raked, and loaded hay; and worked in the garden. Mike paid her for her labor, which made up for not having a teaching salary during the summer.

Emma had the car back in Bolckow on Saturday afternoon. The first fix of the lights had failed, but no mechanic was available. She did use the new ration B coupons for gas.

She spent the night in Bolckow at her grandmother's house. Emma felt her grandmother, who was eighty-two, was aging faster, and she wanted to spend as much time as she could with her. Emma dreaded the day she would lose her grandmother.

By Sunday, Kate had mumps, and the hot weather made her even more uncomfortable. Emma laid linoleum in Kate's kitchen, washed the dishes, and made the beds. Edith got supper for Mike and Kate, for Tommy had been sent to Kate's relatives to keep him away from the sickness.

In the afternoon, Emma drove to Jacob's house. She helped him shell last year's corn, and they ate ice cream. Then she drove home along country dirt roads in darkness broken only by moonlight because her car lights failed completely. Luckily, she knew the roads by heart, having traveled them many times. *I would prefer to have some lights to watch for deer and other critters.*

With the paycheck from Mike, Emma found Peter a birthday present, got her $5.00 car registration sticker, and purchased a new Aladdin lamp. Three letters arrived, so she had enjoyed the day's events.

The next day, Emma drove back to Maryville to pay $3.00 for a car tire repair and $3.28 to have the lights finally correctly fixed. That evening, she helped Owen do chores, then after she enjoyed fried chicken and homemade ice cream, she spent the night.

Melinda came to Maryville with Emma and helped paint the kitchen in the rental house Edith owned. They also painted and moved furniture until late afternoon. After driving home to feed her chickens, Emma cleaned up for a Friday dance in Barnard.

The next day, Emma helped Mae and her family hay. Somehow, a loaded hay wagon turned over when Mae's brother cut a corner too sharply. While it was a mess to right the wagon and reload the hay, Mae and Emma enjoyed teasing her younger brother until he was red-faced. He learned a lesson about showing off how good a farmer he was.

After cleaning up, everyone set off to Maitland for the annual Blue Grass Festival. Emma loved the experience of riding a Ferris wheel and splurged on cotton candy, also.

When she finally returned home in the wee hours of Sunday morning, she found three letters and a pretty card from Peter. How she wished he had been there to take her to the carnival. She wrote him a long letter before finally closing her eyes.

On Monday, July 3, Mrs. Wilkins called to say she would rent Edith's house in Maryville. By Tuesday, Emma and Edith finished painting the kitchen. They cleaned the entire house except for the southeast bedroom, which Mrs. Wilkins had agreed to leave as a storeroom for Edith's remaining furniture.

That evening, although tired, Edith and Emma joined Mike, Kate, and Mae in Savannah to see Heaven Can Wait, a comedy with musical score by Alfred Newman. The film told of a man who had to prove he belonged in Hell by telling his life story. Gene Tierney, Don Ameche, and Charles Coburn starred, supported by Marjorie Main and Spring Byington. *I wish a few people in Hell, like some Axis leaders.*

July had excellent haying weather. Up early, Emma helped Owen rake and bunch hay all day and mowed more hay immediately after supper. The next day, they hayed again, and Emma worked in the loft. As loose hay was forked up into the loft, she pitched it further back, making a pile from back to front. They pitched eleven loads in one day. Emma was covered with tiny hay pieces, which itched and scratched when they slid under her clothes and into her hair. The combination of her sweat and the hay dust made her look a mess by evening.

"I feel like the scarecrow from *The Wizard of Oz*," complained Emma. "I can't wait to take a hot bath and shampoo the dirt and hay out of my hair."

The next day, Emma again helped hay and rode the go-devil.

They celebrated completing the haying that weekend. Her brothers all came to Mike's on Sunday, July 9. The women went to Barnard to enjoy ice cream. Then the entire family had a potluck at a neighbor's house, slurping more homemade ice cream for supper.

After repairing the hay binder by midmorning, Owen began cutting more hay. They also shocked oats all afternoon. Emma ran the binder, which cut the oats and bound the sheaf. Then Owen jammed the sheaf into the ground. He braced two sheaves against each other, then added more sheaves pushed in place to make a nine-sheaf shock that could withstand a high wind. The shocks had to dry before cutting the oats and storing the remaining straw. Then she helped with dinner and washed dishes. She even rode the binder an hour after dinner.

Emma and Owen also helped neighbors shock oats. The weather was such a critical part of haying and shocking oats. The crops had to be harvested before rains came, or the process would be delayed until the plants dried out again. If the rain was too heavy, the hay and oats would become matted to the ground, ruining the crop for that year. Everyone worked from sunup to sundown when the crops were prime for harvesting.

Rain hit off and on all week but was mild. Also, the heavy morning dew had to dry before they could continue work each day. Finally, everyone near Owen's farm had their hay and oats finished. Owen paid Emma $6.88 for her week's work.

Emma celebrated with Owen and Melinda on Sunday, driving them to Hopkins to see *Swing Out the Blues*. The romantic comedy starred Bob Haymes, Lynn Merrick, and Janis Carter. Four struggling musicians decided to perform chamber music at a socialite party. The socialite girl rejected a marriage proposal from a man her dowdy aunt had chosen, declaring to marry the next man who walked in the door, who was the band's leader. Emma laughed as hard as anyone at the story twists, for two hours forgetting her sore muscles and exhaustion.

Bob turned forty years old on Friday, July 21. Emma drove to his house for supper and ice cream. Most of her brothers and their families arrived as an excuse to relax one evening.

On Tuesday, July 25, 1944, the radio blared more good news. Anglo-American forces had broken out of the Normandy beachhead, racing eastward toward Paris. Yes, hard fighting remained, but the Allies controlled more territory in western Europe. The fear was the Nazis would fight even more intensely the closer the Allies came to the German homeland.

Emma joined Mae's family at the Maryville rodeo the next day. Most neighbors attended, for any community event provided a change of pace after spring planting and summer haying. Other crops were maturing. Always farm fences had to be mended, machinery repaired, animals tended, gardens hoed, and food canned. But a rodeo meant playtime for area residents.

That Friday, Edith and Emma officially moved out of their Maryville house. Mrs. Wilkins would move in over the weekend. The rent she paid would be more than the rent Emma paid for her farmhouse. Thus, Edith would still have an income, and Emma would have her mother living with her for company. Edith was sixty-three years old, but her health seemed to be holding steady. Still, Emma preferred to be near her mother, especially when winter icy sidewalks and streets might cause her to slip and fall.

They drove to Rosendale with friends on Saturday afternoon to see *Lassie Come Home*. Roddy McDowall and dog Pal showed the strong bond between a Yorkshire boy and his collie. The movie would be the first of seven Lassie films.

Radio news announced on August 1, 1944, the noncommunist underground Home Army in Poland had risen against the Germans in an effort to liberate Warsaw. The Poles wanted to control their capital before Soviet troops arrived, not wanting the Communists to overrun Poland.

Emma took her niece Alice to the schoolhouse on Thursday. She gave Alice a book to read and showed her the school. Tommy stayed with Emma and Alice that night so the two cousins could play together. The next evening, eight-year-old Alice insisted on going to the Barnard dance with Emma, which would not be an acceptable thing to do. Alice refused to stay with Edith while Emma went, so Emma had to give up going to the dance. But a heavy rain appeared, so nobody got to go.

Mrs. Wilkins called on Saturday. The house sewer line was plugged up. Edith, Mae, and Emma drove to Maryville and called a plumber. The man couldn't do anything until Monday, so Mrs. Wilkins had to use the outhouse. Luckily, it was summer and not winter, so she accepted the situation with fairly good grace. On Monday, the plumber installed new sewer lines to repair the problem.

Emma also visited Mr. Burr, picked up her new teaching unit for the fall semester, and got the book list and her required health certificate. She bought some school supplies from her allotted budget and brought them home.

War events began rapid-fire successes as August progressed. On August 15, radio news came of Allied forces landing in southern France near Nice. They were quickly advancing northeast toward the Rhine River. The Allies would enter the German homeland when they crossed the Rhine. Everyone listening was ecstatic with hope for the war's end by late 1944.

More radio news blared on August 25. Allied troops had liberated Paris. Allied and Free French forces had entered the city. Local citizens had kissed; hugged; waved American, English, and French flags; and provided uncounted bottles of wine to celebrate. Huge crowds jammed the Paris streets, laughing for the first time since the Nazis had captured the city on June 14, 1940.

Emma spent the remainder of the summer on various activities. She sewed clothes for herself for the next school term, including a brown skirt and a new jacket. She cleaned inside the schoolhouse. On August 11, she and Mike's family enjoyed their first home-grown fried chicken meal. She visited friends and family, loving the homemade ice cream and food she didn't have to cook herself. They canned peaches, vegetables, and other foodstuffs and made apple butter. She played cards and dominoes with friends and put together jigsaw puzzles. There were picnics, community fish fries, overnight stays, riding Peter's horse old Beaut, and going to movies.

In Bedford, Owen, Melinda, and Emma saw *A Lady in the Dark*, with lyrics by Ira Gershwin. An unhappy female fashion magazine editor underwent psychoanalysis, with laughs growing out of her experiences. *Most of the world's leaders need mental help from causing a stupid war that's costing so many millions of lives.*

Toward late August, Mike, Kate, and Emma saw Salute to the Marines in Bolckow. The propaganda drama headlined Wallace Beery and Noah Beery, Sr. and was set in the Philippines. When the Japanese invaded, a retired Marine sergeant confronted and strangled a Nazi secret agent, who was spreading anti-American, pro-Japanese views among the native Filipinos. Even realizing the pro-Allies movie slant, Emma could understand the anger and wish to restore life as it used to be before any Axis power had changed the world forever.

Emma painted the schoolhouse hall on August 31. She finished oiling the floor and cleaned the basement. She also finished reading *Bambi, A Life in the Woods*. The 1923 Austrian novel by Felix Salten traced the life of Bambi, a male roe deer, from his birth through adulthood. The book was considered a classic and one of the first environmental novels. Though the story had sad sections, Emma loved the simplicity of the story and viewing life through the eyes of a deer. *If only real life could be as straightforward, but even humans are being targeted by hunters' guns now.*

Emma studied even harder to prepare her lessons. The first teachers' meeting came Saturday, September 2, 1944. On the way home, she stopped in Barnard and bought more paint to finish the schoolroom.

On Monday, she celebrated Jacob turning thirty-seven years old by driving all the way to Lake Contrary near St. Jo for dinner with Jacob's, Mike's, and Owen's families at a restaurant. Later they watched *The Saint Meets the Tiger,* a crime thriller, the last of eight Saint movies, with Templar investigating a body left on his doorstep. The search led him to a quiet seaside village in Cornwall where he pursued a mysterious villain known as Tiger. Emma loved seeing the English countryside, imagining Peter getting to see similar sites, wherever his base was located.

Harmon school began on Monday, September 4. Mary Cooper turned ten, and Shelly Williams was absent in the afternoon, having thrown up during the noon hour.

Peter sent a photograph in one of two letters that arrived on Thursday. Excited, she hurried down to Mike's house to show everyone. Even Edith and Grandmother Bailey were there, so all admired Peter's picture and remarked on how he had changed since he had left Missouri.

More radio good news blared on September 12. Finland signed an armistice with the Soviet Union, exiting the Axis partnership. Four days earlier, Bulgaria surrendered to the Allies and Romania to the Soviets. The Axis alliance was fracturing all around the ever-shrinking Nazi-controlled territory.

Emma's schoolwork continued as if no war existed. She cleaned the blackboard, scrubbed the basement floor, studied lessons, graded papers, and cleaned up after students who became ill. In the evenings, she studied or graded papers and wrote letters to Peter. Life seemed so ordinary in some ways, but the radio and newspaper reports heralded a different reality outside her small world.

Tommy sometimes came after school and helped his Aunt Emma clean up. He was still too young to attend classes, but he wished he could. *I wonder if the war will last so long that five-year-old Tommy will be drafted before it's over?*

Emma played hard with her students at recess. The schoolyard was large enough for most games. Emma managed to hit her first home run of the year on Thursday. She was pleased with her efforts. *Although I had four older brothers, I'm certainly not a tomboy.*

Peter's birthday was Friday, September 15, and one of Emma's students, Linda Cooper, turned twelve that day, too. Emma didn't get to celebrate with either person, since she had a teachers' meeting in Maryville.

But in the evening, Emma got a birthday cake for Peter. She and Gladys ate dinner together, singing "Happy Birthday" to Peter and enjoying part of his cake. They even toasted him with a Pepsi-Cola. "I wish he was here so I could hug him tightly and kiss him once for each year of his life."

On Saturday, Gladys and Emma drove to Pickering to mail Peter his cake. They had cut it down to meet the war mailing size requirements. "I don't care if the cake will probably be petrified by the time Peter gets it. I just want him to know I wished him well on his birthday," she told Gladys.

Unfortunately, Peter's horse, old Beaut, died of sleeping sickness that week. The virus traveled a continual circuit between birds and mosquitoes. After biting an infected bird, the mosquito would then bite the horse, spreading the disease. Some horses had a spontaneous death without any physical signs of illness or behavioral changes. With no treatment available, the mortality rate neared ninety percent. Old Beaut died within a few hours, and Emma knew Gene dreaded having to write Peter about his favorite horse. Peter would blame himself for not being home to care for Beaut, or at least be at his old friend's side. War caused such painful separations, whether it was a relative or a pet that died while the men were overseas.

Owen, Melinda, and Emma attended the Saturday midnight show in Maryville. *The Impatient Years,* a romance, featured Jean Arthur in her final film for Columbia. She and Lee Bowman played two people in court for their divorce. Her father (Charles Coburn) suggested the couple return for four days to San Francisco where they met and retrace all their steps, including getting remarried. *I love the romance but can't imagine Peter and I needing a divorce.*

Emma went with Janie to Sunday School and church in Pickering. They prayed hard for the war to be over soon and Peter to come home safely. For Sunday dinner, Janie splurged on a fresh pineapple. Emma had never tried to cut one, and she discovered how thick the skin was but how wonderful the fresh tidbits could be.

By evening, she met Owen and Melinda and drove to Hopkins to see *Cover Girl.* The musical, starring Rita Hayworth and Gene Kelly, became one of the most popular musicals of the war years. The lavish 1940s costumes, eight dance routines, and songs by Jerome Kern and Ira Gershwin produced a major hit. Rita, a chorus girl, worked in a nightclub owned by Kelly. Otto Kruger played a wealthy magazine editor who offered her stardom. Twists of life produced great entertainment, but Emma knew she would never let Peter go when he got home.

Emma decided to take piano lessons. She practiced her fingering most evenings on the school's piano before going home for supper, and she took lessons on Saturdays in Maryville.

On Tuesday, Mike and Melinda asked Edith and Emma to ride to Guilford for a show. Mike's car ran out of gas on the way, luckily near a friend's house. The neighbor gave them enough from his farm fuel tank to get them to Guilford and back. They saw *Destination Tokyo,* with Cary Grant and John Garfield. The black and white submarine film was based on an original story by a former submariner. *I could never serve in the cramped space of a submarine, for I'm slightly claustrophobic.*

Emma relaxed at her lunch on Wednesday. The children were outside playing and eating. For a few precious moments, she didn't have to talk to anyone or answer any questions. She chewed her sandwich in peaceful contentment.

Then she heard an ear-piercing scream. She dropped her food, shoved back her chair, and ran for the front door and down the few steps. In the schoolyard was a black snake about three feet long. Mary's screams had frightened the snake as much as they had Emma.

"Doyle, get the baseball bat," yelled Emma. When he raced to bring it, Emma took a deep breath before slamming the bat's end onto the snake's head. A few twitches later, the snake lay dead in the grass.

"Good hit, Miss Trotter," approved one boy.

Emma just grimaced, for she disliked killing any animal, even a snake.

"I'll throw it over the fence," the boy offered.

Emma nodded. She really had not wanted to pick up the dead snake. Such was life in a one-room country school.

As Emma drove to Harwood's farm for milkweed pods to decorate the schoolroom, the car began missing a little. She would have to take it back to the mechanic. *Will this car ever quit having issues?* she wondered. Still, she preferred spending the money for repairs to asking friends and family for rides.

Peter's three most recent letters arrived on Friday. In two, he had sent pretty handkerchiefs Emma admired. She wrote another thank-you letter, also telling him about the snake incident.

Mae and Emma drove to Savannah on Saturday. They had to push the car up the crest of two muddy hills but did so without putting on chains. Mae pushed the back bumper, while Emma shoved against the open driver's door while steering with her right hand. They managed to get to the theater on time to see *Frisco Kid* starring James Cagney about the 1850s gold fever in San Francisco and political corruption.

On September 25, Emma built the first stove fire for the term. Shelly

Williams hurt her finger playing baseball. Mary Cooper got her foot caught in the fence wire while retrieving a ball. Mike got the car's spark plug changed, so the car ran well at last. He also bought a bushel of peaches in St. Jo. That evening, Edith cut her finger while fixing carrots for dinner, climaxing an eventful day.

On September 28, Emma got her first pay warrant for the year for $102.60. She felt rich and planned to begin seriously saving her money. The war news, while still serious, sounded more hopeful every day. *Maybe by Christmas the war will be over, and Peter can come home.* Emma wanted to have enough to buy a wedding dress, get a few curtains and such for their house when they found one, and get a welcome home dress so she would look her best when Peter stepped off his final bus. Then she would hug him so tightly he would never want to let her out of his sight again. Ever.

Emma added money at the bank and spent money to get the car's brakes tightened on Saturday. After paying for her second piano lesson, she celebrated with Helen and Alice at the evening Maple Grove school carnival. Emma won a lunch tablecloth and a pie plate playing bingo. They had a great time, getting to talk with friends and the Maple Grove teacher.

Kate had not been feeling well. She had been to the doctor in St. Jo a couple of times. Finally, it was decided she had to have her tonsils removed. Mike took Kate to St. Jo for the operation, which went well. Tommy spent the night with Edith and Emma, sleeping in Emma's bed because he was worried about his mom. The next day, Edith kept Tommy while Emma taught school.

Emma got a ride to Maryville for a morning teachers' meeting, which meant school was canceled. She took a bus back to the Midway corner. She had been running late that morning, couldn't find her overshoes, so she left the house without them. Now she faced having to walk over a mile home from Midway in her sandals over muddy roads. But her problem didn't match Mike's.

As Mike drove Kate home, his car got stuck in the mud a half mile away. He left Kate in the car and trudged through the muck. He got his tractor, then drove back to pull out the car. Kate didn't like to drive, but she had to steer the car while in neutral so Mike could drive the tractor back to the farm.

Two days later, Emma hitched a ride with a friend to Criss's station at the Barnard turnoff. There she took a bus to Maryville for another teachers' meeting. They listened to Roy Scantlin, superintendent of the Missouri State

Department of Education. Emma felt honored that Mr. Scantlin took his time to update Maryville area teachers on new legislation and other issues. The meeting continued the next day, so Emma spent the night with a friend.

They saw the comedy *Mr. Winkle Goes to War* starring Edward G. Robinson and Ruth Warrick. After fourteen years, a mild-mannered forty-four-year-old banker quit to follow his dream to open a repair shop. His status-conscious wife demanded he choose between her and his new career. Before he could decide, the Army drafted him. Emma could never think of quitting a high-paying job like his to begin in a new field with a doubtful salary. *I like having a steady paycheck each week.*

While in town, Emma bought a bath set for Peter for Christmas. The mail system still required sending Christmas packages early, so Emma mailed her gift to Peter on Tuesday, September 25, 1944. *I hope he'll be home before it even arrives in England.*

On October 13, 1944, the radio highlighted exciting news. The Allies had liberated Athens. Allied forces planned to push the Nazis out of Greece by November toward the Balkans, which they still controlled.

The area ladies met at Emma's school and decided to have a carnival, planning the activities and food. Emma worked hard to organize the efforts. Her students made carnival posters to place in local stores in Barnard, Bolckow, Guilford, Midway, and Maryville. Emma worked on invitations.

While in Maryville, Emma shopped for carnival prizes and took her fourth music lesson. She tried to practice after school each day, but sometimes she was just too tired and wanted to get home. She sold her hens' eggs to the Barnard grocer each week to pay for the music lessons.

The radio announced the Hungarian government wanted to pursue negotiations for surrender to the Soviets. But the fascist Arrow Cross movement succeeded in a coup d'état with German support to prevent the shift. Hungary remained in the Axis alliance.

In Savannah, Mike, Kate, and Emma watched *Standing Room Only,* a comedy starring Fred MacMurray and Paulette Goddard. When Fred's secretary was fired, Paulette talked her way into the job, pretending to have secretarial skills. Fred's sweetheart was the company owner's daughter. Paulette's attempts to handle her job produced hilarious results. Sometimes, Emma felt that way about being a teacher. *No one at the college taught me how to kill a snake or wipe up vomit as part of my education courses.*

Emma took her students into Mike's field to pick milkweeds for school decorations, quickly filling two feed sacks. After school, Emma rode with Mike to Barnard, where they paid for coal for Emma's house and school and ordered ice cream for the carnival. The next day, students again worked on invitations and posters. Emma used art class to create the posters.

On Saturday, Edith, Kate, and Emma won prizes playing bingo in Maryville, and Emma had another piano lesson. She also tacked up carnival posters. In the evening, Emma counted jellybeans in a Mason quart jar and wrote the number inside her grade book so she wouldn't forget it before the carnival arrived.

The children gathered more milkweed pods during the week, using Emma's car to bring them back. Also, they worked on a bingo stand made using some boards and egg crates. Emma placed the presents in the bookcase and decorated inside and outside the schoolhouse with milkweed pods.

On Friday, October 27, 1944, carnival day arrived. Mrs. Watson won a beautiful blanket, and Lois Baker got the grocery bag filled with canned goods. The school netted over $84.00, so the school board beamed with pride. Mike took the leftover ice cream back to Barnard late that evening, and everyone cleaned up most of the school grounds. Emma got to bed about two in the morning.

She slept in slightly Saturday morning then met six people at the school at ten. They picked up trash from the yard, mopped the schoolhouse floor, and took bottles and other items to Barnard to recycle to support the war effort. Emma paid the bills in Barnard, then drove to Maryville for a piano lesson. She also cashed her second pay warrant. By dark, she realized she had a head cold.

Even feeling ill, Emma joined two friends to see *Wing and a Prayer* in Savannah. The black and white movie showed the heroic crew of an American carrier in the desperate early days of World War II in the Pacific. Don Ameche and Dana Andrews starred in the classic propaganda movie. *I'm so glad Peter is serving in England instead of aboard a ship.*

Mr. Raskin, a book agent, rode with one mother around the area. They collected $25 in book orders. With the school's portion, Emma bought a set of six nature books.

Emma made it through classes the first two days of the week. Her cold hung on, but she still had to go to Barnard after school for kerosene for her home lamps. While her rented house did have one overhead bulb in each room, the power lines often broke during storms. It usually took the electric company many hours to get everyone's wires repaired, so lamps became backup lights.

Emma had another piano lesson in Maryville and visited Gene and Janie Paxton. They presented Emma with an early birthday present of a lovely white sweater as Peter's gift to her. Emma wrote to thank Peter and received a letter from him.

National election day arrived Tuesday, November 7, 1944. Edith and Emma drove to Mike's for supper then listened to the national broadcasts. Roosevelt was leading over Dewey, and everyone went to bed hoping Roosevelt would win—again. "I can't imagine the country installing a new president with the final war push so near. Roosevelt's been the steady rock through the end of the Depression, the pre-war years, and these frightening war years. He's earned the right to see the war to its conclusion," said Emma to the group.

The next morning, the radio announced Roosevelt had been re-elected, carrying thirty-four states. Emma was thrilled.

At school, she gave out grade cards for her pupils to take home. Her students had worked hard and deserved their good grades. She was proud of them and told them so.

Emma celebrated with Mike and Kate in Savannah by going to see *The Story of Dr. Wassell.* Set in the Dutch East Indies, the film was directed by Cecil B. DeMille. Gary Cooper starred as U.S. Navy Doctor Corydon M. Wassell, of whom President Roosevelt had spoken in a radio broadcast in April 1942. *I wonder how many noncombatants were caught on islands around the world when the war broke out.*

The new school unit on "Land Transportation" began that week. Also, Emma bought material for the girls to learn to make blouses from patterns as part of their schoolwork. The first school term ended the next day.

After spending Friday night at Owen's house, Emma helped drain her car's radiator the next morning. They refilled it and added alcohol to keep it from freezing during the coming winter's cold.

On Monday, Emma thrilled to get five letters from Peter including a V-mail birthday card. She also got the new *Look* magazine and the *Wee Wisdom* children's publication for the school.

Amid cold temperatures and strong winds, the school board held a meeting on Wednesday evening. Emma attended, and they seemed pleased with her work and the carnival funds raised. The book sales money also helped the budget.

The family celebrated Emma's birthday on Monday evening, November 17, three days early. Emma received five cards, the sweater from Peter, a pair of shorts from Edith, and a tablecloth from Ruth Roberts. Everyone devoured the ice cream Mike and Kate brought. She also got phone calls from Mae and Owen.

The first snow arrived with a few flakes on Tuesday, and every student was present. After school, Emma drove to Barnard for a stove pipe for the school. The old one had developed a hole, and the schoolroom kept lightly filling with smoke.

That evening, Mae gave Emma eau de cologne for her birthday. Another couple gave her a picture. Owen delivered a Fiestaware coffee pot, a card, and a birthday cake. She loved her brothers so much, and they took good care of their little sister. They all went to the Barnard carnival that evening, staying out late to celebrate Thanksgiving break.

The family ate Thanksgiving dinner on November 23 with Mike and Kate's family. In the afternoon, Emma helped Mike shuck one round of corn. She bought a bushel and removed the kernels using the hand sheller.

That evening, she drove to Mae's house and on to Savannah to see *The White Cliffs of Dover*. Based on the Alice Duer Miller poem "The White Cliffs," the movie showed Lady Susan Ashwood (Irene Dunne) as a nurse in a British hospital, awaiting the arrival of wounded men. *I want to believe someone nice like Lady Ashwood will be there if Peter ever needs help. But I refuse to think about Peter getting wounded. The war is too close to ending.*

By Friday, school was in session again. Every student except one and Emma had head colds. The daily chills, walking to school in the off-and-on rain, and sitting in class in wet shoes and clothes kept her students' health questionable.

A disagreeable Saturday arrived rainy and misty all day. Mike, Kate, Edith, and Emma drove to St. Jo to shop. Emma bought each schoolboy a new billfold as a Christmas present and paid sixty-nine cents for a new blouse for herself. Driving in the mud tore a car chain coming back, so she and Edith spent the night at Mike's house. He managed to fix the chain on Sunday.

As Emma tried to gather eggs on Tuesday, an old hen pecked her glasses so hard they broke. She taped them together to make it through the school day.

Wednesday evening, Emma got her pay warrant signed. She mailed it in to cover some Liberty Bonds she had purchased on the sixth national drive.

The children practiced for the Christmas program. Emma wrote the parts, and the students decorated thirty-one program covers.

Saturday found Emma in Maryville at her piano lesson, followed by shopping. She had looked all day for new shucking gloves and finally found four pairs. So many farmers were harvesting that stores couldn't keep up. She also bought Kate a pair of overshoes she needed.

The next day, Edith fell on the ice, severely striking her elbow, luckily not breaking it. Emma got breakfast and did all the outdoor work.

Emma was reading *Donald and Dorothy* to her students, which they loved. Mary Maples Dodge, who wrote the book in 1883, was also the author of Hans Brinker in 1865.

Three of Peter's letters arrived Thursday. He had received all three of Emma's packages on November 26. *I've reread his letters so often I think the paper will disintegrate.*

The holidays were nearing. Emma got $4.20 from her eggs sold in Barnard and used some of the money to buy more chicken feed. Despite the snowy roads, she and Mike's family went to Savannah to see *Old Barn Dance,* a Western starring Gene Autry, Smiley Burnett, and Joan Valerie. A cowboy and his buddies had a horse-selling business threatened by a tractor company that claimed horses were out of date. Any time she could see a Western, Emma was happy. They spent the night in Savannah, not daring to travel home on the snow-packed roads.

Everyone around Maryville and the nation felt more lighthearted as the 1944 holiday season approached. The recent war news had been so encouraging. On all fronts, the Germans had retreated, being hammered by Allied bombings and troop advancements. On the east, the Soviets left few prisoners as they pushed forward. The Allies on the west and south headed for Berlin as fast as they could overcome the dwindling German strength. Since the United States had declared war on Germany and Italy on December 11, 1941, hope had been in short supply. Now, hope filled the air, and people looked forward to Christmas much more than any of the last three years.

Hitler, however, was determined to crush the Allies in one final push. On Saturday, December 16, 1944, the Germans fired the first shots in the Ardennes offensive in Belgium to begin the Battle of the Bulge. The military situation in Belgium had been fairly quiet, with troops looking forward to

Christmas packages from home and feeling overconfident of the war's end. Then all hell broke loose on the Western Front, with the Allies almost being surrounded in a surprise attack through the densely forested eastern Belgium region. The Germans intended to split the Allied lines, encircling and destroying four Allied armies. They hoped the move would force the Allies to negotiate a peace treaty in Germany's favor.

On the home front, schoolwork continued, even though the students' minds tended to drift, either outside to the snow piling up or toward thoughts of Christmas presents to come. Still they tried. Emma explained the huge battle raging in Europe to her students, who listened with their parents each evening to radio updates.

A neighbor offered a tree from his field for the school. Emma picked it up on Sunday and a friend set it up. She continued to wrap presents at home and sacked candy for her students. At school, the children also worked on holiday gifts. Everyone continued to practice the play parts and songs.

Finally, on Friday evening, December 22, the program began with one neighbor dressed as Santa Claus. The children remembered all their speeches. The students and Emma had drawn names for class presents. Linda Cooper had Emma's name and gave her a billfold. Each family gave Emma something: makeup, a pair of bookends, stationary, and a handkerchief. Emma was very touched by their thoughtfulness. She truly loved all her students, even the mischievous ones. Mae gave her a Fiestaware gravy bowl and glass candle holders, more to add to her hope chest. Kate gave her a flower. The evening program was considered a huge success.

Emma and Mae finished cleaning the schoolhouse Saturday morning. They even moved the Christmas tree to Emma's house. On Christmas day, the family gathered there for their celebration and gift exchange. Emma felt so grateful for all of her gifts, including a bracelet, a Fiestaware plate and meat fork, a card table, a sweater, pants, hose, a photo of Edith, a Pyrex plate, a jelly dish, and a fuzzy yarn dog. Her family also felt the end of the war was near and were giving her items to plan for her wedding they knew would happen as soon as Peter returned.

Emma came down with another cold, but it didn't stop the holiday fun. Mike, Kate, Edith, and Emma drove to Savannah to see Going My Way. The musical comedy-drama starred Bing Crosby and Barry Fitzgerald. A new younger priest took over a parish from an established older priest. Crosby sang five songs, and the Robert Mitchell Boys Choir was featured. The film became the highest-grossing picture of 1944 and was nominated for ten Academy Awards, winning seven. Emma loved to hear Bing croon every chance she got.

The last day of 1944 was a Sunday. Emma had arrived home from a movie at one thirty in the morning, so she enjoyed sleeping late. After dinner, she worked at school, then studied more at home. All she could think about, though, was how near the end of the war appeared. The Battle of the Bulge still raged, but surely the Nazis would lose the fight and the Allies would continue their march to Berlin. *My only wish for 1945 is for Peter to be safely home and in my arms again.*

Chapter 37

New Year's Day 1945 should have been a true celebration of hope and the end of the war in sight. Instead, everyone became fearful Germany might remain strong longer than anticipated.

The local newspaper carried battle details. In Belgium, heavily overcast skies kept Allied and German air forces grounded. Finally, the Germans' forward momentum stalled, and the Allies reinforced their thinly placed troops. The weather improved, and the far superior Allied air forces attacked German troops and supply lines. The Battle of the Bulge finally ended on January 25, 1945, as the largest and bloodiest single battle fought by the United States during the war and one of the costliest battles in American history.

With the loss of so many troops and huge quantities of war materiel, Germany had no reserves left. The Allied forces began flooding toward Berlin. The closer the Allies came to the capital city, the more fiercely the Germans fought to defend their homeland. With constant Allied bombing of factories and cities, the German civilian population morale dropped to total survival mode. Even German high commanders knew the war was unwinnable, yet Hitler refused to surrender.

The war news developed so rapidly during the first months of 1945 that Emma had trouble keeping up. Each time she listened to the radio or read a newspaper, she knew Peter was closer to coming home.

Emma began the school semester with hope and fear fighting to control her heart. Surely the Nazis could not last much longer, but the Battle of the Bulge would determine the answer. She just wanted Peter safely home and feared the B-17s he maintained would play a key role in the Bulge push. He must be overwhelmed with work to keep the planes in the air. She felt deep sorrow for all the lives being lost by both Allies and Axis personnel, plus civilians caught in war zones.

Her students continued their studies, but they felt the tensions from newspaper reports, radio announcements, and parental conversations about war efforts. The students had relatives and friends overseas. Many local military people had been lost or were now in imminent danger.

On January 12, the Soviets launched an offensive to liberate Warsaw and Krakow, Poland. They captured Budapest on February 13 after a two-month siege. On April 13, they captured Vienna from the remaining Nazi forces.

Leaders of the United Kingdom, United States, and the Union of Soviet Socialist Republics held a final conference in Yalta. From February 4 through 11, 1945, Churchill, Roosevelt, and Stalin debated the post-war peace. The goal was a collective security order and a plan to give self-determination to the liberated citizens of post-Nazi Europe. The result held five Points of Agreement:

- Germany and Austria would be divided into four occupation zones.
- Germany would owe reparations, including using German soldiers as slave labor.
- New borders would be established for Poland and Germany, with the USSR controlling East Poland and Poland gaining East Germany.
- Nazi war criminals would be prosecuted.
- Germany would have to be denazified and demilitarized.

Stalin also agreed to help fight the Japanese to end the Pacific war.

American troops crossed the Rhine River at Remagen on March 7. The Germans had wired the bridge with nearly 6,200 pounds of demolition charges, but only part exploded when the departing troops detonated them. Thus, one of the last bridges across the Rhine was still standing when the Allies arrived to allow rapid transport of five divisions into the Ruhr, Germany's industrial heartland. Finding the bridge intact and crossing it shortened the war.

Emma joined everyone in the United States in shock when President Roosevelt died on April 12, 1945, from a massive cerebral hemorrhage. He had been the only president many citizens had known. He had first been inaugurated on March 4, 1933, when Emma was only twelve years old.

Most citizens knew little about Harry Truman, who had taken the oath as the 33rd U.S. President on April 12. Missourians knew his political background there, but Truman was a total unknown on how he would handle foreign policy, let alone end the war.

On Monday, April 16, the Soviets launched their final offensive and encircled Berlin. Although the city had been bombed almost to rubble, the fierce fighting meant soldiers had to struggle building to building to capture the capital.

The majority of the world rejoiced on Monday, April 30, 1945. Hitler and Eva Braun committed suicide in his Berlin bunker. By May 7, Germany unconditionally surrendered to the western Allies, and two days later, to the Soviets.

V-E Day, Victory in Europe, had finally arrived! The European war was over! Guns ceased firing. Flags waved. Citizens laughed, cried, and hugged each other in delight around the world. Yet the war to defeat Japan would rage until August 14, 1945.

Emma could only rejoice. "Peter's lived through the war and will be coming home!" she laughed to Mae. Now she didn't have to worry any more.

Yes, she realized many logistics had to be settled in Europe before all the troops could head home. Many of the early enlistees or draftees had been gone over three years. American families wanted their fathers, sons, brothers, uncles, cousins, and friends who voluntarily enlisted or had been drafted to be returned home immediately. They were not permanent soldiers, and many had not wanted to be drafted in the first place. "Send our boys home now!" was the prevalent feeling on the home front. The war was over, so let the regular military forces settle the peace terms.

The United States began Operation Magic Carpet, the demobilization of some of the three million military men in Europe. Four unit categories were created. Category I personnel were to remain in Europe, with 337,000 staying in Germany. Category II became one million soldiers who would soon be transferred to the Pacific war against Japan. For Category III, soldiers would be reorganized and retrained before being reclassified into Category I or II. Finally, Category IV troops consisted of soldiers who qualified for discharge under the point system, planned to be 2.25 million between V-E day and December 1946. Upon arriving stateside, soldiers, sailors, and marines would undergo final out-processing at various military bases.

Emma eagerly waited to learn under which category Peter would be placed. She just wanted him home now, not later.

Peter's letters indicated he had spent V-E Day fighting a cold and waiting to hear when he might get sent home. He wrote of wanting to drive down and see Emma and wanted her to continue her music lessons. How he missed his sweetheart and wanted to get home soon.

On May 20, Peter wrote, "So you are keeping your fingers crossed for that homeward journey. Well don't think I haven't. Guess it is all we can do and I am sure hoping." He also kidded Emma about how her young chickens should be ready to fry by now, knowing she loved some of them like pets.

All May, Peter asked about her school and how her brothers were getting along with their crops. The Maryville area had a rainy month, so farmers had to work around wet ground to get crops planted.

Finally, his letter of May 23 sounded more hopeful.

"Well Mom ask about how many Points I had, so expect you wonder the same. I have 81 and there is talk that we will git two more stars wich would make me 91 Points. Don't know if that means any thing or not but may be it will help in time. Here is hoping for I am sure gitting more anxious to git back to Missouri. It sure will take us a long time to git through talking won't it. Maybe as late as it was once on July 4."

Peter was able to get paid and a pass on June 1 to visit London. He saw some shows, walked around a lot, and shot a roll of film. He said the best part was getting back to base and finding five letters from Emma.

Emma had thought about trying to get a teaching position in St. Jo. The pay there was higher, but she would be farther from her mother and family. Even Maryville teachers made more than the country one-room school marms. If Peter were to come back soon, however, Emma wanted to be closer to him near Pickering.

On June 3, Peter mentioned he hoped a certain old maid schoolteacher would be waiting when he got home. Many soldiers were marrying English girls, and he had heard through letters how some Missouri women had not waited for their former boyfriends to return from the war before they had married other local men. Now the European war had ended, everyone felt eager to begin a normal life of marriage, home, and family.

With each letter from Peter, Emma quickly tore it open and read the contents as fast as her eyes could scan the page the first time. She kept hoping for one incredible message telling her he was homeward bound. Her emotions would fall when no news arrived about his leaving England. Then she would reread his letter more carefully, enjoying his words and his future plans for them.

Even the continually rainy month of June brought disappointment to farmers. Peter talked of how he missed working with Owen to bring in the hay and looked forward to it when he got home. He missed home-grown fruits and vegetables.

His letter on June 5 said, "I don't believe I told you about seeing the fresh Peaches in London. I saw a few in windows on display. I Priced them and they were ten shillings each. Wich would be about two dollars in our money. I believe that would be a little high don't you."

Even with the war over, food supply shortages in England continued. At least supply convoys no longer worried about being torpedoed by German U-boats.

Gene Paxton had a new colt that needed breaking to ride. Peter hoped he would be home in time to do the training and get to ride again.

Emma had written Peter about her leading Mike's horse to plow the large potato patch.

Peter replied, "Know what I thought when I read that. Well I thought that is the way these English farm. Always one leading the horse."

Finally, at long last, a letter arrived in early July 1945. Peter had received his orders to leave England! Emma's hands shook as she read his words. He didn't know where he was going, but he would write as soon as he got back to some U.S. base. How he missed her and would settle for a long-overdue furlough. Anything to get closer to her and home. He still didn't know when he would muster out completely.

By mid-July, Peter wrote from Jefferson Barracks, which had been converted into one of the largest Army separation centers, located eleven miles south of St. Louis. Peter wanted Emma to come to see him, since he didn't know when he might get any leave.

Crying with happiness, Emma rushed to telephone Janie. When she heard the news of Peter's location, Janie started crying, too.

"Oh, my dear stars," Janie wept. "He's back in the States! And he's well and nearly comin' home! Oh, my, oh, my dear boy!"

"I'm going to pack my suitcase now and find out how to get to the barracks," Emma laughed. "Do you want to come, Janie?"

Janie started crying harder. "There's nothin' I want more, but I sprained my ankle yesterday and can't hardly walk on it. No way I can make it on and off a bus and all the way clear to St. Louey and back! Oh, drat the luck!"

"Oh, no," sympathized Emma, who knew how much Janie loved Peter. "I'll take my camera and take lots of pictures. At least you'll see he's really alive and well and how much he's changed since he's been gone. I just can't stop shaking from excitement!"

As soon as she hung up, Emma called the operator for the bus company number. She wrote down the times and where she needed to catch the buses out of St. Jo and Kansas City. Then she called her family and notified them of the good news.

"Well, I'll be," exclaimed Owen. "You mean that man didn't wise up while he was gone and still wants to marry you?" he teased. "I'll just have to have a talk with him when he gets here and tell him how you've been a goin' out with other guys while he was gone and how you been a promisin' to marry a bunch of them."

Emma just laughed. "You do that, and I'll make you wish you'd never been born!" she threatened jokingly. "Besides, Peter wants to help you hay and get back to farming as quickly as he can. You might be needing a hired hand and he'd be a good one. That is until we get married and get our own place."

Emma wrote Peter about her plans and mailed the letter special delivery. She had to wait before leaving to see if he could get a pass. Finally, he wrote he could get a one-day pass on July 29, 1945, and told her how to contact him when she got to town.

Driving her car to St. Jo, she parked in the bus station parking lot and rode a bus to Kansas City. There she boarded the St. Louis bus, arriving early in the evening and finding an inexpensive hotel room for the night.

At eight the next morning, Emma exited a taxi at the Jefferson Barracks gate. She asked for Peter, who was waiting nearby. He showed the guard his pass, walked through the gates, and threw his arms around Emma, pulling her off her feet and swinging her in a circle so many times she felt dizzy.

"Oh, my sweetheart," Peter gushed. "How many times I done dreamed of doing that over the last two years!"

Emma couldn't breathe from his tight squeeze, but she didn't care. She just held his face between her hands and began kissing him. He finally eased up on his grip and ran one hand onto the back of her neck, pulling her closer for a deeper kiss. He didn't care about the whistles from other soldiers also leaving base.

"Let's get some privacy," he urged, leading her to where several taxis waited. "Take us to the nearest park," he told the driver.

At a small park, Peter paid the cabbie and, gripping her arm, led Emma along a path overlooking the River Des Peres. They found a secluded bench, but quickly embraced again before they sat down. They just clung to each other, kissing and touching.

"Oh, you're real and here and not injured at all," whispered Emma.

Peter alternately squeezed her tightly and then released her to give her a deep kiss. They couldn't let go, trying to convince themselves they were truly together again.

"I was sort of afeared you wouldn't want to wait for me," Peter said. "I kept a hopin' but couldn't a blamed you if you hadn't. I know there was guys at home that must of ask' you out a lot."

Emma stared straight into his eyes. "You're the one I want," she replied. "Sure, my girlfriends and I went to some dances and enjoyed ourselves. But I kept wishing the guy I was dancing with was you," she said sincerely.

"But you don't listen to Owen when he tells you I've been going out with other guys!" she laughed. "He threatened to tell you all kinds of lies, but you know he's just teasing us both!"

Peter threw his head back and laughed heartily. "Well, I'll just have to have a good talk with him and see whether I believe him or you! I've heard stories about how few guys were left a' home and how the gals was chasin' all of 'em."

"Well," Emma coyly replied, "some of the sailors at the college did look really great in those white uniforms! And some were pretty good dancers! But I was waiting for you to get home. I didn't want to be dancing with any-one but you, Peter."

Peter grabbed her again, breathing in the scent of her perfume and the feel of her next to him. "Well, those guys are gone now, and I'll be home soon for good. And I think my shotgun is still a sittin' in the closet at home. If any of those boys stray onto my property and try to take what's mine, I'll just have to show 'em they's wrong."

Emma smiled. She was so proud of Peter for following his heart and enlisting, even if it did mean they had been apart far too long. He looked so handsome in his uniform, having filled out even more muscles and matured some in his face since she had last seen him. But his eyes still twinkled when they looked at her and his arms said he wanted her as his own.

They spent the entire day talking, catching up on things they couldn't put into letters the war censors might have read. They talked of home life and base life and the crazy world and all the things Peter had done while in the military. He had not been allowed to tell in letters what his job had entailed due to the threat of alerting the enemy if some spy had intercepted the mail packets.

He told of the hours at the English base near High Wycombe spent repairing planes all night trying to get enough flightworthy by morning to meet the number of planes needed for each day's sorties. Almost daily, the B-17s had taken off, missing only when clouds enveloped the English countryside or European bombing site. Often the number of planes departing did not match the number of planes returning. Each plane carried ten men, so the loss of life was great when one went down. Yet each day the weary flight crews bravely mounted the planes and soared into the peaceful blue sky. Peter admired their courage, realizing his job was much safer.

Emma recounted her joy at teaching and the perils of dealing with mischievous children. Her stories of killing mice and snakes and cleaning up vomit had Peter laughing. She told of her lack of confidence in writing plays and her struggles to make good grades in her college courses. She spoke of how lonely she felt at times, not having any family members to advise her on what college courses to take or to help with homework. Her honesty in telling about being slightly envious that many of her friends were married and settled in their homes touched Peter.

"We'll be talkin' more about what we both want for the future," Peter said, "when I finally git let go from the Army. I want us to git to know each other again, to be sure we're still thinkin' the same thing before we take a big step. My folks been happy for a lot of years, and I want that whenever I get hitched."

Emma nodded. "I think it's a good idea. We didn't get to date very long before you left, but I'm pretty sure I know how I feel about you. You're a good man, and your mom has talked so much about you and how you were growing up I feel I may know more about you than you know about me.

"Besides," she grinned, "you may have picked up some really bad habits in the Army. Like drinking and gambling and running around, despite what your letters said!" she teased. "I want time to check you out and see if you're still the gentleman I knew before you enlisted!"

Peter pulled her close and kissed her hard. "Well, I'll just have to court you right and proper so you'll believe I don' do none of those things," he laughed.

Emma had purchased a sack lunch for them from a nearby café before she left the hotel. They enjoyed their first meal together in many months while watching the river flow serenely past them. All too soon, the afternoon sun started dipping lower in the sky.

Slowly, they rose from the bench, still linking arms, and headed for a gas station outside the park. They called a taxi, because Emma's bus left St. Louis in the early evening. They wanted a nice meal in a diner before Emma had to depart for Kansas City and home.

Arriving home after two bus rides and driving from St. Jo, Emma briefly called Janie. She told her how wonderful Peter looked and how eager he was to be heading home, free of the Army. Janie was thrilled to think she would soon see her boy. Then Emma said hello to Edith before collapsing into bed for some much overdue sleep.

Peter wrote her the same day. "It hasn't been but a few hours since I saw you but it seams like a month or more. It ment a lot to me just to have you there and thanks." Emma could feel his emotions as he wrote the words.

They were back to playing the Army game—hurry up and wait. The Army had moved Peter quickly to Missouri after his arrival stateside. He had gone by train from the east coast to Jefferson Barracks, then had to wait before his official release.

Both Peter's and Emma's frustration appeared in their letters. The hot July ended with these words from him: "Had to stand in line three times to git all through for had this month, back Pay, travel and ration Pay to git. And wish I could spend it for gas to go to Barnard, a malted milk. I can git malts here but they are a lot better when we can drink them together. Well Sis I don't know how much longer I will be here so don't write till you hear more."

On August 1, Peter and a bunk mate had been discussing the women in their life. Ray Johnson was married and having problems, but he commented about Peter and Emma.

"He ask me if you were my wife. Said he thought sure but what you were. Has any one down there thought that about you. Ha."

Oh, how I wish we were, thought Emma. *I can't wait for our wedding!*

Another letter talked about Peter not going to town much.

"It is rather lonesome here to-night. Most the boys have gone to town. I am the only one down stairs. Ray went to town to-night for the first time. I could of went but didn't want to. Was afared I would be by myself. While he has never did any thing out of the way while with me but think he aimed to drink some beer and I don't care to and I have just about decided he is not just as true to his wife as he might be. But he has all-ways been fine to me. I hope things never happen between you and I that I am afared has between them."

Yes, Peter was the type of man Emma wanted, someone loyal and dependable. She felt proud to have waited for him to return.

On August 3, his letter brought Emma some hope. "Well Sis we git the stars at the next stop and ever one seams to think we will git the extray points. I saw the captain that was over us mechanics. He seamed to think we might git out. That is the ones with high points. I am most afared to plan on it to much but am sure hopeing. I hope they send me right back for that discharge."

Both felt the sweltering heat of August was more oppressive due to their personal uncertainty. High temperatures made them even more anxious to get Peter's discharge.

With no official duties to perform, Peter spent his days sleeping, wandering the post, drinking malted milks, and writing letters home. He still didn't want Emma or his folks to write, since he felt he might be moved soon to a final post before discharge. Always the goal was "soon, soon" but never reached "now"!

Peter's friend Johnson continued having marital troubles. Peter wrote, "I made a few trips to the P.X. for a malted milk. Wish we were going to drink one together. Just a week ago to-night since I saw you but say it seams like a long week. I heard Johnson say to-day that he wished he was single. I hope neither one of us is able to say that for I don't think that would be a very happy way to live do you."

"I swear the moment Peter drives up to this house, I'm going to grab his arm and drive him right over to the preacher's house," Emma declared to Edith one day. "He wants to marry me, and I want to marry him. Enough of this waiting! Let's do this and start our future together."

Edith laughed at her impatience. "Lordy, gal, he won't know what hit him. But I think he'll enjoy ever' minute of it!"

Peter's letter of August 5 came from Jefferson Barracks, but his August 8 letter carried a Sioux Falls, South Dakota, address. Emma could start writing again. On his train trip there, Peter had seen a lot of good corn crops, but many fields remained unplanted due to wet ground.

"See a lot of good oat fields around here and I guess help here is like ever where else hard to git. One fellow said in a station we came through that men to shock grain cost from 75¢ to $1.00 a hour."

Farm labor remained in short supply since many men had not been released from military duty or had been shipped to the Pacific to fight the

Japanese.

On August 9, Emma's hopes hit bottom. "Will be moved from here to another base and will wait there until my turn for a discharge. Might be 3 months 6 months or a year. That is the way I understand it and you know things can be changed awful easy. So don't tell to many I will be discharged soon. But unless things are changed a lot from what I was told will stay in states."

"Oh, blast the Army!" yelled Emma in frustration. "I didn't want to teach this fall if Peter was going to get home soon. Now I don't know what to do!"

His letter continued, "A lot of the boys got married while on furlough. One boy said never git married while in Army for you sure have a lot of papers to sign when you do."

"Well, Peter should just start filling them out if the Army is going to make us wait much longer," Emma said as she stamped her foot. "I may just have to move closer to him and get married at the base pretty soon."

They both followed the latest radio war news, hoping the end of the war with Japan would speed Peter's release. "Well Sis how does the news sound to you. It sure sounds good to me and I sure hope it is soon over. Think if it would end that it wouldn't be long until I would be home soon to stay. Have they teased you quit a lot the past two weeks. Most all the boys ask that question if I am still single. What makes people git those ideas. Ha!"

"Yes, you need to be home to stay," a frustrated Emma exclaimed to Peter's photo. "I need you near me. Letters just aren't the same! We both want to get married now. The European war is over, and you're just sitting around a barracks, and the Army isn't using your skills, so why don't they release you?"

On August 12, 1945, Peter's letter arrived. "Did go to the PX and git a milk shake this after noon but such lines as you have to wait in. I don't think I ever want to see another line when I git out so don't ask me to stand in line to go to a show."

The Army finally did put him to work the next day in the mail room.

On August 14, Emma lost more hope. He wrote, "I would like to git to where I am going next for if I understand right that will be my last stop until I go back to Jefferson Barracks for that discharge that have been waiting so long for. Also if I understand right that next stop isn't to be very far from Missouri."

"Another move!" shouted Emma. "Why keep moving him around with no duties to do, just for the fun of moving guys around! That makes no sense."

Peter heard when Japan surrendered on August 14, 1945. "Boy that news just came. May be it won't be so long now until I am back to Missouri I hope."

By August 16, Peter's letter was addressed from Pratt, Kansas. He had left Sioux City the previous afternoon, riding all night. They had had supper at Esterville, Iowa, and breakfast in Kansas City. Peter heard gas and tire rationing had ended. He still didn't know when he would be discharged. The Army had assigned him to check clothes and help set up beds. Also, he was missing regular letters from Emma and his folks. The moving around had delayed his mail deliveries again.

Three days later, Peter wrote, "Well I guess our records are here and we will start having our records checked and I suppose git assigned to a job. I wish they would assign me to farming back in northwest Missouri. I suppose a week from in the morning you will start back to work. Or is it two weeks. Is Tommy still anxious for school to start. I bet he steps big that first morning.

"Do you have that sewing all done. If you have you can sew some for me. Have to put on some sholder patchs and the strips on two more shirts. Guess the 8th air force goes on the right shoulder and the 2nd on the left now." He closed with "Love with a world of Kisses."

Mike served on the Harmon School Board. He had persuaded the board members to hold off signing a different teacher to Harmon, hoping Emma would again teach there. With Peter's delays in getting discharged, Emma reluctantly signed the contract. She had hoped to be married by now and to teach school closer to Peter's farm near Pickering.

Peter updated Emma on August 20. "Well I hear they got word to discharge those with over 85 points at sioux falls. If that is so I wish I was still there.

"Yes I got my records checked to-day and assigned to another job. You better set down for if you don't you will fall. For they assigned me to M.P. duty. Think it will mostly be checking passes at gate and such as that. I don't hardly believe it is going to be so awful long until a lot of us is discharged and I don't feel like I will be so far down the line I hope. They said there was so many mechanics they didn't know what to do with them all. I think will just take time to git ever thing set up then look for things to move fairly fast.

Of course not fast enough to suit us.

"One thing I am glad of and that is that I have my over sea time in. Didn't want to go but sure glad it is over with now."

Two days later, Peter described his Military Police duty. "Well I got by as an M.P. allright I guess. I drove the officer of the day most of the forenoon. Had a four door Ford for that and had a jeep to drive this afternoon. It wasn't such a bad job and didn't have to pinch any one.

"Say my moral is still higher again to-night. They called all of us with over 85 points up to head quarters to-day to check if they had our points right and to give them our home address. Now I think we will be divided into groups to go to different seperation centers (I go to Jefferson Barracks) and the officer I was driving this morning said he wouldn't be surprised if I wasn't gone from here by the end of the week. But I don't hardly look for it that soon. Some think about two week. And one thing sure when they say go it won't take me long to pack. That will be one time I can be ready quick. Just keep your fingers cross but don't let your eyes cross for I want to know when you are looking at me." He closed with "Yours forever with Love."

Emma hugged the letter to her chest. *Maybe we're getting closer to getting him home.*

The next day, Peter continued his good news.

"The latest rumor I have heard is those with over 85 points will be out of here by the first of the month. That is just a rumor but here is hopeing it is true for the quicker I leave here the quicker I will git out. I don't think they hold you but a very few days at the seperation center. I am thinking I will see you before so awful much longer. Heres hopeing any way. Am hopeing to celebrate my next birthday in Northwest Missouri."

Peter explained his job checking clothing in his next letter.

"Well there was several of us working at a counter. They would come through and put all there clothing on the counter and it was our job to check and see that they had what there were supposed to and take some away. No there was no WAC's to be checked but several working and one checking right with us. And I think she got away with about as many cigarettes as any one else. And if things didn't go right she could use some rather strong language. Now see why I didn't want you to be one."

Sunday, August 26, found Peter working the night M.P. shift.

"Was rather busy last night. The officer of the day and I had to go around and close the different clubs up at 1:30 last night. Some of the officers didn't want to close theres up very bad but didn't have much trouble. But say I bet some of there caps is small this morning. Some of the women weren't in as good a shape. Saw them carry one to the car.

"Say that is what you think that I wouldn't give you a ticket. But expect it would take a long time to write it out and then could tear it up. That away we could talk couldn't we. Ha."

His next letter was full of hope.

"Oh boy my moral is high. How about a date for a week from Sunday night. I don't know just when I will leave here for J.B. but am fairly sure it will be soon. And then it will depend on how long they hold me at J. B. and I don't think it will be long there. And Sis I don't believe there is much use you writing any more after you git this for think I will be gone before I git them. I am hopeing to talk to you soon if the old Chevrolet can find that Harmon school house. Ha."

Peter turned in most of his clothing two days later. He expected to turn in more clothes at Jefferson Barracks. His excitement was contagious, for Emma found herself planning to get her hair cut and permed, deciding what dress to wear, and checking everything off her list a girl had to do before her guy came calling. She felt giddy and young and free again.

A letter on letterhead from the Service Men's Club in Kansas City at 15 Pershing Road arrived dated August 30.

"Thursday morning and here I am with a little time in Kansas City MO so will try and drop you a line so you will know where I am and of course you know where I am headed and for what. Have heard several rumors that not long at JB. I have hopes that I will see you a week from Sunday but can't say for sure.

"I hear they have lifted the speed limit so don't know just what it will do when the Chevy heads that way this time. Had to use my breaks the other time (believe it or not).

"Love and a world of Kisses."

Kansas City! Peter was so close Emma could almost feel his thoughts. If only the Army would let her drive to KC and pick him up. It would save the government the cost of sending him to Jefferson Barracks and then back to Maryville. Now "soon" was really going to happen!

His next letter said he had made it to St. Louis. His paperwork had to be checked before he could get his final discharge.

Emma didn't receive a letter for several days. She was beginning to worry something had caused a glitch and Peter was too upset to tell her he would be delayed.

After supper on Monday, Edith helped Emma clear the table when the wall telephone rang. Emma answered.

"Well, hi, Sweetheart," came a male voice. "Have you saved me some supper?"

Emma held her breath. "Peter? Is that you? You've never called me before while you've been in the Army! Is everything okay?"

Peter laughed, "This is such a special occasion I decided to splurge and call you. I got my discharge, honey! I'll be home on the bus early Friday evening to Maryville! Know any old maid that might wanna pick up a soldier?"

Emma started to cry. "You mean it? No more Army? No more separation? You're really coming home?"

Edith rushed into the room and hugged Emma.

"Yea, I'll be the good-lookin' guy in a uniform gittin' off the bus first thing. You 'pose I could get some gal to go on a date Friday night?"

"You try and pick up some other gal and you'll see her get shoved out of the way! I'll be on the front row to greet you. Oh, I can't believe it's finally over and you're coming home."

Peter laughed. "Believe it. I know it's been 'bout a month 'n half since I seen you, but I reckon I still remember what you look like. You're the blond gal I used to date, ain't you?"

"Oh, you soldiers," she exclaimed. "So many girls at each base you can't keep them straight. But don't worry, I remember what you look like, so handsome in your uniform. I'll find you if you don't see me."

"Well, I better git off this phone 'n save some money for those malted milks we're gonna share. Sweetheart, I love you and I'll be home Friday. I've saved a bunch of kisses for you and don' expect to git home early from all the talkin' we're gonna do."

"Okay, Peter," Emma replied. "I'll be at the bus station Friday evening. I can't wait to see those discharge papers to be sure you're not just going AWOL to get home!"

"Well, it'd be worth it if I was AWOL. See you in four days!"

Emma hung up the receiver, turned, and hugged Edith. "Oh, it's finally over. He'll be home Friday. I'll never make it through the school week because my mind won't be on teaching. It's a good thing we have a long Labor Day weekend."

Edith's eyes teared up. "Well, now, I think we best be lookin' for a wedding dress for you real soon. If that boy is as eager as he sounds, it won't be long before you're both hitched."

Emma spent every moment she wasn't grading papers or making lesson plans to prepare for Peter's arrival. She pressed her clothes, got her hair done, and painted her nails bright red to match the red on her letters to Peter. She knew he would understand the joke.

Chapter 38

Thursday evening, the telephone rang.

"Honey, it's me," said Peter. His voice sounded strained, and Emma waited for him to continue.

"What's wrong, Peter?" she asked. "You don't sound right."

"I know. My stomach is aching purdy bad. It may have eaten somethin' I ate. I don' wanna get on a long bus ride and lose my food all over. I think I'll wait until Saturday to take the bus. I'm sorry to miss our Friday date, but I don't want to give you something."

Emma stifled her disappointment. "Peter, the only thing important is you being healthy. You just take care of yourself. Have you seen a doctor?"

"Think I might head over to the base clinic now. My stomach hurts so bad. Maybe he's got somethin' for it. I'll call you as soon as I feel better."

"Alright, Peter. Just take care and I'll be waiting whenever you get here. Call me soon. I love you. Good night."

Emma hung up the receiver but couldn't hide her feelings from Edith. "He's sick with something, so he's not coming until Saturday."

Edith tried to be practical. "Well, it'll just give us an extrey day to git ready for him. We'll make his favorite cake and have it sittin' on the table when he arrives."

The students on Friday were not in a mood to study due to the three-day weekend ahead. For once, Emma didn't try to engage them. She used a field trip to study plants and insects as a change of pace to teach science.

Emma closed the school quickly that afternoon, not waiting to grade papers. She wanted to get home and relax and see if anyone had heard from Peter. The telephone rang about four.

"Emma," a female voice sobbed into the mouthpiece. "Emma, it's Janie."

Emma felt her insides tighten with fear. "Janie, what's wrong? Is Gene alright?" Gene had not been feeling well about a week ago, but she had thought he was better by now.

"No, Gene's fine. Emma, it's Peter. He's ..." Janie completely broke down. Emma heard the receiver bang against the wall. Then Gene spoke.

"Honey, it's Gene. You know Peter ain't felt good for several days now. He'd been poorly since Wednesday, but he didn't want to worry you. So he didn't call you 'til last night."

"Okay," Emma softly replied, waiting for the rest of the story.

"Well, Peter went to the doc last night. They put him in the hospital, but his appendix burst during the night." Gene started to cry. Emma felt herself hold her breath, not wanting to hear anything more.

"His docs tried real hard all day, but they couldn't save him. Peter died about two thirty this afternoon. We just … we just don' know how to … Oh, Emma dear, we'll call you later with more details." Gene hung up.

Emma managed to replace the receiver on the hook before she felt her back slide down the wallpaper. Her legs collapsed under her, and she squatted on the floor. For a long minute, nothing happened. Then a long, gut-wrenching sob burst from her lungs.

"NO!" was all she could say. She buried her head in her hands and her hands against her bent knees. Slowly she rocked back and forth, crying for all she was worth.

Edith heard her scream and rushed in from working in the flower bed. "Emma, Emma, dear, what's wrong?" she said as she brought over a chair to sit near her.

Emma could only shake her head, tears flying off her checks. "Peter's dead. His appendix burst."

Edith sat stunned, feeling helpless. She let Emma sob for several more minutes, then slowly reached both arms to pull her from the floor. Emma could hardly walk, leaning on Edith's shoulder until she collapsed on the sofa.

Edith grabbed some dish towels, for a small handkerchief would not contain the amount of tears Emma was shedding. Having lost a baby girl and her husband, Edith knew what Emma was feeling and just let her cry. She rubbed her back and forehead, uttering soothing sounds she knew Emma barely heard.

"You've got a right to cry, so let it all out. That's the only thing to do right now," Edith said.

And cry Emma did, not knowing she had so much water in her entire body.

"He didn't come home to me, not like we wanted. And we were so close to being together! No, this can't be happening!" Emma blurted out at one point.

After more than an hour, Emma drifted into a semi-conscious stupor. Edith turned the fan so it would blow gently across her body to cool her emotions and the early September heat.

Quietly, Edith slipped out of the room, turning off the telephone ringer. She didn't want anyone disturbing Emma. She knew some neighbor on the party line had probably listened to Gene's call. Soon the entire area would know of Peter's death, and folks would be calling in sympathy. Those calls could wait until later. Right now, Emma needed whatever peace and quiet she could find.

*****

They shipped Peter's body back from St. Louis. Price Funeral Home, which had handled Daniel's burial, received his coffin. Knowing Gene and Janie could use some financial help, several neighbors and friends donated what money they could. Together with their funds, his parents were able to have Peter placed in a nice metal coffin.

The small church in Pickering overflowed with mourners on Labor Day. Emma sat on the front row with Gene and Janie, since they had considered her their daughter-to-be. People had made beautiful flower bouquets, mostly from their own gardens and lovingly assembled for the sad occasion.

Emma felt numb. She made it through the church service without breaking down. Actually, she barely remembered what was said or done. From now on, she would only see Peter's smile in his photographs.

At the Maryville Cemetery, the burial plot rested under the shade of an oak tree on a slight rise. *From here, Peter can look over the countryside to the east and north,* Emma thought. The line of cars driving from Pickering to the north Maryville site stretched nearly half a mile. The Paxtons were well-respected and well-known in the area, plus people wanted to honor Peter's extended military service. Emma stared ahead most of the time, but lost control when they began laying flowers on the coffin before lowering it into the ground.

As she started to collapse, Owen grabbed her shoulders to hold her up. She laid her head against his good suit and softly cried into her handkerchief. He just hugged her tighter, telling her it was okay to cry. Being her closest brother in age, Emma felt a strong bond with Owen, so she appreciated his strength now when she had none.

Finally, the military gun salute and taps ended the graveside service.

Mourners came by to pay final condolences, then quietly filed back to their cars. Janie, Gene, Davie, and Emma rode away in the funeral home's limousine, the first time she had ever ridden in one.

Chapter 39

Emma was unable to teach school the next two weeks. The school board managed to find a substitute teacher, a woman with previous experience who was waiting for her husband to get his Army Air Corps discharge. Emma helped her as much as she could to develop lesson plans, but her heart wasn't in it.

Mostly Emma sat and stared at nothing. Even when her father died, she had not felt so lost. The two men she had truly loved in her life were both gone, buried under the black Missouri soil they had tilled so many years. She just couldn't get her mind to focus on anything.

Edith noticed her daughter's weight loss. Emma had always been slender, but now she looked gaunt. Whatever Edith baked of her favorite dishes, Emma just dabbled at eating, taking only a few bites before pushing away her plate. Knowing each person grieved in her own way and time, Edith tried to be patient. As the days extended with no improvement, Edith became seriously worried. She just didn't know how to help Emma.

Two weeks after Peter's death, Emma sat in a chair in the sunshine, staring at the ground. Edith had insisted she get some fresh air and daylight on her skin. While Edith pulled weeds in the nearby flower bed, she watched Emma from the corner of her eye.

Standing to stretch her back and legs, Edith pulled another chair next to Emma's. "I want you to think about what I got to say," she began, putting her finger under Emma's chin, turning her head to face her mother. "You've had a terrible loss. No one's gonna deny it. You and Peter had plans that ain't gonna happen now. You can't change that."

Emma felt tears running down her cheeks.

"Now think about this. You was luckier than most gals who lost their men in the war. Their men died somewhere overseas. Most gals hadn't seen their boyfriend or husband for ages, some nearly four years! They hadn't heard their voices or felt their guy hold them in their arms. You did. You got to see Peter for an entire day! You and he got to talk about your plans. You got to hear his voice. You got to hold his face in your hands. And you got to talk to him on the phone twice before he died. Do you know how many girls would've give anythin' to do that? To have talked to their man or held him just once more?

"You know how Peter died and where. So many other gals never knew. They just got some telegram saying, sorry, but your man's dead. And you can visit Peter's grave. You can put pretty flowers on it and talk to him. These other girls can't. They don't know where their guy is buried. Lots of their men never even got a burial, 'cause they was blown apart in too many pieces to count."

Emma felt her tears flow even more freely. At least she had begun to listen to Edith's words.

"I done buried a baby girl and a husband. I know what that pain is like. And soon I'll be a burin' my momma, too. It's just like them flowers over there. We plant the seeds in the spring, and they sprout up real nice. Then they get the purtiest blooms, and we bring 'em in our house and enjoy their beauty.

"And then the heavy frost comes and freezes 'em to death. And we start all over in the springtime. We plant new seeds and watch them grow. That's just the way life is."

Edith patted Emma's arm, then rose and headed back to the flower bed. *Women know how to handle grief,* Edith thought. *We clean something or cook something or plant something. Anything to keep busy.*

*****

Emma dragged herself back to school the third Monday in September. Her heart wasn't in her teaching, but she needed to do something, anything. She faced her students who had all heard why she hadn't been at school. For once, they all behaved and were extra studious.

As she watched their faces, Emma felt the loss of any children she and Peter might have had. She had wanted her own children's faces smiling up at her from the breakfast table before they left for school. Now that would never happen. She had to strictly control her emotions to make it through the day.

She managed to finish the week, painting a semblance of a smile on her face each morning. Going through the motions, she moved her pupils along each required curriculum path. When Friday came, her relief at having made it through the week only got her as far as home. She ate a quick supper before collapsing in bed, sleeping nearly twelve hours.

The telephone rang mid-Saturday morning. Emma had grown to dislike its sound, for she couldn't take one more word of sympathy from well-meaning friends. She let Edith answer the call.

"Hello," Edith spoke into the mouthpiece.

"Edith? This is Janie."

"Oh, Janie, nice to hear your voice. How you folks holding up?"

"Well, we're tryin'. Each day's a challenge, but we got Davie to think about, and he's takin' it purdy hard, too."

Edith nodded. "I know. Emma's not doin' too well either. Too many plans got ruint."

"Are you two gonna be home this afternoon? Gene and me thought we'd drive over if you're gonna be there."

"I don't think we're goin' anywhere," Edith replied. "Emma hasn't been out of the house except to teach this week, and she don' seem like she feels up to goin' anywhere soon. Come on over."

At two o'clock, Peter's old Chevy pulled into the driveway and parked next to the back door. Edith stepped onto the porch, opening the screen door.

Gene, Janie, and Davie stepped out of the car. They had polished the old Chevy, trying to make Peter proud they were keeping it up so well.

"Come on in," Edith offered. "I've got a fresh pie baked, and I know a boy who's always hungry," she said as she smiled at Davie. "We got a good fan that turns round and round to move the air some. It sure makes the warm fall days seem a little cooler." Any small talk was welcome, since Edith sensed the Paxtons' emotions.

Emma combed her hair and joined them in the living room. Everyone took a seat, waiting for one of the Paxtons to start the conversation.

Janie held her handkerchief between her hands. Her eyes showed she was having trouble trying not to cry when she talked.

"Well, Emma, we wanted you to know how much Peter thought of you. He was just as proud as he could be of you bein' a teacher. And he figured you'd be a wantin' to keep on teachin', at least for a while, after you two was married."

She paused to catch her breath, and Gene continued.

"He was always braggin' 'bout how hard you was workin' on gettin' your teaching degree. He wanted you to git it, even if it meant you went to school after you two had married. He was set on you havin' it.'"

Gene took a deep breath. "Well, Peter had signed some papers so his Army life insurance was to go to me and Janie as his folks. We just got the check this week. And we thought real hard 'bout what Peter would want."

Janie jumped back into the conversation. "We know he'd a wanted you to finish your schoolin'. So we want you to have some money to pay for one year's tuition and books and such for your college next year. You've signed your teachin' contract this year, but we was hopin' you'd take next year off and really git a bunch of them credits toward your degree."

Gene went on, "Peter always said how he wanted yours and his kids to have better schoolin' than he'd had. He wanted you to help your own kids with homework and such. And he knew how high esteem other folks thought of you as a teacher. So we want you do to this."

Shocked, Emma could only stare at them. With Peter gone, they would have to keep paying a hired man to work their farm. Davie wouldn't be any use for nearly seven years, so Emma knew they could use all of Peter's insurance money to keep their farm going.

"Oh, I couldn't," Emma insisted. "You need the money, and I make enough teaching each year to pay for summer school. I can get my degree that way."

Janie and Gene shook their heads. "Nope. We've made up our minds. It's what Peter would've wanted. And you got to honor his memory for us by goin' to school more. Goin' just in summers is gonna take you a heap of years to finish."

Emma glanced at Edith, who nodded her head. "Yes, I think Peter would want this."

Staring at all of them, Emma started to cry in earnest. Their generosity was overwhelming, and she was so touched she couldn't speak.

"'Sides," added Davie. "I always thought I'd git you for a teacher when I got to school. That way, I knowed I'd git good grades since you was Peter's gal and I'm so cute and his brother and all."

Everyone looked at Davie, then had to laugh a little at his frankness. Out of the mouths of babes comes pure logic.

"Well, Davie," Emma managed to say. "Maybe you could be a teacher some day yourself. I believe Peter would think it was a really good idea."

"Nah," exclaimed Davie. "I ain't got the patience to put up with a bunch of brats all day!"

Emma studied his face. He wasn't trying to be smart. He was just being honest in his opinion.

She thought back to other moments in her classrooms when youngsters had made astute observations about life. They often showed wisdom beyond their years. That part of teaching she had always treasured, when students finally grasped a difficult concept or saw the world in a bigger picture beyond local opinions. Expanding minds was the reason teachers taught. It was why Emma had always wanted to teach.

Smiling softly, she gathered Davie into her arms and hugged him ntil he wiggled to be set free. She felt like she was hugging a little part of Peter.

Emma now realized that she was one of thousands of young women whose world had changed forever. She would have to discover her new future without Peter in it. Emma decided for the time being to focus on teaching and getting her college degree. Maybe later the innocent wisdom of her school children could heal her heart enough to look forward to a new future.

ABOUT THE AUTHOR

Ilene W. Devlin was born in Winterset, Iowa, the actor John Wayne's hometown. She lived in Macksburg and Winterset and often visited relatives in northwest Missouri. Attending the University of Iowa, Devlin obtained a BA in anthropology and an MA in archaeology and a minor in museum training. Afterward, she worked in museums in Nebraska, Tennessee, and Alabama.

Since 1986, Ilene Devlin has lived in San Antonio, Texas. Her freelance articles and essays have been published in newspapers in San Antonio and Iowa. *Emma's World: A World War II Memoir* is her second book. Her first book, *Cherry Tree Dares: Essays on Childhood,* was published in October 2020.

Made in the USA
Monee, IL
23 December 2020